Luminos is the Open Access monograph publishing program
from UC Press. Luminos provides a framework for preserving and
reinvigorating monograph publishing for the future and increases
the reach and visibility of important scholarly work. Titles published
in the UC Press Luminos model are published with the same high
standards for selection, peer review, production, and marketing as
those in our traditional program. www.luminosoa.org

The publisher and the University of California Press Foundation gratefully acknowledge the generous support of the Anne G. Lipow Endowment Fund in Social Justice and Human Rights.

The Big Gamble

The Big Gamble

The Migration of Eritreans to Europe

———

Milena Belloni

UNIVERSITY OF CALIFORNIA PRESS

University of California Press
Oakland, California

Suggested citation: Belloni, M. *The Big Gamble: The Migration of Eritreans to Europe*. Oakland: University of California Press, 2019. DOI: https://doi.org/10.1525/luminos.82

Library of Congress Cataloging-in-Publication Data

Names: Belloni, Milena, author.
Title: The big gamble : the migration of Eritreans to Europe / Milena Belloni.
Description: Oakland, California : University of California Press, [2019]| Includes bibliographical references and index.
Identifiers: LCCN 2019021373 (print) | LCCN 2019980901 (ebook) | ISBN 9780520298705 (paperback) | ISBN 9780520970755 (ebook other)
Subjects: LCSH: Eritreans—Social aspects—Europe. | Africans—| Migrations—Social aspects.
Classification: LCC DT16.5 .B44 2019 (print) | LCC DT16.5 (ebook) | DDC 304.8/40635—dc23
LC record available at https://lccn.loc.gov/2019021373
LC ebook record available at https://lccn.loc.gov/2019980901

28   27   26   25   24   23   22   21   20   19
10   9   8   7   6   5   4   3   2   1

CONTENTS

ACKNOWLEDGMENTS

This work would have not been possible without the help and care of my Eritrean informants, whose real names have been changed to protect their safety. They are the protagonists and the soul of this book. Among them I would like to mention my friends Violetta, Johanna, Lwam, Alazar, Adonay, Gabriel, Esther, Saba, Baba, Gebreyesus, Samuel, Michael, Paolos, Noah and his Kunama family, Maria, Sister Kudussan, and Sister Lethe Brahne and the nuns of her congregation, whose work is of immense relief to many. It is to all of them that I dedicate this book.

I am obliged to Ambassador Renzo Rosso for providing me with institutional support while doing fieldwork in Ethiopia, and to Dr. Fekadu Adugna and the Department of Anthropology of Addis Ababa University for facilitating my local academic affiliation. I am also deeply indebted to Martina Messa, who welcomed me in Asmara, Ernesto Molinari and his family in Addis Ababa for their support during the initial phases of my stay in Addis Ababa, and to Khaled Mohamed for facilitating my entering Sudan. I owe a special thanks to Ephrem Tadesse for his logistical support in Shire and to Mohand Hassan Fadeel for his priceless help in Khartoum.

The writing process has been long and strenuous and would have not been possible without the encouragement of my family and friends. But money also helps, and I am indebted to the American Academy in Rome for awarding me with the *Italian Fellowship in Modern Italian Studies* and providing me with the perfect environment and means to complete the first draft of the book. I am especially grateful to Eric Cazdyn for pushing me to get to the core of the ideas that inspire this book. At the University of Trento, I would like to thank Paolo Boccagni for his patient comments and Giuseppe Sciortino for his wise jokes, which made my doctoral time much more inspiring. Finally, I would also like to thank Jørgen Carling, Nauja Kleist, Michael Collyer and Anna Triandafyllidou, who encouraged me to turn my thesis into a book, and the anonymous reviewers who critically assessed it.

PROTAGONISTS

NOTE:	All names have been changed to protect the anonymity of my informants. Ages are given here ca. 2014.
Alazar:	a 30-year-old ex-military refugee, originally from Asmara, my main contact in Eritrean informal networks in Rome.
Senay:	Alazar's friend and age-mate, my host in a Roman squat.
Kibreab:	my main informant in a Roman shantytown inhabited by Eritreans in transit to other destinations.
Ogbazgi:	a 25-year-old refugee living in Sicily whom I met in Ethiopia on the occasion of his marriage. I also visited his family in May Nefas, a village in the southern region of Eritrea.
Gabriel:	my 28-year-old main informant in Milan, who facilitated my stay at his aunt's place in Asmara.
Ester:	the head of the family who hosted me in Asmara.
Salam:	Ester's youngest daughter, who shared her room with me during my stay in Asmara.
Johanna:	Salam's friend and neighbor, who became one of my main informants in Eritrea.
Lwam:	Gabriel's younger sister, my main interpreter during my home visits in Asmara.
Minia:	Alazar's mother. I met with her family in Asmara and then in Ethiopia after their escape from the country.
Sister Kudussan:	an Eritrean nun who had lived in Addis Ababa for more than three decades, where her small convent was a meeting place for young Eritrean refugees.
Hagos:	a 30-year-old refugee from Mai Nefas and main spokesperson among the group of Catholic refugees I met in Addis Ababa

Violetta: my flat mate in Addis Ababa.
Adonay: a 28-year-old refugee student at Addis Ababa University.
Jeremiah: a 40-year-old translator and informant in the Adi Harush camp
               in Ethiopia.
Noah: a 25-year-old Kunama translator and informant in the camp of
               Shimelba.
Tsegay: the middleman I interviewed in Addis Ababa, who became a
               people smuggler to earn a living and pay for the migration of
               his siblings.
Maria: my 28-year-old host in Khartoum. I lived with her and her
               8-year-old daughter, Anna, for over a month.
Michael: a 23-year-old successful broker of people smuggling in
               Khartoum.

Introduction

It was 2016. Surrounded by the perpetual noise and relentless coming and going of Termini Station in Rome, my friend Alazar and I were drinking coffee at our usual meeting point.

"My brother is saying that I should join him in Canada . . . ," Alazar said.

"How is that possible?" I answered, surprised.

"My brother said not to worry . . . that he will find a way for me," Alazar replied quietly.

Alazar, whom I have known since he sought asylum in Italy in 2008, had finally found a job in a local restaurant and seemed to be feeling quite at home in Rome. After surviving a war when he was only eighteen, enduring a troublesome Mediterranean crossing, and spending a few years of unstable existence between Italy and the few countries in which he had sought asylum afterwards, Alazar had finally found some stability, I thought. He had a full international protection, a lot of friends and spoke some Italian. Apparently, however, he was not yet at his final destination as far as his relatives were concerned. Life was not easy for Alazar and many of the other Eritrean refugees I knew in the city. They often lived in poor housing and had few, irregular jobs. But I nonetheless had trouble understanding how Alazar's brother could even think that moving to Canada, probably through an incredibly dangerous and expensive crossing of the Mexico-U.S. and then the U.S.-Canada borders, could be a good idea. Why gamble resources, time and energy again for an unsure outcome?

Such situations were not new to me. The restless search for a suitable final home in spite of all obstacles characterized the trajectories of most of the Eritreans I met during my research across Eritrea, Ethiopia, Sudan, and Italy. The dream of fulfilling family expectations and finding not only a safe haven but some degree of socioeconomic and existential stability at one's next destination was typical of the stories I collected. My Eritrean interlocutors felt that migration, no matter how risky, was their best option if they were to change their lives and those of their families. Their resources, time, and energy were all invested in this, the big gamble of the protagonists of this book, in which the stakes are incredibly high and the outcome extremely uncertain.

Through the hardships of the national service in Eritrea and the adversities of exile in refugee camps and peripheral neighborhoods in Sudan, Ethiopia, and Italy, *The Big Gamble* investigates migrants' and their families' fears, dreams and stratagems in navigating the opportunities and constraints produced by national migration policies and the international asylum regime. Besides describing their experience of deprivation and violence, I reconstruct the *choices* faced by my research participants at each stage of their migration. In each site, I account not only for the importance of socioeconomic resources for geographic mobility, but also for the role of shared moralities (that is to say, shared conceptions of what is moral and immoral), transnational expectations and imagination in the decision whether to stay put or move on. In each site, I illustrate the cumulative impact of previous emotional and material investments to reach the desired destination.

In a nutshell, *The Big Gamble* seeks to show the space of refugees' agency—to explore the paradox of choice for those who are defined by the lack of it. In so doing, I break with long-standing assumptions, criticized but never really overcome, that reduce the explanations of refugee movements to push factors and confine the debate about them to the paradigm of emergency and exceptionality. By considering the role of aspirations in the context of chronic crisis, the influence of families on refugees' decision-making long after they left home and the emic perception of risk in dangerous border-crossings, this book shows the relevance of concepts developed in broader migration studies for the theoretical interpretation of refugee movements. In particular, building on long-standing debates on imaginaries, culture of migration and transnational moral economies, the idea of cosmologies of destinations, explained below, is for me a way to understand the interplay of mobility and immobility by analyzing how shared moral norms, personal aspirations, and collective emotions shape refugees' choices for mobility and their directions.

After introducing the idea of cosmologies of destinations and placing it within the larger debate over mobility and immobility, this introduction briefly revisits the history of refugee and forced migration studies and shows the theoretical as well as political importance of blurring the boundaries between research on forced and voluntary migrations. Then, it explains the significance of the Eritrean case in today's scenario and provides a historical overview of the country. Finally, I present the main features of my multi-sited ethnography across four countries and a summary of the book chapters.

MODERN COSMOLOGIES

Since starting to work with Eritreans in 2008, I have come to realize how the desired outcomes of their migration trajectories are patterned along a geographic hierarchy, with Canada, the United States, and the Scandinavian countries at the top and Eritrea at the bottom. In the middle, countries like Ethiopia, Sudan, and even Italy were perceived only as transit places, unsuitable for long-term settlement. Although individual preferences, family connections, rumors about recent policy changes, and other contingent circumstances could orient choices of a final destination—"Is it better to go to Sweden, Norway, or Switzerland?"—Eritrean refugees I encountered seemed to share common perceptions about the levels of safety, individual freedom, and labor market opportunities in different countries both among themselves and with their relatives around the globe. Far from being simply a configuration of geographic imaginaries, this hierarchy—which I define as a *cosmology of destinations*—also reflects a pathway of moral achievements and recognitions. Migrants' journeys are constructed as more or less successful, depending on the final country of settlement.

In anthropology, cosmologies are conventionally defined as widespread representations of the world as a hierarchically ordered whole.[1] Traditionally pertaining to the vocabulary of religion studies, cosmologies have progressively come to refer more generally to systems of classification and their related moral and emotional attitudes. Although for a time, this concept has been regarded as an outdated and ethnocentric notion, it is nevertheless an important heuristic tool for linking representations of reality with perceptions of morality and prescribed actions.[2] The concept of cosmologies has recently been used, for instance, to talk about social security conceptions in South Africa ("cosmologies of welfare"),[3] to refer to the capitalist system and its encompassing narrative,[4] and to denote the system of religious values underpinning the economic transactions involved in irregular migration from Fouzhou in China ("cosmologies of credit").[5] Cosmologies are crucial in Liisa Malkki's *Purity and Exile,* a founding text in refugee studies. Malkki illustrates how the *mythico-historical* reinterpretation of the Burundian genocide—a cosmology in its own right—shaped refugees' understanding of daily life in the camps and oriented their interactions with locals. Hutu refugees regarded intermarriage with locals and residence outside the camp, in particular, as threats to the purity of their identity.[6]

Whereas Malkki's *Purity and Exile* examines the cosmological beliefs of a limited number of refugees living in a confined camp, *The Big Gamble* aims to make sense of transnationally diffused worldviews among migrants in transit, their families back home, and their relatives and friends in the diaspora. Their views emerge not only from a national history of the Eritrean people as colonial subjects, war martyrs, and sacrificial migrants, but also from the wider effects of global cultural circulation on local cultures of migration, imaginaries and aspirations.

These concepts have previously been examined in the context of voluntary labor migration, but rarely in that of refugee flows from areas of chronic crisis. However, as described by Alessandro Monsutti in the context of Azhara migration from Afghanistan, long-term violence and related disruption of livelihoods often lead communities to reorganize, not only practically, but also morally and symbolically, around geographic mobility as the only significant means to survive.[7] The social expectations related to migration can be no less widespread in communities that have experienced a long-term outflow of refugees than in those of labor migrants.

Concepts such as aspirations, cultures of migration, and imaginaries crucially relate to the idea of cosmologies of destinations. However, there are some differences among them. Aspirations have become an especially crucial concept in migration studies thanks to the work of Jørgen Carling, Hein de Haas, and Ellen Bal and Roos Willems, among others.[8] The analysis of migration aspirations generally defined as "the conviction that leaving would be better than staying" has contributed to overcoming the simplistic understanding of migration as economically driven. Specifically, as argued by Jørgen Carling and Francis Collins, "unlike alternative terms, such as 'intention', 'plan' and 'wish', 'aspiration' marks an intersection of personal, collective and normative dimensions."[9] As such I consider aspirations as a crucial manifestation of the socially shared and individually incorporated set of images, norms, and symbols that I call "cosmology of destinations."

A culture of migration designates a widespread societal orientation to geographic mobility.[10] The idea of a cosmology of destinations adds more specificity, implying that mobility desires can be differentially addressed to specific locations, historically, culturally, and economically linked to the contexts of departure. These locations are typically ordered along a hierarchy of preferences, which are by no means fixed. Their order continually shifts, owing to feedback mechanisms between individuals living in different countries as well as popular images, which are at the same time rooted in specific historical experiences. In this sense the concept of cosmologies of destinations resounds with one of the geographic imaginaries that, as several scholars notice, often tend to be hierarchically ordered according to a wide range of social, historical, and economic factors.[11]

However, if imaginaries are mostly representational systems, cosmologies are by definition symbolic, and moral constructions. They are not only sets of images, but include emotional attitudes and moral orientations, which encompass those who are on the move as well as those who stay put. More specifically, within a vision of a hierarchically ordered world, the desire to move to another location that is deemed safer and more conducive to socioeconomic—and existential—stability, also implies a specific moral understanding of what it means to remain stuck in one's own place. Although moralities and emotions have certainly been touched upon by those studying migration imaginaries, they are not explicitly connected to the concept of imaginaries. The idea of cosmologies of destinations instead provides a frame in which the symbolic, emotional, and moral dimensions of migration can be systematically interpreted. This allows me to account for the role of community pressures and the moral obligations as well as the emotions involved in migrating no matter the cost.

While systematically linking images of the outside world—and different destinations within it—with the subjects' perception of their own position, the concept of cosmologies of destinations thus enables me to analyze different dimensions of mobility and immobility. Besides physical "stuckedness," I unfold the different meanings of mobility and immobility from my informants' point of view—that is, their protracted and reproduced *sense of being trapped* at different stages of their trajectories. Without reconstructing the worldview that defines Italy exclusively as a transit country, for instance, it would not have been possible for me to understand why Alazar was still perceived by his family as "being stuck" in Rome. This is only one of the many different instances of *being* and *feeling immobile* that I document throughout the book.

BEING MOBILE IN AN IMMOBILE WORLD

Immobility has in the past few years become central to the debate on migration.[12] While scholars usually consider sedentary populations as the norm and simply focus their attention on migrants, some have argued that immobility and its factors must also be analyzed. Individuals often aspire to migrate, but are prevented from doing so by restrictive immigration and emigration policies, the devastating effects of wars,[13] or the disempowering effects of poverty.[14] Limitations of mobility are reproduced along the complex trajectories of refugees and migrants, who may get stuck in transit, stranded at the edges of Europe, at the Mexico–U.S. border, or in between the European legal and jurisdictional boundaries of the asylum regime, trapped in locations from which is hard to move either ahead or back.[15] Protracted displacement—defined as the lack of prospects of return to the homeland, resettlement in third countries, and local integration for those who are in extended exile—has become the most typical and intractable issue of today's refugee scenario. Protracted displacement has become normalized for 78 percent of all refugees—15.9 million people—leading to decades spent in first countries of refuge.[16]

The analysis of such involuntary immobility is crucial in the study of what is normally defined as "forced migration." Refugees' access to mobility is not only stratified along socioeconomic, age, and gender lines—as discussed, for example, by Nicholas van Hear and S. C. Lubkemann[17]—but also depends on the availability of transnational kinship and community networks and the ability to mobilize them. While exploring the structural circumstances that reproduce my informants' immobility along the Eritrea–Europe corridor, the analysis points to the paradox first made explicit by Lubkemann's work: mobility, even in highly constrained circumstances, represents an expression of agency, of capability to act upon one's own situation. Involuntary immobility is rather the condition in which the powerless and most vulnerable end up being—repeatedly—trapped, whether in their own home countries or in transit after crossing their national borders.

However, immobility is far more than a physical condition.[18] As scholars have pointed out, using terms such as "waithood," "existential immobility," "chronic crisis," and "stuckedness," people are stuck not only because they are not able to migrate, but because they cannot reach a socioeconomically recognized position. They are unable to become the men and the women they wish to be and to grasp the future they aspire to for themselves and their families. This feeling of immobility is widespread among youth living in a context of protracted crisis all across Africa. Achille Mbembe,[19] James Ferguson,[20] Alcinda Honwana,[21] and Henrik Vigh,[22] among others, have documented in various ways in which young Africans' aspirations are often frustrated by the structural incapability of postcolonial African economies to accommodate a new labor force, by the wider effects of corrupt political establishments, the failures of developmental measures, recurrent conflicts, and deteriorating climatic conditions. Although specific in many regards, Eritrean migration also represents the response to similar frustrated aspirations—especially among the youth—in a context of chronic crisis, stagnant economy, and political stasis. Such a context where different aspects of being forced and being willing to move—or to stay—continuously intertwine, defies the boundaries of forced and voluntary migration.

REFUGEE AND FORCED MIGRATION STUDIES: ON BLURRING THE BOUNDARIES BETWEEN TYPOLOGIES

Article 1 of the Geneva Convention (1951) defines a refugee as someone who "owing to a well-founded fear of being persecuted for reasons of race, religion, nationality, membership of a particular social group or political opinion, is outside the country of his nationality, and is unable to, or owing to such fear, is unwilling to avail himself of the protection of that country."[23] In spite of later modifications of the Convention and the establishment of a set of juridical tools aimed to protect refugees and expand the Geneva definition—such as the Organization of African Union (OAU) Convention (1969) and the Cartagena Protocol (1984), not to mention national legislation and, in the European Union, the regulations established since the early 1990s[24]—the 1951 Convention is still the most widely recognized one. In fact, it is the text of refugee law on which most national and international legislation is based.[25]

This juridical framework shaped the early development of refugee studies as a discipline. Refugees have long been analyzed as an intrinsically different category from voluntary "economic" migrants. In 1973, for instance, E. F. Kunz claimed that refugees' migration is triggered by push factors alone, with a complete absence of pull factors.[26] B. N. Stein has similarly argued that the refugee constitutes a distinct social type, and that the main common characteristics of the "refugee experience"—that is, loss of social ties and trauma—can be delineated.[27] The refugee condition has been regarded as exceptional in the migration scenario, as well as the responses required. Even today, refugee policies still have an emergency, humanitarian character that does not reflect the systematic and structural nature of refugee problems.[28] This is reflected in a theoretical segregation of the field of refugee studies from the broader debate of migration studies.

However, the contemporary asylum/migration scenario has dramatically changed in the past sixty years and calls for new interpretative tools. At the end of World War II, beneficiaries of international protection were perceived to be from Europe and victims of the recently ended war and of national ethnic cleansing. More than sixty years later, the world refugee population mainly originates from Africa, Asia, and South and Central American countries.[29] Most refugees come from countries marked by chronic low-intensity conflict, state fragility, livelihood disruption, human-rights violations, and protracted socioeconomic crisis, such as Afghanistan, El Salvador, Eritrea, Guatemala, Honduras, Myanmar, and Somalia.[30] Moreover, refugees are not alone in their dangerous journeys. Many migrants, hardly definable as refugees in a conventional sense, are ready to take enormous risks to reach Europe or other developed countries. Whatever the reason for leaving their country, conventional refugees and other categories of migrants may accumulate the same vulnerabilities and share a similar need for protection. The multiple, interlinked motivations that push migrants and refugees to embark on high-risk journeys are reflected in concepts like "the asylum-migration nexus"[31] and mixed-migration flows.[32] This points to the difficulty in distinguishing between refugees and purely "economic" migrants, since causes of forced mobility, such as wars and human rights abuse, are often linked to failed development and poverty. This has led to a reexamination of previous categories that were crucial to the birth and development of refugee studies as a discipline.[33]

It is no surprise, then, that the international asylum discourse has progressively multiplied labels for vulnerable individuals in need of protection, variously called IDPs (internally displaced people), environmental refugees, cultural refugees, gender-based persecuted refugees, and so forth. Some academics have proposed new categories such as "survival migration"[34] and "crisis migration,"[35] which may be more inclusive than previous ones.

As the legal and humanitarian regime concerning asylum was looking for more encompassing definitions and new grounds to provide protection, another category, that of the "forced migrant," has become prominent in the academic debate since the mid-1990s. This has come to include and replace the label "refugee" in the literature. The definition of forced migration, although far from well delimited and clear, mainly refers to all people who leave their homes owing to forces beyond their control. It includes legal categories such as IDPs, environmental refugees, and other less well defined populations of migrants.[36]

However, the shift from refugee studies to forced-migration studies has not corresponded either to a substantial shift in the theoretical development of the field or in the global political agenda. The change has, rather, been a superficial, nominal one. Even today, in the literature and especially in policy documents of humanitarian agencies, it is not rare to encounter the commonsense assumptions that "refugees have no choice but to leave," "forced migration is a reaction to a sudden threat," "political refugees are intrinsically different from economic migrants," and so forth. Even the most recent international policy developments, represented by the Global Compact on Migration[37] and the Global Compact on Refugees (2018),[38] adopt a binary approach (migrants vs. refugees) that does not address the asylum-migration nexus. As a result, in spite of their structural existence and their repeated patterns, refugee movements keep being defined as emergencies, exceptions in migration scenarios.[39]

In sum, although the category of forced migration has its own merits, including that of showing the limits of previous definitions, it does not seem to be a solution in itself, inasmuch as it reproduces a binary distinction between those who can and those who cannot choose. Such clear-cut distinctions have been widely criticized in the past decade by scholars from different disciplines, such as law, anthropology, political science, and sociology.[40] Marta Bivand Erdal and Ceri Oeppen argue, for instance, that although the forced/voluntary dichotomy may serve migration-management purposes, it does not reflect the complex reality of migration decisions.[41] To define a migration flow as forced does not clarify under what circumstances it takes place, or how it is distinguishable—if at all—from other kinds of migration, and to what extent constraints, personal agency and enabling resources interact to produce mobility. Finally, this dichotomy between forced and voluntary migration tends to reproduce limited access to protection rights for some groups, who are deemed to originate from safe areas or not to fit the label.

However, when stating the continuity between forced and voluntary migration and the space for choice in migration dynamics, researchers may face a major ethical dilemma. On the one hand, we are afraid to undermine the system of categories that protect research participants. On the other hand, we feel the need, as Thomas Faist puts it, "to challenge the power of categorization which oppresses the subjects we talk about."[42] The more the distinction between economic migrants and refugees gets blurred; the higher the risk of moral and political claims for international protection losing momentum and cogency. The cynical but not implausible question could then be, if refugees are not fundamentally different from voluntary migrants, why should an international legal system to safeguard them be maintained at all? In the European political arena (and Europe is not an exceptional case), xenophobic declarations are popular, and fears focused on migrant populations orient the political agendas of leading parties. It is therefore understandable that providing scientific foundations for such an argument is a cause of concern for academics, myself among them.

Presenting my work to a diverse audience of students, practitioners, and refugees, I found out how unsettling the statement "economic migrants and refugees are not categories apart" can be. In one occasion, one refugee auditor exclaimed that while I was talking, "people who need protection and have the right to be saved" were dying at sea. Others, mainly practitioners, told me that I should not mix "bogus refugees" with "real ones." The former felt that my argument was questioning refugees' entitlement to be protected and welcomed in Europe; the latter felt that I had perhaps missed the point, and that the people I was talking about had in fact *no* entitlement to international protection. These comments shocked me: Was I saying that my Eritrean informants, my friends, in fact, had no proper right to obtain asylum in Europe? Although I felt that some of my critics' associations of ideas were off-target, their comments made me think of the potential implications of my own argument.

For me, rejecting the dichotomy between forced and voluntary migration means contesting the exclusion and illegalization that inevitably derives from a stereotyped understanding of reality. Instead, the focus on mobility and immobility in their manifold aspects across borders enables the researcher to untangle factors underpinning migration pathways. It allows us to go beyond depersonalized accounts of forced migration, whether humanitarian or security-oriented, and to provide insights into how gender, age, class, cultural, and social background influence not only the possibilities but also the desire to be mobile and the experience of being immobile. Together with scholars such as Faist, Erdal and Oeppen, and Sandro Mezzadra,[43] I believe that the debate on refugees and migration calls for creative solutions to interpret mobility going beyond the categorization of forced and voluntary. There is a need to think out of policy-driven categories, to portray real stories in their complexity, to account for vulnerability as much as for capabilities, aspirations, and desires in migrants' struggles for mobility. These struggles over mobility reflect more or less implicit political contestations about the nature and the fairness of borders, migration regulations, and related distribution of rights.

WHY ERITREA?

Although specific in many regards, Eritrean migration is a typical response to the constraints and opportunities produced by the contemporary asylum regime in its interaction with national migration policies. Its analysis can illuminate the effect of this system on the daily lives of millions of refugees, as well as its consequences on their mobility choices. At the same time, Eritrean pathways respond to a distinctive structure of opportunity. Emigration is severely restrained by the Eritrean government, which grants its citizens passports only after they have done their national service. However, even those who are legally permitted to leave the country often cannot move to their preferred destination. Visas to study, work, or visit

Western countries are extremely hard to obtain for those coming from developing countries, and even more so for those who originate from a refugee-producing country like Eritrea. Western embassies tend to believe that Eritreans applying for temporary visas are unlikely to return home on expiry of their permission of stay. Those who manage to leave Eritrea, with or without authorization, usually end up in Sudan or Ethiopia, with limited possibilities for legal and socioeconomic integration there.

Since resettlement rates are extremely low—less than 1 percent of the refugee population worldwide—and work and study visas are hard to obtain, most Eritreans, like most refugees in the first countries they reach—usually low-income nations—live in encampments with few prospects of long-term solutions. Those who do reach developed countries usually have wider prospects to study, work, and enjoy a decent life—although other forms of deprivation may be present.[44] The repeated migration attempts I document in the book mirror the contradiction between the immobility of substantive rights and the physical mobility required to gain access to them.[45] It is important to note that, although things could quickly change, Eritreans, unlike other nationalities, have high rates of recognition as "legitimate" refugees in Europe. As Erdal and Oeppen point out, it is important also when analyzing forced migration to keep in mind "the anticipation" by migrants "of the particular labelling by immigrant authorities in Europe."[46] This is crucial, inasmuch as it provides them with some prospects of access to legal and social protection once arrived in Europe, unlike those migrants whose asylum applications are typically rejected based on the fact they come from what are deemed "safe areas."[47]

Eritreans were one of the main national groups of the 2015–16 European refugee crisis. UNHCR estimates that the number of Eritrean refugees, asylum seekers, and other categories of concern was over half a million at the end of 2017, making Eritrea the ninth-greatest source of refugees worldwide, with one of the relatively most numerous diasporas in the world.[48] Although statistics on the Eritrean population are largely unreliable and out of date, it is safe to say that there are at least a million and a half Eritreans who live outside their country, out of a total population of fewer than five million.

Aside from its timeliness and statistical significance, the theoretical relevance of this case has primarily to do with the state of chronic emergency that characterizes not only Eritrea but most "refugee-producing countries." In spite of its contemporary momentum, migration from Eritrea is much more than a simple reaction to an individual life threat. Rather, it is a historically developed communal strategy against hardships. As such, it represents a key case to understand how concepts, such as aspirations, imaginaries and transnational moralities, originally elaborated in the study of labor migration can apply to the research on refugee movements.

A History of Migration

Geographic mobility is ancestral history in the Horn of Africa. Different ethnic groups have long moved from one area to the other in search of better pastures for their animals, to find better lands to cultivate, to escape violence, to take control of the resources and the people of other regions. For some ethnic groups, especially pastoralists, systematic and periodic geographic mobility has been a normal part of their social organization and livelihood strategy in facing harsh climatic conditions. However, it was at the end of Italian colonization that Eritreans systematically started traveling across national and international borders.

The history of Eritrea is not a unitary tale of a people on a delimited territory. As revealed by archaeological findings at the ancient Red Sea port of Adulis in the northeast of the country, the Eritrean coast was part of the kingdom of Axum, which flourished from 100 to 800 CE. The Axumites spoke a Semitic language, adopted Christianity, and had a sophisticated political system and trading relationships with India, China, the Black Sea region, and Spain.[49] When the coast was invaded by Arab expansion in the eighth century, the kingdom of Axum was cut off from trade and its decline became inevitable. After the fall of Axum, the region became politically fragmented: people from Sudan and Egypt occupied the coast and the western lowlands, while in the highlands mostly Tigrinya and Amhara local rulers based in different regions competed for power until the nineteenth century.[50]

Although the Eritrean highlands have often in the course of history been a partly independent province, they have historically been linked to the Ethiopian highlands. Alemseged Abbay speaks of a trans-Mereb identity (the river Mereb marked the Eritrean and Ethiopian border in colonial times) founded on precolonial institutions,[51] which would have included the Coptic Church and its monastic culture, the linguistic roots of the Amharic and Tigrinya languages in the Ge'ez script, the land tenure system, and the feudal political order of the several regional kingdoms. The self-designation "Habesha," used both by Tigrinya-speaking Eritreans and the inhabitants of the Ethiopian side of the plateau, such as Tygraians, Amhara, and Oromo, is evidence of this ethnic, cultural, social, and political connection.[52]

Eritrean and Ethiopian Tigrinya speakers and the Amhara (Coptic Christian Amharic speakers), who inhabit the more southern Ethiopian highlands, have historically been the dominant political groups of the area.[53] In Eritrea, lowlanders are usually Muslim nomadic pastoralists (with several exceptions among the Kunamas and the Bilen groups, who are agriculturalists and often non-Coptic Christians). They belong to different ethnic minorities (see "Eritrea at a glance").

The history of Eritrea as one country begins with Italian colonization (1889–1941).[54] Italian occupation lasted for almost fifty years and had a profound impact on the country, especially on the highlands.[55] Many Italians came to settle in the

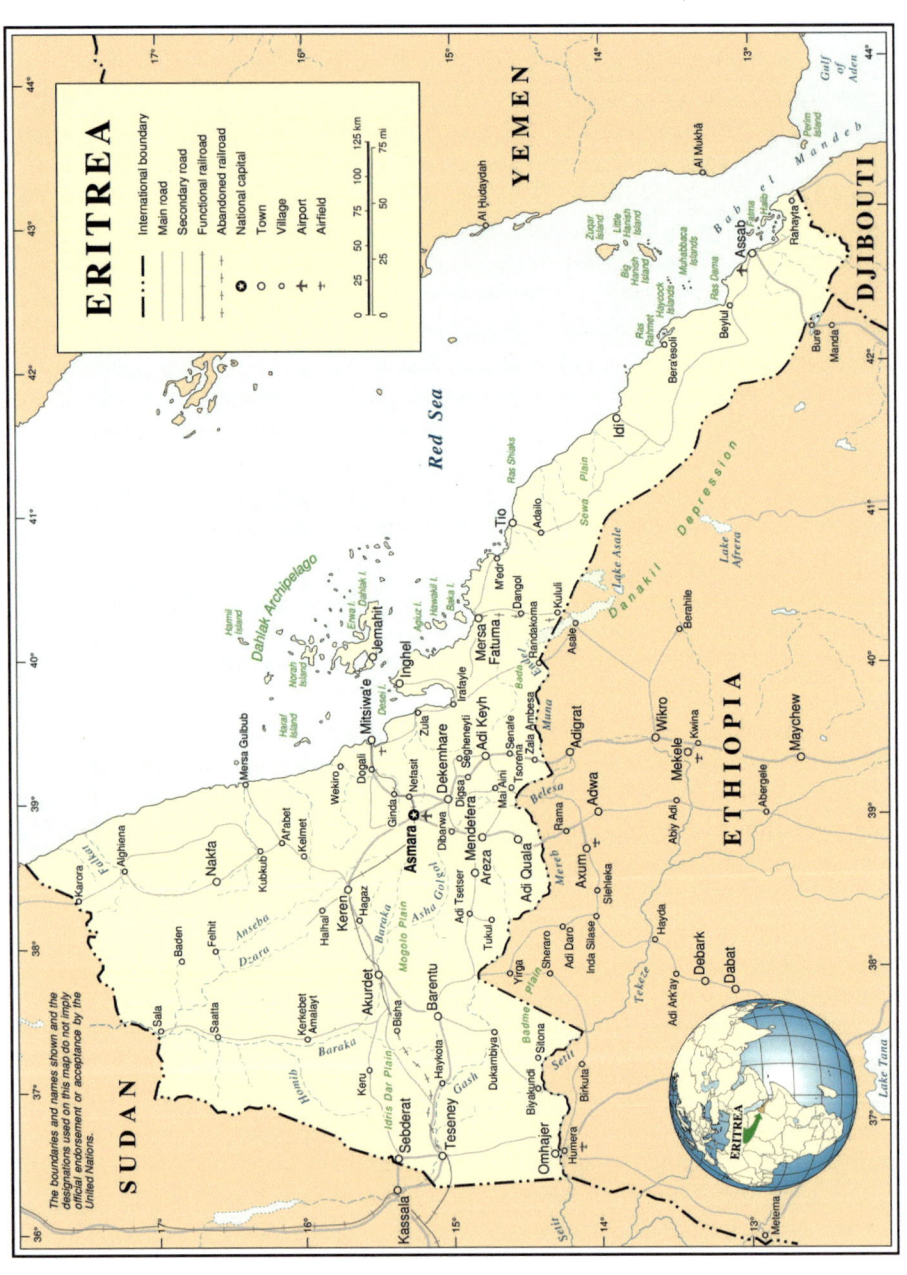

MAP 1. United Nations map of Eritrea

ERITREA AT A GLANCE

Population: The United Nations estimate is five million, but Fusari 2011 suggests 3.2 million, taking into account the emigration rate and decreased fertility since the 1980s. The only available census dates from 1993.

Geographic features: The southern and central regions of Eritrea are dominated by Ethiopian north-south trending highlands, which descend on the east to the coastal desert plain, on the northwest to hilly terrain, and on the southwest to plains.

Climate: Eritrea consists of a hot, dry strip of desert along the Red Sea coast, cooler and wetter central highlands (rain falls mostly between June and September), and semiarid western hills and lowlands.

Capital: Asmara, recently listed as a UNESCO World Heritage site.

Main religions: Muslim (47%), Christian Orthodox (39%), Roman Catholic (5%), Evangelical Protestant (1%), vernacular religions (2%), other Christians (4%). There are groups of Pentecostals, Jehovah's Witnesses and other Christians in the country, but they are not institutionally recognized.

Main ethnic groups: Tigrinya (50%), Tigre (27%), Saho (5%), Afar (5%), Hidareb (4%), Kunama (3%), Bilen (2%), Nara (2%), Rashaida (1%).

These percentages are provided by the Eritrean government (www.eritrea.be/old/ eritrea-people.htm).

Languages: Tigrinya and Tigre are the main spoken languages in the country. Like Amharic (the main spoken language in Ethiopia), they derive from ancient Ge'ez. Arabic and English are also widely spoken. Ethnic minority languages are also studied in school and widely spoken.

Essential timeline:

- 1000 BCE: Semitic peoples from the South Arabian kingdom of Saba' (Sheba) migrate across the Red Sea, absorbing the Cushitic inhabitants of the Eritrean coast and adjacent highlands.
- 100 to 800 CE: Emergence and fall of the Axum empire, a strong trading and political power that developed around the port of Adulis. Christianity becomes the area's main religion around 300 CE.
- 9th–19th centuries: Arabs invade the coast. Solomonic dynasties rule in the Ethiopian highlands, with Eritrea the northern province of their kingdom. The western lowlands are controlled by Sudanese empires and the eastern lowlands mostly by Afar rulers. From the 16th to 19th centuries, the coastline around Massawa was part of the Ottoman empire.
- 1869–1944: Italian colonization. The Genoa-based Rubattino shipping company buys the bay of Assab from the local Afar sultan and Italians progressively expand their control as far as the Mereb River.
- 1941–52: After Italian defeat in World War II, Eritrea becomes a British protectorate.
- 1952–62: Ethiopia and Eritrea are federated but maintain a degree of political and administrative independence.

- 1961–62: Following forcible annexation of Eritrea to Ethiopia under the emperor Haile Selassie, a liberation struggle starts in the lowlands.
- 1974: Haile Selassie is overthrown in Ethiopia by Menghistu Haile Mariam, who establishes the Derg regime.
- 1983: Conflict between the Eritrean Liberation Front (ELF) and the Eritrean People Liberation Front (EPLF). The EPLF defeats the ELF and becomes the only militant Eritrean front.
- 1991: De facto independence. EPLF and TPLF (the Ethiopian Tigray People Liberation Front) enters Addis Abba and overthrows Menghistu's government. The EPLF becomes the Party for Freedom, Democracy and Justice (PFDJ), which has ruled Ethiopia since then.
- 1998–2000: Conflict with Ethiopia, allegedly for disagreement on border demarcation around the village of Badme.
- 2000: The Algiers agreement. A period of "no peace, no war" between the two countries begins. Diplomatic and trade relations are blocked.
- 2018: Peace process between Ethiopia and Eritrea. Ethiopia recognizes that Badme belongs to Eritrea, and the newly established Ethiopian prime minister, Abyi Ahmed, pays the first Ethiopian diplomatic visit to Eritrea in eighteen years.

country, where they were given land confiscated from the local population; cities, roads, and other infrastructure were built and several industries were established around the region. The colonial rulers imposed a hierarchical system that systematically limited the rights of the indigenous population. Under racial laws passed in 1935, indigenous Eritreans were allowed to study only up to fourth grade. At the same time, new modes of production, the introduction of modern technology in agriculture, and the construction of urban centers deeply influenced the traditional social structure of Eritrean society. Local imaginaries, aesthetic tastes, and cultural models were also significantly shaped in those years, with long-standing implications for contemporary politics, Eritrean people's horizons of meaning, and migration pathways.[56]

In 1941, Eritrea then became a British protectorate. The British dismantled industries and infrastructure such as the Asmara-Massawa Cableway, built by the Italians, as war compensation. They also lifted the ban on higher education for indigenes and allowed the growth of a free press and political parties. This was a period of lively political activism, from which the protagonists and ideas of the later independent Eritrea sprang.[57]

Starting in the 1950s, many Eritreans who had been working for Italians moved to Addis Ababa. Others, mostly female domestic workers, followed their employers back to Italy. Still others, mostly Muslims, left for the Arab world (mainly

Sudan, Egypt, and Gulf countries) to work and pursue further education.[58] Then, with the beginning of the thirty-year-long war against Ethiopian rule, Eritrean international migration skyrocketed.

In 1952, Eritrea was then federated to Ethiopia, but kept most of its political, administrative, and judicial autonomy. In 1961, however, the emperor of Ethiopia dissolved the Eritrean parliament and unilaterally annexed Eritrea. Hamid Idris Awate, a former *ascaro* (indigenous soldier in the Italian army), fired the first shot against Ethiopian occupation in the western lowlands on September 1, 1961, launching the country's long independence struggle.

The seeds of crisis: the independence struggle and "no peace–no war"

The Eritrean independence struggle has complicated historical roots in ethnic conflicts, regional instability, and political claims, which have been thoroughly investigated by several historians.[59] In fifty years of Italian colonization, Eritreans had developed a separate political identity from their Ethiopian cousins. Moreover, Muslims, traditionally marginalized by Christian highlanders, interpreted the annexation to Christian Orthodox Ethiopian rule as a new attempt to subordinate them. It was mostly owing to them that the independence struggle started. The Eritrean Liberation Front (ELF), initially constituted by Muslim lowlanders, began the rebellion in the western plains, triggering retaliation by the imperial army against civilians in those areas.[60] This led thousands to cross the border with Sudan in search of refuge.[61] In 1974, the Derg, a military regime led by Menghistu Haile Mariam, overthrew the Ethiopian emperor and the war spread to the highlands and the cities. Thousands were killed and more were displaced throughout Africa, the Middle East, Europe and the United States, creating the bulk of the numerous, worldwide population of Eritrean origin that was a crucial ally for the liberation fronts in the war and for the government subsequently.[62] In that period, moreover, the original liberation front—the ELF (the Eritrea Liberation Front)—and a newly emerged Eritrean People Liberation front (EPLF) came into conflict (1982), which resulted in further displacement.

In 1991, the military regime in Ethiopia was defeated by an alliance of Ethiopian and Eritrean liberation fronts and Eritrea gained its de facto independence under the rule of the EPLF. Since then EPLF cadres have ruled the country through the PFDJ (People's Front for Democracy and Justice) party. Initially enjoying widespread support among the population and the Eritrean diaspora, this regime was praised by the international community for its progressive agenda on social and economic development and gender equality. Some Eritreans who had fled decided to return home, and the fragile economy of the country seemed to benefit from government intervention and foreign investment.

This illusion lasted only until 1998, when a new conflict broke out with Ethiopia. Allegedly, the war was triggered by an issue of border demarcation around the small town of Badme, but the reasons behind it are far more complicated and range from the control over the ports to deep-rooted ambitions in regional politics.[63] Around a hundred thousand Eritrean and Ethiopian soldiers died, and hundreds of thousands of people were displaced. At least seventy thousand Eritreans were expelled from Ethiopia in 1998, and thousands of Ethiopians were forcibly returned from Eritrea.

The conflict officially ended in 2000, when the two countries agreed to a ceasefire. The UN Eritrea–Ethiopia Boundary Commission (EEBC) ruled that Eritrea had a legitimate claim to Badme, and that Ethiopia should withdraw its troops from the town, but Ethiopia never respected this decision. Although the war had ended, hostilities continued. Diplomatic and trade relationships ceased, with negative consequences for both countries. Ethiopia lost cheap access to the sea, and Eritrea lost its natural trading partner. Moreover, Eritrea has progressively become isolated on the international scene, owing partly to bad relations with all its neighbors and partly to a deep-rooted mistrust of the international community.[64]

Eritrea's economic and political efforts at self-reliance since its independence have reflected a wary anti-colonialist mentality, reinforced by the fact that whereas Ethiopia's noncompliance with the UN recommendation over the border issue was not followed by international measures, Eritrea has been a target of UN sanctions since 2008. Although these sanctions have mainly been an embargo of weapons and freezing the financial assets of the Eritrean leadership, these measures arguably had a widespread negative effect on the Eritrean economy, discouraging investors, increasing the diplomatic isolation of the country, and thus indirectly worsening the living conditions of the population.

Twenty years of cold war and isolation have recently been interrupted by a drastic change in regional politics. In July 2018, following a shift of power in the Ethiopian leadership, the newly appointed Ethiopian prime minister Abyi Ahmed withdrew Ethiopian troops from Badme. This has led to the peace agreement between the two countries and the reopening of the border between them. Since then, families who had been separated for decades have able to meet again, and trade and diplomatic relations have resumed, decreasing the cost of living and leading to renewed hope among Eritreans at home, as well as fear among those who sought asylum in Ethiopia, who wonder about their safety. The short- and long-term implications of this radical change are still hard to forecast.

Whether it is simply revealing its true nature, as some believe, or reacting to the constant threat from Eritrea's more populous and powerful Ethiopian neighbor, the repressive attitude of the PFDJ has remained unchanged since 1998. Eritrea has not had free elections since its independence, the Constitution has never been ratified, and all of the PFDJ's political opponents have been eliminated as supporters of the Ethiopian enemy.[65] There is no free press, and religious and cultural liberties have been severely curtailed. Parallel to this political atmosphere, development efforts have mostly fallen on the shoulders of young citizens, who are obliged to work for years in different sectors of public interest—education, health service, defense—with little or no pay. This is the background of the stories I tell in this book.

A MOBILE ETHNOGRAPHY:
THE ERITREA-EUROPE CORRIDOR

As a twenty-three-year-old student at University of Siena, I met Alazar, an Eritrean who had been rescued from sea in November 2008, at a temporary asylum center in the nearby tourist town of Follonica on the Tuscan coast. My classmates and I visited the center twice a week for three months, and as a result of the friendship that developed between us, the stories of Alazar and the other young Eritreans I met in the center became part of my life.

When I began researching Eritrean migration in 2012, Alazar became my point of reference for the community of refugees living in Rome, who wanted to move on. In June–December that year, living in squats typical of those inhabited by many Eritreans, I explored the contradictions of their daily lives and also paid regular visits to other informants I had come to know in Genoa and Milan. Most of my research subjects in Italy were Christian Tigrinya men (some of them Catholics, others Orthodox) in their late twenties, who had come to Europe by crossing the Mediterranean.

At the beginning of 2013, to explore the conditions underpinning my informants' decision to leave home, I asked them for contacts among their families in Eritrea. For three months, I subsequently shared the everyday life of a family in Asmara, hanging out with young men and women I met there and visiting the families of other informants in the Eritrean capital, as well as in rural areas.

As many of the young people I encountered in Eritrea wanted to escape to Ethiopia, I continued my fieldwork there from September 2013 to March 2014. I was familiar with the country, since I had lived there for four months in 2011, and I already had some local contacts among local humanitarian workers, Italian diplomatic officers, Eritrean families, and relatives of my friends in Italy. Through these already established and newly emerging relationships, I conducted ethnographic research in refugee camps in Tigray (northern Ethiopia) and lived with a young Eritrean doctor, Violetta, in a neighborhood of Addis Ababa with a high concentration of Eritrean refugees. It happened to be the period of the year when most of our neighbors were planning their departure via Khartoum to Libya.

Khartoum then became the last site of my fieldwork (March–April 2014). There I lived with Maria, a young Eritrean and her eight-year-old child, Anna, in a shared house with four other Eritrean refugee families. While hanging out with her refugee friends from Asmara, I came in touch with a middleman facilitating illicit border crossings through the Sahara and his colleagues. This enabled me to explore the hidden world of smugglers from an inside perspective. Being in

MAP OF FIELDWORK LOCATIONS (2012-2014)

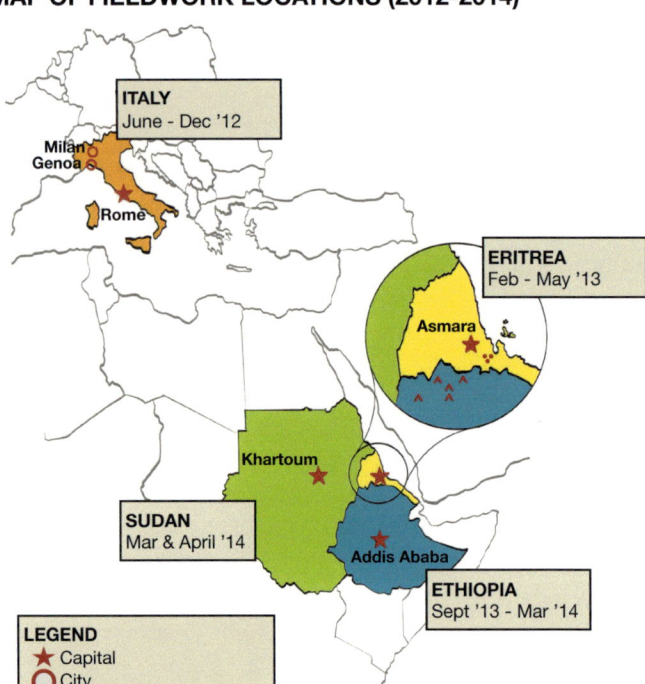

MAP 2. Fieldwork locations (Designed by Sarah Anschütz)

Khartoum also allowed me to catch up with other informants whom I had met in Eritrea and Ethiopia. The main locations where I conducted my research are shown in map 2.

Multi-sited ethnography seemed to me an obvious choice to investigate mobility practices and related transnational societal spaces.[66] My mobility was the result of a cumulative, open-ended research design—one that was continuously constructed with my informants, depending on contingent field circumstances. I progressively extended my fieldwork boundaries to the main nodes of the migration corridor connecting Eritrea with Europe. I could not include Libya owing both to time and energy constraints and to the extremely unsafe conditions there in the period in which the research took place. This corridor connecting Italy with Sudan, Ethiopia, and Eritrea can be seen not only as a geographic route but also as an imaginative pathway for families, friends, and co-nationals living in different locations, who exchange expectations, aspirations, desires, and ideas using media, internet, and mobile communication.[67] The observation sites I chose along the way were not only key locations to explore migration, but also fields of social relationships that I navigated along with young refugees and their families and friends. The observation of specific sites was as important as grasping the interactions between them, and within them, at different but interdependent points of the migration corridor.[68] Sharing my informants' everyday life in their home country as well as in exile allowed me to appreciate the role of interpersonal micro-dynamics—such as family ties, peer pressure, and social expectations—in producing and reproducing refugees' movements.

In my research, multi-sited ethnography did not mean only conducting participant observation in different countries and at different sites within the same country, but also simultaneously engaging with diverse social and ethnic networks in different sites within the same country. In Eritrea, I did research in several towns and cities; in Ethiopia, I resided in Addis Ababa and visited the camps of Tigray; in Sudan, I lived in Khartoum; in Italy, I conducted participant observation in Rome, Milan, and Genoa. This plurality of sites included an even larger variety of informants, gatekeepers, and subjects of research. Several networks of religious, ethnic, geographic, and family affiliations gave me access to different perspectives and diverse experiences of living in the same place and connected me with other cultural environments, which I would have not been able to explore if I had only stuck to one gatekeeper or a "clique." Although most of my observations pertain to Tigrinya Eritreans, the dominant and most numerous ethnic group in Eritrea, the multiplicity of sites and networks I navigated allowed me to meet Eritreans from minority backgrounds (Saho and Kunamas, for instance) and from rural areas. Moreover, during my research I would often hang out with locals—Sudanese in Khartoum, Ethiopians in Addis Ababa. The interactions that I involuntarily created between locals and refugees worked as sorts of experiments—I put in touch two worlds that rarely interface. This enabled me to observe how trust and distrust among locals and refugees play out in real encounters and how conflictual these relationships can be.

The above considerations show that my presence in the field was far from being a neutral one. My relationships with informants were characterized by reciprocal emotional engagement, prolonged involvement in each other's lives well after the formal end of the research—sometimes, even despite me. Friendship, care, unparalleled expectations, love, and disappointment were all ingredients of my fieldwork in ways that I could not anticipate at its outset. This allowed me to gain insights that would have been hard to attain otherwise, but that also exposed me to ethical dilemmas. Throughout the book, I mention these aspects when they are relevant for the interpretation of my observations, but I have restricted discussion of the main methodological and ethical challenges of my fieldwork to the Appendix.

Although I did not "follow people" in a literal sense, the very fact that I was moving within the same geographic and imaginative space as my informants enabled me to come across the same individuals at different stages of their migration process. For example, in Ethiopia, I encountered families whom I had previously

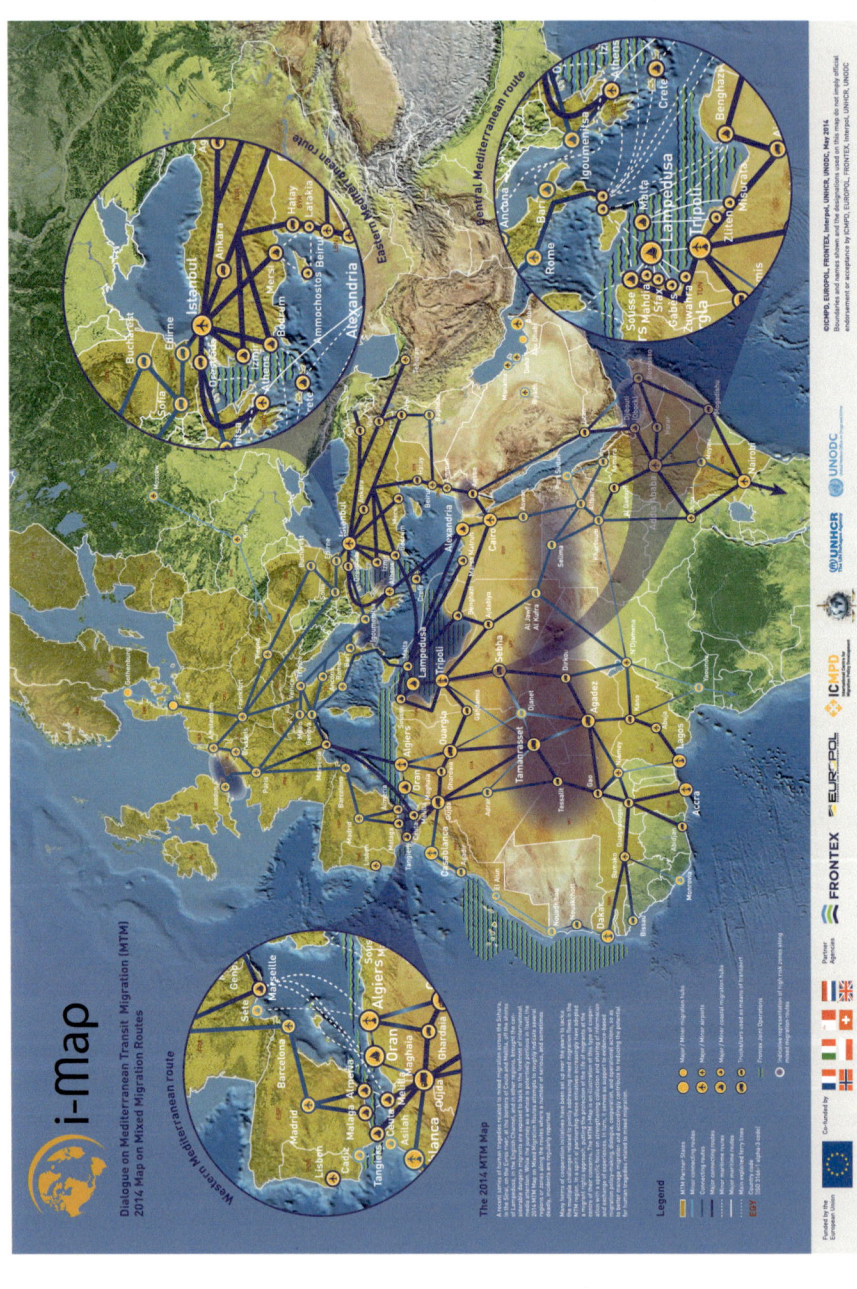

MAP 3. Migration trajectories (IMAP 2014)

met in Eritrea; likewise in Sudan and in Italy. Moreover, even after the end of my fieldwork, my informants and I have kept in touch, and many of them contacted me when they reached Italy to ask for help or simply to let me know that they had arrived in Europe safely. Sometimes they preceded me and sometimes I preceded them in the corridor, but my informants and I were following the same steps of the journey. Following a corridor rather than a group of people enables a researcher to see who, at each step, can move on and who has to wait or simply stay. This allows one to account not only for differentials in capabilities (based on access to legal migration, economic resources, and social networks), but also for their will to do so or not, in the presence of incredible risks. Within the current debate about mobility and immobility, this is a crucial option for advancing the state of the art on these underinvestigated issues.[69]

The Eritrea-Ethiopia-Sudan-Libya-Italy corridor's existence should not be considered permanent, but fluctuating on the basis of policy changes, border control practices, and geopolitical arrangements in the countries of transit, origin, and destination.[70] Moreover, this corridor is only one of the many possible pathways taken by Eritreans to find a new home. The route through Egypt to Israel, for example, used to be extremely popular until 2013. It is estimated that close to forty thousand Eritreans reached Israel by way of Egypt's Sinai Peninsula between 2006 and 2012. Then, in 2012, Israel implemented a series of border controls and progressively restrictive measures on illicit migration and resident asylum seekers that practically stopped arrivals.[71] Other Eritreans moved on to other less predictable destinations, such as Uganda, Angola, and South Sudan (until civil war broke out there in December 2013). Still others have reached countries in the Middle East, such as Dubai, Saudi Arabia, and Qatar, which have been historic destinations of the diaspora since the 1960s.[72] The fact that I encountered only a few Muslims during my research may also reflect the historic trend of Muslim Eritrean minorities' migrating to the Middle East rather than to Europe. It is important to take these considerations into account so as not to generalize about the migration practices of an extremely diverse population of migrants from Eritrea.

At this point, it is important to advance a few epistemological considerations that have oriented the analysis of my data. In interpreting my observations and my informants' narratives, I considered what Frank Salamone, following Georges Condominas,[73] calls the *preterrain,* that is to say, the preexisting structural relationships that underlie, and possibly shape, research settings and interactions. For Salamone's study in Nigeria, the preterrain consisted of colonial-related inequalities in power distribution. In my case study, not only postcolonial relationships, but also the social dynamics produced by the international asylum regime had to be taken into account. Doing research with asylum seekers and refugees, in particular, has meant entering into a shifting constellation of roles where refugees, framed (or framing themselves) as victims, right holders, and resource recipients, interact with border guards, asylum practitioners, and resource providers.[74] In this game I could often be identified with the latter group. This was especially—but by no means exclusively—the case in highly controlled research settings such as refugee camps, where I was doing on-the-spot interviews with informants I had just met, with whom I had not been able to build reciprocal trust.

Attention to structural circumstances and power dynamics of the field have informed not only the analysis of my data, but also the way I reached out to my informants in the field. I have systematically tried to navigate the informal networks of my Eritrean informants to meet other informants and access the field, although several choices have been constrained by circumstances beyond my control. Although I also interviewed humanitarian workers, diplomatic and government officers, and local NGO staff, I rarely relied on them for access to the field or to introduce me to refugees and locals. This has facilitated a closer, less institutional relationship with many of my informants and has enabled me to observe refugees' attitudes both "onstage" and off.[75]

This book gradually moves from the alleys and sitting rooms inhabited by Eritreans in their home country via Ethiopian tent camps and lively neighborhoods in Addis Ababa and Khartoum to the crowded squats some of them occupy in Rome. From Eritrea, through Ethiopia, Sudan, and Italy, the first three chapters geographically follow my informants' main pathways to reconstruct the bundle of desires, fears, and pressures that push them across borders in spite of mounting risks.

Chapter 1 investigates the aspirations of young men and women trapped in the hardships of national service in contemporary Eritrea. Drawing on ethnographic research in urban and rural areas, the chapter illustrates how, in a context of chronic crisis, emigration has become normalized even in its most dangerous and tragic aspects. Many young Eritreans and their families tend to perceive migration at all cost as the only alternative to a life "without a future." While investigating the daily struggle of young men and women to escape social, generational, and geographic immobility, this chapter also accounts for the importance of aspirations and imaginaries in young Eritreans' desire to move elsewhere. By elaborating on the concept of cosmologies of destinations, this chapter describes widespread hierarchies of preferred destinations ordered along the perceived possibility of achieving freedom, stability, and self-realization there.

Based on participant observation in Ethiopian camps, Addis Ababa and Khartoum, chapter 2 illustrates why most Eritrean refugees are determined to move onward. Eritreans face several challenges in their first countries of asylum, ranging from their limited freedom of mobility outside camps to the lack of opportunities in local labor markets. However, their desire to move on does not only emerge from this disadvantaged socioeconomic context. Collectively shared and transnationally diffused sets of memories, norms, and images also define Ethiopia and Sudan as undesirable destinations. While describing how the desire for

migration is continually reproduced in camps and shared accommodations in cities, the chapter accounts for the matrix of socioeconomic and cultural conditions
that stratify possibilities and aspirations for geographic mobility. Most refugees
were stuck in spite of their will to move on, and some chose to stay put, awaiting
eventual return to Eritrea.

Chapter 3 investigates the reasons why many Eritrean refugees try to move
north from Italy. Drawing on ethnographic fieldwork with refugees in Rome,
Milan, and Genoa, as well as with their families in Eritrea, this chapter shows the
role of family expectations, peer pressure, and individual aspirations in Eritreans'
repeated attempts to seek asylum in northern European countries in spite of policy
obstacles. Preexisting aspirations to further mobility are reinforced and kept alive
for Eritreans living in buildings illicitly occupied in Rome in a context of substantive deprivation and marginality. It is argued that refugees' decision making has to
be studied in a larger transnational frame, which includes families back home, as
well as relatives and friends in northern Europe.

Chapter 4 explores the roles, social mechanisms, and emic moralities involved
in illicit border crossings, perceived by the main protagonists as legitimate ways
to attain freedom. Building on refugees' narratives and on ethnographic research
with two smugglers in Ethiopia and in Sudan, the chapter describes the complex
world of the professionals of illicit migration and the moral and social embeddedness of their business in these refugees' communities. The chapter then goes on
to illustrate the complex of affection, economic interest, and desire for mobility
among transnational refugee couples. Partly emerging from the reproduction of
traditional marital arrangements and partly from business opportunities, transnational marriages are mostly perceived as legitimate mechanisms to help compatriots pursue further mobility.

Chapter 5 revisits migrants' complex trajectories and illustrates how they, like
gamblers, become at each stage more likely to bet their resources and lives in
onward migration. It brings together the findings and observations made in the
previous chapters to develop an analytical framework of Eritrean refugees' mobility. Borrowing the concept of entrapment from gambling studies, this chapter
shows that in Eritreans' migratory decisions, as a sequential process, each stage is
marked by a cumulative set of psychological and social pressures to make a further
move, even at the price of risking everything yet again. In fact, every stage makes
interrupting the journey more difficult for both structural and symbolic reasons.
The concept of entrapment not only helps us understand what immobility means
from a cognitive point of view, but contributes to the analysis of high-risk stepwise migration. This analytical framework promises to feed into a more refined
understanding of the motivations of high-risk migrants, which have, until now,
been studied without the sequential nature of their movements being considered.

In the Conclusion, after summarizing the main findings of my case study, I
outline its implications for the general debate on refugee studies. I argue that the

concept of cosmologies of destinations is a promising tool for analyzing underinvestigated aspects of migration dynamics from areas of protracted crisis. Then I reconnect the notion of cosmologies of destinations with the other main theoretical contributions of my ethnography to the literature. In particular, I focus on the following major issues: the importance of moral, imaginative, and social aspects in the analysis of refugee movements; the dialectic relation between mobility and immobility and its manifold meanings; the normative aspect of unauthorized migration, in particular the unwritten moralities that underpin it; and the idea of entrapment and the cumulative aspect of migrants' high-risk journeys.

The methodological Appendix revisits the main challenges of the research, reflecting on the difficulties in gaining access to refugees and their living environments, and in building mutual trust, as well as managing the expectations emerging from complex and unbalanced fieldwork relationships. Drawing from field experiences, the Appendix elaborates on the researcher's positionality in terms of gender, age, and sexuality, narrating significant episodes of conducting covert research in an illiberal political environment, avoiding authorities' scrutiny in refugee camps, and deconstructing refugees' self-representations. Finally, it discusses ethical issues concerning the researcher's accountability to his/her informants, as well as the moral and political role of research in the larger debate on asylum.

When Migration Becomes the Norm

Ingredients of an Ordinary Crisis

Refugee flows do not always originate in areas of violent crisis. They are some-times, indeed frequently, rooted in countries marked by decades of social, politi-cal, and economic deprivation. In these contexts, migration is rarely a traumatic novelty, but rather a multigenerational experience and an everyday reality. Geo-graphic mobility is the norm, not only because it is recurrent in people's lives, but also because it assumes a crucial symbolic, moral, and socioeconomic role in the organization of society. Eritrea is one of these cases.

The study of voluntary migration has usually documented the socioeco-nomic and cultural transformation produced by long-term migration under the heading of "culture of migration." However, scholars have rarely considered how migration can become a normalized experience even in areas from which refugees originate. By "normalized," I do not mean to say that it is not tragic or problematic. Instead, I want to point to the abilities of individuals, groups, and communities living in chronic crisis to reorganize their living by imagining and pursuing a possibility of life elsewhere. Following Henrik Vigh's definition of "crisis as a context"—that is to say "a terrain of action and meaning rather than an aberration,"[1] I describe the process of routinization of suffering, hardships, and risks among my informants. At the same time, I account for their ongoing efforts to make sense of their everyday lives by imagining the outside world as a place of hope and achievements.

In contexts such as the Eritrean one, marked by a stagnant economy, political stasis, it is crucial not only to account for the everyday violence experienced by different individuals in the past and in the present, but also for their dreams, desires, and aspirations for the future. Since the lack of positive motivations to leave the homeland has been considered one of the defining features of refugees compared with voluntary migrants, the cultural and moral mechanisms underpinning their migration have typically been neglected by scholars. However, these aspects, I argue, are crucial for understanding mobility from areas of protracted crisis. Drawing from my ethnographic fieldwork in Eritrea, this chapter shows how conventional push factors are tangled with social, moral, and symbolic features that encourage and direct emigration. Here I develop the idea of cosmologies of destinations, not only as socially shared geographic imaginaries, but also as a set of moral obligations and expectations that tie migrants to their immobile kinship circles.

A LAND OF MARTYRS AND MIGRANTS

When I visited Eritrea in 2013, the visual references to war were still omnipresent in the landscape. Rusty old tanks lay overturned on the side of the road or in the middle of dry, stony fields. The massive deforestation carried out in the 1980s has left hills naked, with a few sporadic trees. People in the countryside still were holding old Kalashnikovs to shoot hyenas or to fire a few shots during marriage celebrations. As a reminder of the defeat of the *Derg* and the magnitude of the struggle, old Ethiopian warplanes were parked in the middle of Asmara's public gardens.

Thirty years of war have had a huge impact on the country and its inhabitants. Not only has Eritrea arguably never fully recovered, but its people still painfully feel their private losses. All the families I met during my fieldwork had to face the death of at least one beloved family member during the struggle, as well as the absence abroad of many others. "In every Eritrean family, there has been at least one martyr and one migrant," Eritreans told me whenever I asked if they had relatives elsewhere in the world. The Eritrean family who welcomed me for over two months in Asmara was no exception.

When I decided to move to Eritrea after having conducted research in Italy for several months, I asked to my Eritrean friends and informants if they could give me contacts among their families or friends there. Some of them were reluctant to do so,[2] but others did not hesitate to help me. Twenty-eight-year-old Gabriel was incredulous—likely thinking *why does this girl want to go to a place from which I did my best to escape?*—but suggested that I could be his family's guest in Asmara. Gabriel had been my guide for a few months in Porta Venezia, the neighborhood historically inhabited by Eritreans in Milan. When Gabriel phoned Ester, his aunt in Eritrea from a call center in Porta Venezia, she seemed initially worried to have a stranger in her place, but I was ultimately welcomed.

FIGURE 1. Mixed traffic in Asmara (photo by the author, 2013)

FIGURE 2. Road in Asmara (photo by the author, 2013)

Asmara is not one of the chaotic capitals typical of developing countries today. It has around three-quarters of a million inhabitants. Cars are not very numerous and streets are not very noisy. Old red buses run alongside well-dressed people walking along the tidy central avenue of the city center—Godena Harnet (or Freedom Avenue)—and drink *macchiato* in the famous cafés around the majestic cathedral built during Italian colonization. Little of the everyday hardship of the country and its people can be guessed at first sight. Moving to the peripheries of the city where Ester's house was located, however, those material and inner hardships were more evident. As in many other neighborhoods, our district of Petrosia was experiencing continuous power cuts and water shortages. Early in the morning, a long queue of women wrapped in their *nezelas* (traditional cotton shawls) and young boys and girls would stand with big bright blue barrels and rusty metal ones waiting for the municipal water truck.

Five residents occupied the house where I spent almost three months: Ester, the fifty-year-old head of the family; her late husband's father, Baba; her younger sister, Saba; her twenty-four-year-old daughter, Salam; and Lwam, Gabriel's sister, who had come to Asmara to do the compulsory military training of Ministry of Agriculture employees. My everyday life in Asmara was divided between the time I spent at home chatting with Baba, Saba, and Ester, and home visits to other informants' families. The rest of day I hung out with Salam, Lwam, their friends, and other young Eritreans. Getting to know them and their stories, I soon realized the extent of the impact of war and displacement on their intimate family history.

Ester had moved to Ethiopia to attend school as a teenager, but after twenty years there, she, her husband, their three kids, and the grandfather were forcibly returned to Eritrea at the start of the 1998–2000 war.[3] Most of Ester's siblings had also been migrants. Her older brother had gone to Saudi Arabia in the 1980s; Saba had worked in the Gulf for ten years before returning in the late 1990s to take care of Ester and her displaced family. Ester's older sister had migrated to Ethiopia and from there to Germany, where she still lived with her children. Some among Ester's siblings had instead remained to fight for national independence. "We were so hungry and our bare feet were bleeding, but we had to walk across the mountain to escape our enemies!" Candle, Ester's sister, and ex-*tegadelit* (female partisan), told us once during a visit. Their eldest brother had died in the war.

Displacement due to war characterized not only the family's past—it was an ordinary aspect of my hosts' present as well. Ester's son had escaped a few years before to Angola. Her nephew, my friend Gabriel, was already in Milan. Salam and Lwam were constantly planning their departures. This was common among the families I met in Asmara and in villages. Their sons aged twenty and older were often outside the country.

The ghost of war was an omnipresent feature of my informants' daily lives. The whole population is often required to engage in periodic military training, like the course Lwam was doing during my stay in the country. Rifles had been distributed to all able-bodied citizens a month before I arrived. Elderly people were also required to take up arms again, triggering a sense of endless war, lack of prospects, and continuous repetition of past struggles. "They gave me a rifle at my age! Can you imagine?" a sixty-five-year-old refugee in Addis Ababa told me. "I was in the independence struggle in the 1970s, and now I have to carry a rifle again. There is no peace in our country."

The identity of Eritreans as a people and as a nation is built around war and displacement.[4] Martyrs and migrants are national symbols, publicly celebrated in memorial days, popular songs, and governmental pronouncements. In propaganda, Eritrea as a nation was made possible through the sacrifices of the Eritrean freedom fighters who gave their lives for independence—the martyrs—and the sacrifices of Eritreans in diaspora who selflessly supported the struggle from afar.[5]

But not all migrants are good ones in the public narrative. Whereas the government celebrates previous generations of refugees as national heroes, current refugees have generally been defined by national media, the president and his supporters, as "economic migrants," "traitors," and "deserters." From the perspective of the regime, most refugees nowadays are evading their duty to serve the nation (i.e., do national service), and if caught, they are severely punished as traitors.[6] Fugitives picked up by the army may be jailed, sent to a training center, or even executed, much depending on whether one is a civilian, student, or soldier.[7] There can also be consequences for the families, who often have to pay a very high fine for every child who leaves the country.[8]

Not everyone who left did so without permission, but at the time of my research, exit from Eritrea was mostly achievable through irregular means. Leaving the country illegally was a political act, "voting with one's feet" against the policies of the government and evading one's duty to defend the homeland. Although people might not have migrated because they were political opponents of the regime, the very reason of having escaped made them such. Moreover, crossing the border into Ethiopia and seeking asylum there amounted to siding with the nation's historical enemy. Returning to Eritrea was and still is extremely unsafe for all of them.

This is why the current exodus is publicly sanctioned and references to it are largely absent from public space and popular culture in spite of its magnitude and relevance. In past many famous songs, such as "Zemen"—"time," in Tigrinya—by the widely celebrated singer Yemanie Baria, evoked the experience of exile and migration, but today's songs rarely address these issues, unless they are released by musicians who already live abroad. The same goes for novels, movies, and plays.[9]

In the Eritrean "culture of migration," the regime ambivalently promotes migration and, at the same time, forbids it.[10] Emigration is pervasive and systematic, as in other regions of intense out-migration, but the professionals who facilitated it are hidden. The migration industry and desire for mobility, which in other contexts are manifest and widely marketed, remain underground in Eritrea. Most of my informants in Eritrea, especially the young ones, knew the escape routes, how much money was needed, and sometimes the names of the smugglers, but this information remained highly confidential.

SACRIFICE AND OPPORTUNITY: THE TWO FACES OF MIGRATION

In the ambivalent symbolic, social, and economic organization of Eritrean society, migration is both a sacrifice and an opportunity. The two faces of migration, are manifest in both the external and domestic landscape of Eritrea. Desirable houses in well-to-do areas of Asmara like Tiravolo and Indabonda are known to belong to wealthy Eritreans who have been living abroad since the 1970s. Other residential areas, built in the past twenty years are called Endo German (Germans' houses) and Enda America (Americans' houses), referring to the country of residence of the Eritrean owners. In Massawa, a popular beach holiday destination for returnees, imposing villas, originally built by Italian colonialists, lie deserted for most of the year except for the black crows cawing loudly on the rooftops, until their owners come back for the summer break. Even in villages, *hudmos*—traditional huts made of stones—stand alongside more modern-looking constructions owned by the families of those who have emigrated. The village of Barur, which I visited in May 2013, is an example of how migration abroad has changed the traditional landscape of some rural areas.

Located thirty kilometers away from Asmara, more than 2,500 meters above sea level, Barur has traditionally survived on subsistence farming. In the past decade, many inhabitants of the village have migrated to Israel. Since then, families known by other villagers to be *mesakin*—unfortunate and poor—have been able to build houses, indicating their new social status. A woman from the village noted, for example, "There was a family in the village that had nothing, absolutely nothing. Two twins were even brought up by the nuns because they could not feed them. Then the eldest son was able to migrate to Israel. Now they have built a house that is worth at least two million nakfa [about 33,000 euros, or U.S.$37,000]!"[11]

While walking on the streets of Barur, the distinction between those families who had members abroad and those who did not was evident. The former had houses with corrugated iron roofs and whitewashed cinder block walls; the latter had traditional stone houses with thatched roofs. The cinder block houses were looked upon as a demonstration of wealth and success due to emigration and were objects of desire for neighbors and relatives.[12] The subtext of this landscape of "remittance architecture" is, however, deeply ambivalent.[13] The newly built houses not only indicate success, relative wealth, and ongoing transnational connections between migrants and their families, but also absence and family fragmentation.[14]

Photographs in the houses also told an ambivalent tale: the celebration of the migrant and the mourning of his/her absence. The sitting rooms of the Eritreans families I visited were a mosaic of colorful religious images, certificates of military distinction, and family pictures. Often many of those portrayed there had left the country.[15] The triumphant pictures of the young graduate son with his black mortarboard and new diploma before emigrating would be side by side with framed official acknowledgements of those who died during or bravely participated in the independence struggle. Jesus Christ, the Virgin Mary, or St. Michael with his sword unsheathed against the devil would surround the images of the absent ones, watching over them. These decorations certainly tell intimate tales of separation, and also suggest how migration has become a legitimate—at times encouraged—way to achieve respect from one's own family and the community at large.

Migration has historically been a well-established, socially legitimated strategy for support of those left behind. Uncles, aunts, or other relatives who lived abroad helped kin when things were going wrong in Eritrea during the war. For many of my informants, "the uncle abroad" was almost a legendary character, to whom they had addressed letters during their childhood asking for dolls or toys. Often "the uncle abroad" was more educated and seen as someone who had experience of the world. When he came back to visit the family, big parties were organized in his honor. This is the cultural environment in which young Eritreans grew up learning the value of migration.

With the current lack of economic opportunities in the country, having or not having relatives abroad is a critical element in the socioeconomic stratification of the Eritrean population. Sometimes, it is the only defense against starvation. As locals told me in Barur, malnourished children receiving assistance from a humanitarian program mostly came from local families who did not have any close relatives abroad. Even when families are better equipped to survive, remittances are extremely valuable, given the gap between the average salary and the increasingly high cost of living owing to inflation and the weakness of Eritrean economy.[16] Although scarce and not detailed, the available data show the Eritrean economy to be heavily dependent on private transfers.[17] At the national as well as household levels, emigration provides the basic resources for the survival of families and of the country itself.

Engraved in the landscape as well as in domestic space, emigration in its positive and tragic aspects is not only *normalized* as an everyday reality and crucial resource of Eritreans' daily lives. It has also become normative. As widely documented in other regions characterized by protracted political stagnation and economic uncertainties,[18] emigration may become the norm, that is to say, *expected* by families and the community at large. This was illustrated for me by my encounter with Alazar's mother, Minia, and the other members of his family.

THE LAST SON LEFT BEHIND

Minia's family was a prime example of the diasporic engagement of Eritreans. Most of her siblings were scattered around Europe and the Middle East. Two of her sons were in Israel, one was in Italy, and another in Sweden. When I met Minia, she still her twenty-five-year-old son Robel and her sixteen-year-old daughter Lula living at home with her and her husband, but by the time I left the country, the two had already fled to Ethiopia. Minia and Alem followed them two months later.

Sitting on the small stool in front of the stove preparing traditional coffee, Minia asked me how Alazar was doing. I was glad to tell her that he had finally found a good job as a barman in Rome; he had many friends, and was generous with everyone. Minia's big brown eyes lit up with pride:

> I have no words to describe what Alazar is for me. When he was a child he used to ask me for some food from the doorstep of the house. But often there was not enough food. Then a gesture of my hand was sufficient, and he would run off without saying anything. Alazar has always been strong, but he was not good at school. He was only sixteen when he went to defend our country. He was wounded then and imprisoned in a camp in Ethiopia for years. We thought he was dead . . . but then he came back to us.

Looking at Robel sitting on the sofa, she exclaimed: "Alazar is different from this one . . . that has no salary and is still at home with us!" Robel laughed, a bit embarrassed.

Compared to Alazar, who had had to cope with poverty since he was a little boy and had been a soldier and a prisoner of war, Robel was still a bit spoiled. Later, when Lwam, my translator for the occasion, and I were walking away from the house, she commented that Robel must have felt very ashamed for being the only one left in the house, unable to help his family.

As Robel's subtle stigmatization illustrates, migration has become especially expected of young men, since the ability to support one's parents and provide for one's wife and children is the most basic element of Eritrean masculinity and adulthood.[19] However, young women may also feel the pressure to leave Eritrea so as to provide for their families. Lwam, for example, felt extremely responsible for her parents, who were farmers in the south of Eritrea and had suffered through recurring droughts. Since her brother in Italy had been unable to support the family back home, she was determined to take his place and make her father's dream to see Massawa come true. "My father has never even seen the sea," she said. "Can you imagine? Everyone comes from abroad to see Massawa, but my family has never been there. When I have some money, I'll take him there. You can be sure of that."

Mainly due to the constraints produced by the indeterminate national service, which I describe in detail in the next section, achieving a recognized social status becomes impossible for most young men and women unless they leave the country. As widely highlighted by scholars of Eritrea, abiding by the government rules not only implies economic dependency on others, but also a life of "social liminality.[20] Since national service, which is intended to be a sort of initiation period necessary to join the national community and reach adulthood, has been indefinitely prolonged, young people are prevented from becoming adults in both symbolic and practical ways. Most of them are trapped in a state of perennial adolescence.[21]

Their forced permanent adolescence can also be negatively sanctioned as a failure by families and peers and turns into a condition of "social death." Conventionally used to define the status of slaves as those who do not belong to a community,[22] the descriptive "social death" is also the condition of those individuals who break a taboo and are therefore condemned to social exclusion, sometimes even to physical death.[23] In migration studies, it more generally refers to those who are excluded/or who risk being excluded because of the impossibility of fulfilling the social expectations—concerning remittances[24] or the passage to adulthood[25]—of their community back home. Migration thus becomes a necessary passage to overcome this condition of social liminality and to gain the appreciation of one's own family and friends. As I show in the following chapters, the desire for positive social status with the family and community left behind is also crucial for understanding my informants' motivation to keep moving after having reached Ethiopia, Sudan, or Italy, and for those who had arrived to support the migration of their kin.

Family expectations certainly mirror an economic strategy of survival,[26] but it would not be correct to reduce them to economic interests. Parents' encouragement to migrate are also animated by the desire to see their children settled in a better and safer place. Eritrea is perceived as a place without a future, and the outside world is represented one of happiness and stability. Families share with their young members hierarchies of possible destinations—*cosmologies of destinations*—classified according to the deemed availability of economic and educational opportunities and freedom. At the time I met Minia, for example, she did not really need more money. Three of her sons were already abroad and regularly remitting enough to ensure a good standard of life to those left behind. However, Minia firmly believed that Eritrea could not guarantee a future to young people. In particular, she did not want her only daughter to go through the challenging experience of training in the Sa'wa military camp (see later).

Although parents usually believed that life abroad would be good for their children, they were also aware that migration can have tragic consequences.[27] Given this tension, the decision to flee or to stay was mostly left to their sons and daughters. Indeed, families were often unaware of their sons' and daughters' migratory plans. Most of them come to know about their children's flight after it has already happened, by receiving a call from their son/daughter or from a relative abroad.[28] Except in a few cases, migration from Eritrea is young people's business. As

UNHCR data show, most part of those who leave the country today are young (sometimes very young) men and, to a lesser extent, women.[29] This is because the young are those of whom the Eritrean state has demanded the most sacrifices over the past twenty years.

CONSCRIPTED FOREVER

Self-sufficiency, defending Eritrea against Ethiopian invasion, and making it a modern country are among the main official justifications for the mass mobilization of the population aged over eighteen in the military and in the execution of public tasks.[30] This mobilization has mainly been enacted by modifying the original terms of national service. According to 1995 proclamation, national service was to be for eighteen months in all: six months of military training and one year of "active military service and development tasks in military forces for a total of 18 months" (Proclamation of National Service No. 82/1995, art. 8).[31] All citizens had to serve, except for people with serious disabilities and those who fought in the liberation struggle.

From 1994 to 1998, this was the case, but when the 1998–2000 border conflict started, the population was massively drafted into the army. At this point, the draft was often voluntary, since many Eritreans, animated by patriotic feelings, were willing to fight to defend the country. However, when the war ended, the expected demobilization never occurred. On the contrary, in 2002, the so-called Warsay-Yekealo campaign was launched. This campaign targeted young people on the basis that they (the inheritors, or *warsay*) should learn the attributes of self-sacrifice and resistance of older generations of freedom fighters (*yekealo*) to use them in the development of the country. In practice this meant that national service became open-ended, and that education has been increasingly militarized.

Since 2002, in fact, after having reached eleventh grade, all boys and girls have had to do their last year of school in the Sa'wa military camp. Although its infrastructure has been improved over the years, Sa'wa is known for being a hard place. My young informants told me about the harsh climate, the strict training sessions, and the inadequate food and facilities.[32] During this year, they both attend regular classes and undergo military training.[33] At the end of this last year, all students take a matriculation exam. If they pass, they are allowed into a university or professional curriculum, according to the marks they obtained during the exam; if they do not pass, they start their national service. Located in the dry hot region of Sahel, the traditional stronghold of the EPLF during the struggle, Sa'wa has been developed, not only to provide military training, but also to teach younger generations the values of national companionship in spite of ethnic and religious differences.[34]

FIGURE 3. Students celebrating Independence day (May 24) before their departure for Sa'wa (photo by the author, 2013)

In the early 2000s, following student protests, the internationally recognized University of Asmara was closed down and regional colleges were established in which students have to observe strict military discipline under soldiers' control.[35] Successful matriculants are admitted to one of these.

Those who do not pass the matriculation exam usually become soldiers or join specific ministries to carry out lower tasks. As soldiers, young men, and to a lesser extent women, are sent to Barentu, Assab, Tsorona, and other more remote areas, usually to patrol the border or to build roads, dams, and other infrastructure of public interest for little remuneration: a common soldier used to earn 400 nakfa a month—about U.S.$8.

Once college students finish their education, they are assigned to a specific ministry and start their year of "community service," for which they used to receive 175 nakfa (less than $4) per month. After that year, they start working for a salary in the ministry to which they have been assigned. Salaries used to range from 450 to 800 nakfa per month (~$9–16). Doctors exceptionally earn 1,500 nakfa a month (about $30). Given that rents and food and commodity prices are increasing exponentially, it was extremely hard for people to survive on such low salaries. Although educated Eritreans are mostly employed in administration, education, and the health sector and other services, the majority have never been released from military duties.[36]

FIGURE 4. Young conscripts headed for the Independence Day parade (photo by the author, 2013)

FIGURE 5. Independence Day parade in Asmara (photo by the author, 2013)

The indefinite extension of national service has now been in force for almost two decades. Among the many social and economic pitfalls, this measure has produced generations of young men and women who do not have the freedom to work, to earn a decent salary, or to enjoy a family life.

TRAPPED AT HOME: THE LIVES OF YOUNG ERITREANS BETWEEN NATIONAL SERVICE AND SOCIAL IMMOBILITY

In the house I lived in, twenty-four-year-old Salam and I shared a double bed, and I often lay there writing up my notes, waiting for her to finish her prayers or to come back home from a date with her boyfriend, Gaim. Once, it was already late at night and I was dozing on the bed when Salam walked into our bedroom in tears:

Me: "What happened, Salam *sukhor?* Are you okay?"

Salam: "It was so bad, Milena. The police took Gaim."

Me: "They took him?

Salam: "Yes. We were waiting for the taxi . . . you know there, on the way to the *shouq.* The police came and asked for his papers. He did not have them . . . they took him away."

When Salam's boyfriend got caught, she started calling people who might be able to help get Gaim out of prison. She was worried he was going to be sent back to his military placement, very far away from Asmara. "If you have contacts, you can pay and then they will set him free," Salam told me. "If you don't have contacts, you cannot do anything. . . . They are too stupid. . . . There is no freedom in this country. It is not possible to live here."

Gaim was a deserter. Like many other young people in Eritrea, he had decided to stay away from his assigned employment in a faraway military location in the north of the country. Since he did not have his *menqasaqasi* (documents), the police had arrested him, but he came from a wealthy family and had some good contacts in the right places. Not long after the above-mentioned episode, he was let out of jail and apparently released from national service too.

Obtaining a release not only means freedom from indefinite national service but also has many other implications. Unreleased citizens cannot obtain passports and thus cannot travel; their salaries are (even) lower than those of released citizens; they cannot obtain a license and open a private business; finally, graduates are not given their official transcripts, which would allow them to use their qualifications abroad. Holding or not holding a release paper is one of the main factors (together with remittances from abroad) influencing the socioeconomic stratification of the Eritrean population.[37]

Obtaining a release is not easy. Rules are not clear and often change. In general, one can obtain this document only if one can be shown to be suffering from a severe sickness. The chances of release were significantly higher for a woman than for a man. Women can obtain a release if they get married, have children, or have extremely worrying family problems. But some ministries are known for being stricter than others. Young women who worked for the ministries of Health or Education, like our neighbor and friend Johanna, were extremely unlucky. The chronic shortage of teachers and health professionals in the country has made release mostly unattainable for women working in these fields. During one of the many evenings that Lwam, Johanna and I spent chatting in the darkness of the house (there were regular electrical blackouts), they explained that each case could be different depending on the supervisors and the ministry. For example, Lwam, who had worked for the Ministry of Agriculture for three years, was applying for a military release from her regional administration. She was planning to claim that her free work outside the ministry was vital for her family's survival. The claim seemed a bit weak to me, since this condition was shared by most Eritreans I knew. Lwam was confident, however, and a year later, she actually obtained her papers and legally left the country.

For men, a release is so difficult to obtain that it had become the subject of much sarcasm among my informants.[38] In the villages that I visited in the southern highlands, I was told that some sixty-five-year-old men were still serving in the military. In Asmara, I met only two young men who had been released from national service: one suffered from a serious form of mental retardation; the other was Salam's boyfriend, who, after having been incarcerated, was released from the military owing to high-level contacts in the army. "Nothing is impossible if people have good contacts and money," one of our common friends commented when I reported what happened to Salam's boyfriend. I was told many stories of young men who managed to avoid the military service because the parents had close contacts within the PFDJ party, or because they had a relative with an important position in a ministry. All the others had to take informal jobs while dodging the draft.

Since the cost of living is extremely high in relation to the average government salary, the young people I met in Asmara had second, and sometimes third, more profitable jobs. Our neighbor Johanna taught in a public school, for example, but also privately tutored children on the side in order to make some money. Her younger brother, Paolos, should have been teaching in a technical school far from Asmara, but he was working as a truck driver while keeping an informal agreement with his supervisor at the school.

Johanna and Paolos are good examples of those who remain stuck at home despite their desire to leave it. In spite of long years of service and a difficult family situation—their mother had died and they rarely saw their distant father—they could not get a release from the Ministry of Education. Neither could they leave the country, given their limited economic resources. Johanna dreamt of pursuing her passion for painting in an art school in Italy, but could not get her relatives to pay for her. Her brother was also desperately trying to leave the country, but could not afford a safe and reliable getaway. He had already tried to escape the country three times. As a result, he had been caught and imprisoned for more than a year—an experience he did not want to talk about with anyone. As they did not have any other option, Johanna and Paolos did their best to put up with their everyday economic constraints and public duties as *agelgalitat* (conscripts), by playing small tricks on the system, or simply by working very hard.

Johanna and Paolos are "displaced in place." As Stephen C. Lubkemann observes,[39] the ability to move is stratified according to individuals' and families' socioeconomic resources, educational background, and physical capabilities. Johanna and her brother were well informed and fit enough to cross the border, but could not afford a safe way to do it (see "The Cost of Safety" text box at the end of this chapter). Conventional categories of refugee studies are overturned here: refugees are usually defined by their lack of choices, but cases like Johanna's illustrate that the ones who have no choice are those who stay behind. From this perspective, becoming a refugee is not an involuntary act, but a demonstration of individual possibilities.

However, staying can also be a matter of choice. Loyalty to the political project of the government and the strong commitment to develop their country have certainly led some Eritreans, even those who had been serving the nation for decades in return for insignificant salaries, to stay put. In fact, the tension between their migration and their duties to the nation was often present in the narratives of the young Eritreans I met. Brought up as patriots, young Eritreans often view migration through the same categories as government discourse.[40] In a way, my interlocutors often felt that migration was a sort of treason. Even for Johanna, migrating would have conflicted with the patriotic values that her father and her mother, both ex-guerrilla, had taught her.

No matter the reason for which young Eritreans I met were still in the country, their life was full of hardships. Johanna and her brother were lucky enough, like many of those living in urban areas, educated and employed as civilians by the ministries, to find time and space for other income-generating activities. Other conscripts especially those who serve as soldiers in remote areas, can only choose between corvée labor for the state or a life on the run.

EVERYDAY FUGITIVES

Desertion is extremely widespread in Eritrea.[41] Sometimes individuals decide to evade their assigned job out of necessity. Married men, who have the responsibility to support their families, may desert to earn more. Others, usually young men and women, often choose to desert hoping to find a way out of the country, even if this may take years. Still others, especially young women, decide to hide from the system—dropping out of school, Sa'wa military camp, and national service all together—until they are automatically released by getting married and having children. It goes without saying that these tactics of evasion have an impact on wider societal dynamics, such as the rate of female education and the availability of labor, as well as on the everyday world of families and individuals constantly living in a state of existential suspension and anxiety.

Deserters have a hard time dealing with continual controls and round-ups (*geffas* in Tigrinya). As often reported, the ordinary quiet of Godena Harnet, the main central avenue in Asmara, was often shaken by the tumult of soldiers checking the documents of all young people sitting in cafés or walking in the streets.[42] Those found without papers could go to prison, as in the case of Salam's boyfriend, or were sent back to their military placement to be punished there.

Geffas were also common in the villages I visited in 2013. "Last time soldiers came to our village, they could not find the young people," one of my informants in Mai Nefas reported. "So they took the elders and made them march in bare feet to punish their connivance with their draft-dodging sons." According to my informants there, villagers had a complex system of information sharing via contacts in the police, which gave them notice that soldiers were coming.

Like the young black drug dealers studied by Alice Goffman in a Philadelphia ghetto,[43] Eritrean *koblali* (a negative word referring to draft-dodgers in Tigrinya) develop "an art of running." They learn how to live unpredictable lives always on the run, periodically escaping *geffas,* avoiding soldiers, not sleeping at home, suspecting neighbors and fellow villagers of being spies for the government. For many, this becomes a way of life. Some draft-dodge only for a few months, but others do it for years, and evasion becomes the norm. While dodging soldiers, many deserters date their girlfriends, work, get married, bring up their children, and start new businesses. One of my informants had been a draft-dodger for more than seven years before being caught while trying to escape the country.

Eritrean draft-dodgers live in constant fear of being caught, David Bozzini emphasizes,[44] but it was the normality of living as a deserter that amazed me. By "normality," I do not mean to say that their lives were simple. The very possibility to feel at home was crumbling due to the fact that they often had to sleep outside their home, and that their families were covering for them. However, many young people I met seemed to see living their lives as fugitives as something "normal," and as Salam put it once, "people can get used to the most terrible things." For example, Robel, Alazar's brother, had been absent from his teaching post for over five months, yet he often risked meeting me in the center of the city, walking with me through streets frequented by police. Likewise, Salam's boyfriend used to hang out with her in city center and go out almost every evening in busy bars. The night Salam came home in tears, they had, in fact, been close to the center. What appeared to me as a situation of extreme risk, crisis and hardship had become the normal background for their daily activities. *Aren't they worried about going to jail?* I always used to wonder to myself. When I asked people, they usually answered with a bitter smile and no clear explanation, but once Salam replied in a way that threw some light on my question:

> They [young people] have no other way. They escape for a while, then the police catch them and they go to prison. Then, when they are out, they will once again try to escape from the military. What can they do? Anyway, to be in this country is like being in a prison. We call it "free prison" because it is like a big prison from which nobody can easily leave.

Salam's representation of Eritrea as a big prison symbolizes well the different aspects of immobility experienced by young Eritreans. First, her words suggest that staying in or out of prison was not so different from young Eritreans' point of view: neither prisoners in a jail nor young Eritreans outside the prison have a future. Both are condemned to live in an eternal present where the past is continuously reproduced without any significant prospect of change. This was not only because the whole country was stuck in an endless repetition of the past and its tokens— the struggle for independence, its martyrs and its heroes—but also because young Eritreans are stuck in a condition of generational and social liminality.[45]

The whole country was perceived as a huge prison: it is hard to escape, and individuals have no control over their lives. Young people felt locked away from the outside world, seen as the site of happiness and possibilities. The risk of being sent to prison was thus no scarier than the certainty of remaining stuck in a temporal, geographic, social, economic, and existential state of immobility. Against the risk of being "the living dead," a person had no other alternative than to try to escape as many times as possible. Desertion is in fact one of the tactics to resist the forced stasis and try to advance one's life, to reinstate a kind of normal course of "social becoming" even in a context of chronic uncertainties.

EVEN DESERTERS MARRY: ORDINARY STORIES FROM THE COUNTRYSIDE

This forced social and existential immobility is even more striking for Eritreans in the countryside. While many young men in the city manage to keep their formal employment while also having more profitable jobs, individuals from rural backgrounds are usually sent far away from their villages to remote military outposts. This prevents them from accomplishing their familiar duties, ranging from plowing the land to providing for their elders and forming new families. This was the case for many young men I met in a group of villages in the southern highlands. Many of my friends and informants in Italy—mostly the Catholic ones in Rome and Genoa—were originally from that area. Ogbazgi, in particular, a twenty-five-year-old refugee living in Sicily at the time, was from Mai Nefas.

Like most other families in the village, Ogbazgi's family were farmers. Their *hudmo*—a typical stone house—was set in a landscape of huge, smooth, round rocks, surrounded by tall cactuses half-eaten by local camels put out to pasture. When I went to visit them, Ogbazgi's seventy-eight-year-old father, Abraha, welcomed me with a toothless smile. Although thin as a matchstick, he was strong and agile, and still able to work in the fields for an entire day. Ogbazgi's youngest sister was sitting in front of the coal stove preparing coffee and eggs. The other members of the family were not around: Abraha's sons were abroad and his daughters had married and were living elsewhere in the country. The eldest brother, Tewodoros, was the only one left, but he was out in the fields. That was the period of transhumance and plowing in the nearby lowlands, where it is rainy between November and March, while the highlands remain dry and dusty. Abraha told me that Tewodoros had been a soldier for more than seven years. The ministry sent him to Assab, "a very bad place" according to Abraha. It was too hot there, and soldiers were not given enough food and water. They did not hear from Tewodoros for five years, but finally he had recently managed to return home and had married a young woman from a nearby village.

In the evening, Tewodoros came to see me to give me the video recording of his marriage to pass on to Ogbazgi. After congratulating him on his wedding, I asked him about his plans for the future. Smiling like a child who has just done something naughty, he told me he would not go back to the army any time soon. Being the eldest son and the only one left in the country, he bore the responsibility to help his old father with the crops and to support his new family. At the age of thirty-two, national service having delayed him in all main steps toward male adulthood, draft-dodging was his only way to become a respected son and a husband.

However, perpetual desertion does not free young Eritreans from a stressful life of suspicion and unpredictability. Many men whom I met in Mai Nefas did not sleep at home, fearing that soldiers would come at night to capture them. While deserting might allow them to get married and meet some of the traditional expectations, life would remain a matter of subsistence—a life "without future" as my informants put it. This "lack of future" in my informants' view not only stems from the limitations to their personal freedom and the lack of long-term prospects in the country, but also from the perception that a better life is possible elsewhere. Not unlike many other young Africans, most boys and girls I met during my fieldwork expressed the desire to leave the country in order to be part of "modernity"—which they see as a bundle of freedom, possibilities, and consumeristic wealth, seemingly so far from daily life in Eritrea.

STRIVING FOR MODERNITY

Most explanations of Eritrean migration have mainly focused on conditions of structural oppression hindering the ability of young people to fulfil traditional sociocultural expectations.[46] The complexity of Eritreans' aspirations to migration has remained hidden by the static portrait of a closed traditional society. However, this image is far from reality on the ground. The appeal of "modernity" is, here as elsewhere, crucial in understanding how young Eritrean men and women perceive their own situation and how they project their futures into specific destinations in the "outside world." Eritrea is often compared with North Korea in journalistic accounts, and people themselves feel locked away from the real flow of life, but contacts and interactions with the outside world are numerous. Social remittances, cultural products from abroad and images spread through the media shape young Eritreans' "global subjectivities".[47]

As widely highlighted in the literature on the topic, modernity is far from being a clearly defined concept, but it may mean different things for different actors in different places. The many dimensions of modernity—colonial, postcolonial, neo-liberal, developmental, consumeristic, gender progressive, democratic—are often mixed in social imaginaries and personal aspirations.[48] The modernity inspiring my informants' dreams reflected an intricate bundle of colonial stereotypes, postcolonial development ambitions, consumeristic images, gender models, and democratic aspirations, locally experienced, imagined, and reinterpreted. In my informants' eyes, the possibility of belonging to a modern world meant many different things. It not only represented the chance to access material development and the availability of more or less technological, luxurious or basic consumer products. "Modernity" for them also meant living in a place where they could enjoy personal freedom, social rights, and enhanced status in their families. The pursuit of the "modern world" in its material, social, and moral attributes was one of the important ingredients in my informants' hierarchical categorization of their most desired migration destinations.

Concerned as I was about rendering an accurate image of my informants as legitimate refugees, I often wondered whether portraying their desires for "modernity" might have undermined their claims for safe refuge in Europe. Finally, dissatisfied with simplistic accounts reducing refugee flows to their structural factors, I decided that there was no reason to deny prospective refugees' "capacity to aspire." Although oppressed, my Eritrean informants could envisage better futures outside their home country—unlike "the poor" portrayed in Arjun Appadurai's book *The Future as Cultural Fact*.[49] Aspirations to modernity (conventionally considered pull factors) are, I argue, crucial not only for the study of voluntary migration but also for understanding of the trajectories of those who come to be labeled refugees.[50]

As a matter of fact, Eritreans are immersed in global modern culture as much as most other peoples in the world. "Global modern culture" here does not necessarily mean capitalist Western culture, even if consumerism is a big part of it.[51] It rather consists of a plurality of mediascapes from different parts of the world that are received, absorbed, and manipulated in a variety of ways.[52] Mobile phones, international TV channels, and the internet (widely uncensored) are available to Eritreans, although information and communications technology infrastructure is often poor. Almost all the houses I visited had a television set. Even in the poorest neighborhoods, satellite dishes spring up like mushrooms from the roofs of the houses. Bollywood movies, Arabic shows, and American and Turkish TV series are among the most popular cultural products, along with the national news and local music. In Ester's house, for instance, whenever electricity was available in the evening, the women would gather in the living room to watch a Turkish family saga called *Jemilah*. Later at night, Salam would follow some American series, and Ester, if free in the afternoon, would watch news on ERITV or other international channels, such as MMC (Dubai), Al Jazeera (Qatar), or the BBC (UK).[53]

Salam, as well as most my other young informants in the country, was active on the internet and social networks. While sitting close to Salam in busy internet cafés in the center, I could glance at her friends' Facebook profiles. The pictures of her male friends in the United States and Europe showed them in suits or fashionable clothes, leaning on flashy cars; her female friends would be smiling in their bikinis from swimming pools, while others hugged their new friends in luxurious shopping malls in Dubai. Along with religious representations, spiritual proverbs, and family images from their past, what Eritreans abroad mostly share are sanitized images of their new life. These widespread images of the outside world were a constant reminder to those still stuck in Eritrea of the life they could have if they left.

Often the many dimensions of my young informants' unsatisfied desire for modernity were crystallized in a lack of "things". Issues like the lack of fuel, electricity, technological facilities, good clothes continually came up whenever my informants described why life in Eritrea was unbearable. These "things" were much more than material objects; they symbolized their feeling of being trapped. My informants' lives in Eritrea were continually compared with lives outside the country as depicted by returnees and in electronic images. Eritrea was perceived as an unchanging land, stuck in the past. The First World was the future.

PRICKLY PEARS AND ROOTED TREES: MOVERS AND THEIR LEFT-BEHIND COUNTERPARTS

It was a beautiful, starlit night, made all the more noticeable by the complete electrical blackout in Asmara. Lwam, Johanna, and I were sitting in a taxi going to a bar in town. The taxi driver was keen to chat with us and explained to me: "Eritrean people can be divided into *beles* and *shibaha*: *beles* [prickly pears] are those from abroad who come to Eritrea on holiday, spend their money in clubs and hook up with beautiful Eritrean girls; *shibaha* [a kind of tree] are those who have never left; they are always here no matter what." The taxi driver was laughing but Johanna did not find his explanation funny: "I get very angry if someone calls me *shibaha*," she commented. "It is not my fault if I am stuck here and I can't leave this country!"

The Eritrean rainy season lasts from July to September. The land, usually arid, deserted and stony, becomes covered with shiny, green grass. Thorny cactuses produce glossy red prickly pears—the *beles*—blanketing the valleys with red, to the delight of children and the elderly. The rainy season is not only the period of the year when the country revives, but also the time when Eritreans from abroad come back to their home country. Their presence represents a moment of rebirth for Eritrean society. Families can embrace their sons who live abroad; old friends who live in different parts of the world can meet again; girls wear their best dresses, hoping to meet the love of their lives. Their presence also shakes the stagnant local economy: emigrants import foreign currency, spend their money in clubs and restaurants, and bring gifts to their families and friends.[54]

In the eyes of the locals, *beles* are rich, well dressed, and free to travel. Girls like to imagine what their lives would look like if they married a *beles*. Mothers keep the best picture of their daughter in case a *beles* asks about the possibility of marriage. Boys dream about the cars they will be able to buy if they manage to work abroad.[55] "When my friends come back from abroad, they invite everyone to dinner and spend more money than I earn in a month," Salam once told me while we were sitting in our pajamas in front of an episode of *Pretty Little Liars*. "I'm twenty-five and I still live at home with my mom. I can't even help her as I would like to. I have to leave." Most of Salam's friends had already left the country; some of them were in Dubai, others in Kampala, Uganda, and still others in Europe. She could not wait to join them, even though she knew that it would be difficult at first. Her friends had told her that she would be lonely and have to work hard. However, her life had to change; staying put was not an option.

Yet, migration was not a leap into the void for Salam, or for most of my informants. Many young women and men I spoke to had quite a clear idea about their desired final destination. This is not to say that everyone who leaves Eritrea knows where he/she will end up and may not change his/her mind.[56] However, as a result of TV news, transnational contacts with friends and family connections, young Eritreans commonly imagine different destinations as hierarchically ordered along more or less objective assumptions about work possibilities, social and political freedom and attractiveness of their inhabitants. Their cosmologies of destinations were subjective, since they reflected personal aspirations, but, at the same time, they were fairly standard across young people and their families. They represent the shared imaginary and moral contexts in which migration is fostered and pursued.

THE FIRST AND FIFTH WORLDS: COSMOLOGIES

I heard one of the clearest cosmological formulations from a taxi driver in Asmara. While he was driving me, he started complaining about the situation in Eritrea, saying:

> Italy, Europe, and America are the First World. India and South Africa are the second world; the Middle East is the Third World. . . . Eritrea is the Fifth World! In the First

World people are brilliant. It does not happen that there is shortage of electricity, or no water supply. They have good public management. Here in Eritrea we do not have fuel, no water, no electricity, even though we have the resources! . . . but the government is corrupt and there is no positive result for the people. . . . It's so bad. But if I go to Switzerland, Sweden, Norway—they even give me money to support myself. . . . That is First World!

Although this hierarchy of countries was the taxi driver's own categorization, his words express ideas widely shared among Eritreans. There are good, developed, civilized countries and bad, underdeveloped, corrupt countries. Most notably, desires and aspirations of freedom and self-realization are typically related to the United States, Canada, Australia, and Europe (Italy was probably included in the First World by the taxi driver only out of respect for me). Eritrea belongs to the group of hopeless countries. These worlds are inhabited by people who are given specific, essentialized attributes (the inhabitants of the First World are "brilliant"), and each of them presents well-known opportunities and difficulties as regards the climate, legal context, labor market, and so on.[57] Moreover, this hierarchy entails a temporal dimension, which is crucial for interpreting the way Eritreans see migration. The First World represents the future, while the Fifth World represents the past.

Other scholars have noticed how migration aspirations are often associated with a hierarchical vision of the world. Erind Pajo's work on Albanian international migration, for instance, documents his informants' hierarchical world visions and their aspirations to migrate to certain places.[58] In his investigation of urban youth in Bissau, Henrik Vigh also talks about "an understanding of a world order consisting of societies with different technological capacities and levels of mastery over physical and social environment, as well as the spaces and social options which are open or closed to persons of different social categories within it."[59] Not unlike young Eritreans whom I encountered, Vigh's informants constantly felt "humiliated" in what they perceive as a developmental void of their home and imagine the positive prospects awaiting them in certain destinations imagined as more developed, more technological, more modern. As James Ferguson noticed, these categorizations reflect the developmental model, which since the 1970s has distinguished among so-called First, Second, Third, and Fourth worlds, in a sort of spatial and temporal scale of progress.[60]

But there is more to it. Eritreans' hierarchical cosmology includes cultural assumptions and moral norms about places and people inhabiting these worlds. While people in the First World are perceived as progressive, free, and responsible,[61] there is general distrust and suspicion of Ethiopians and Sudanese. These assumptions about different nationalities indicate that cosmological views are not only the result of the developmental discourse. Rather, they stem from historically stratified conceptions, which have been variably documented in the literature on Eritrea,[62] and ongoing cultural circulation among left-behind Eritreans and those living in different parts of the world. Precolonial, colonial, and postcolonial experiences, such as deep-rooted interethnic relations, Italian racial discrimination,[63] and the 1998–2000 war with Ethiopia feed into common stereotypes about places and their inhabitants. Besides these collectively stratified historical experiences, information, images, and values absorbed through the media and continually exchanged with friends abroad, as noted above, contributed to shaping my informants' expectations of suitable future destinations.

Cosmologies of destinations, thus, could be considered as simultaneously long-standing and flexible constructions. Although some assumptions may be resistant to reality checks due to the unparalleled nature of transnational communication and its related moral obligations, they can also shift due to changes in the objective structure of opportunity or to the power of media images and rumors. For example, Salam thought that migration to Europe was not such a good idea anymore: "Now everyone knows that Europe is finished. It is better to go to Dubai, where there is a good international community and you do not need a visa to enter. If you know somebody who can find work for you, you are fine. In Africa, there is work, in Europe, there is crisis, they also said it on TV." Salam portrayed Eritrea as the bottom of possible choices, and Canada as the most desirable final destination; but other African countries were described as possible good places to live. Through her friends, Salam had gathered a very specific idea of alternative destinations, together with their pros and cons: "In Juba [the capital of South Sudan], if you have some money to start an activity, you can make a lot of money. A friend of mine has opened a supermarket there . . . but it is not safe there and it is too hot. In Kampala, instead, the climate is good and the people look beautiful with their dark and shiny skin—men look also handsome –you can enroll as a refugee there and wait for resettlement to Canada."

Salam's words represent an interesting instance of how imaginaries of possible destinations can quickly shift and over the long term produce a change in the moral expectations shared by migrants and families. However, I would argue that if ideas about destinations may be easily transformed by rumors and widespread images, it takes longer to influence the moral expectations connected to these destinations. To put it differently, potential and current migrants may be relatively fast to pick new information up and adapt to new obstacles and opportunities, but societal and family expectations of what migration to certain countries entails in terms of family status are more resistant to change. I return to this point in following chapters. This is where the concept of cosmologies may be more suitable than imaginaries, as it encompasses not only the symbolic, but also the deep-rooted moral aspects that produce and reproduce migration.

The combination of different memories, images, and rumors has produced multifaceted hierarchies of destinations, which cannot be reduced to one single dimension. The most salient axes for analyzing my informants' cosmological beliefs

THE COST OF SAFETY: HOW TO ESCAPE ERITREA

The safest way to leave Eritrea is by obtaining release from national service. Passports and exit visas can be bought for 400,000 nakfa (around U.S.$7,000), with half of the money going to the broker and half to a Ministry of Emigration official. However, money is not enough. According to Valentina (May 2013), it was crucial to good strong contacts in the Ministry of the Emigration and perhaps to know someone able to facilitate departure from the airport.

The second safest way to leave the country costs 300,000/200,000 nakfa (about U.S.$5,500–3,500). This is a direct journey. Escapees are picked up in Asmara by ministerial land cruisers and are directly dropped off in Khartoum. These kinds of journeys are managed by people who work in security, who have all the permits to cross freely to Sudan without anyone asking them for further explanations. This was considered a comfortable journey, but, according to Valentina, there had been frauds.

For 150,000/180,000 nakfa (around U.S.$3,000), it is possible to exit the country by car, but the journey is not direct. From Asmara customers are driven to Tesseney; from Tesseney a second vehicle takes them to Kassala in eastern Sudan (see map 1). For this kind of journey, it is necessary to bribe the general at the check point with 60,000 nakfa per car, while 60,000 goes to the driver and the remainder to the smuggler. From Kassala, customers are driven to Khartoum. This was the option that Valentina considered most convenient for her. Michael, who arranged this service, told me that it included a seven-hour walk across the Eritrean-Sudanese border.

Tsegay was able to provide passage from Eritrea to Ethiopia for U.S.$1,800, plus a commission of U.S.$300 for himself. The customer has to get from Asmara to Mendefera, where he/she is met by the pilot (guide). Some pilots can drive customers to Adi Quala, others accompany them by bus. From the town of Adi Quala, it takes about half a day's walk to cross the border. Pilots usually leave from Tigrayan camps and pick up the customers in Mendefera.

The price from a border town, such as Tesseney, Sa'wa—on the Sudanese border—or Adi Quala, Tsorona—on the Ethiopian side, is significantly lower. However, prices vary significantly depending on the route, the origin, the destination, the relationship between the customer and the pilot, the size of the group led over the border, the season, the specific agreement with the middleman, and so on. Michael told me that for 60,000 nakfa (about $1,200), he could facilitate border crossing on foot from Tesseney to the Wodi Sherife or Shegerab refugee camps in Sudan. This usually took a full day's walking. Sister Leterberhan had heard that the trip on foot from Adi Quala cost around 70,000 nakfa. Another man I interviewed in Ethiopia told me he paid 80,000 nakfa from Adi Quala. Sister Leterberhan told me that she could have got a good deal from Decamhare for her nephew for 10,000 nakfa (about $200). To get to border towns is not easy, since there is no free movement inside the country and there are many checkpoints, especially on some roads and at some times of the year, and doing so without documents can imply higher risks.

Rashaida smugglers in Massawa charged 70,000 nakfa (about $1,400) to convey migrants along the coast into Sudan. According to Sister Leterberhan, this kind of journey had been dramatically cheaper in 2010—45,000 nakfa, she said—and was very popular until the government started patrolling that side of the border more closely.

Finally, it is possible to travel by sea from Massawa or Assab to the coast of Yemen for 30,000/40,000 nakfa (about $700) per person.

Would-be migrants can also cross the border by themselves provided they know the way, but this was less common among my informants.

NOTE: These prices are highly volatile and continuously change according to the demand of movement, the offer of services and the circumstances of the journey (more or less control, more or less danger). These prices are updated to 2015. I collected this information all along my research, but my main informants on this topic were: (a) Valentina, a 25-year-old woman who had been trying to leave the country for long time; (b) Sister Leterberhan who was closely in touch with young people in different parts of Eritrea; (c) Michael, the smuggler I met in Khartoum; and (d) Tsegay, the smuggler I met in Addis Ababa. While in Ethiopia and Sudan, I also collected private accounts from escapees.

might be the following: freedom/lack of it; access to resources/lack of resources; social fairness/corruption; moral righteousness/moral decay. These dimensions were variously reproduced by my informants, depending on their gender, political attitudes, and age, to mention only the most important factors. I encountered several other parallel and related dichotomies such as clean/dirty, personal freedom/social and religious restrictions. For instance, reaching Europe did not have the same value for my young male and female informants. By accessing freedom and a better-paid job through migration, young men mostly aspired to become breadwinners, get married, and help their families back home. My young female informants—mostly highly educated and from urban backgrounds—did not only want to migrate to Europe to support their families. They were also searching for the social freedom to pursue their dreams. Not satisfied with the traditional conception of women as wives and mothers and rejecting the model of female freedom fighters promoted by government propaganda, they were looking for new ways of realizing their modern womanhood.[64]

The above considerations show that shared hierarchies of destinations assume different subjective meanings, gender implications, and generational values. What is crucial to highlight now is that these symbolic and moral structures deeply influence the way in which Eritreans understand migration and their efforts to reach specific countries.

Hypermobile and Immobile

*Diverse Responses to Protracted Displacement
in Ethiopia and Sudan*

Refugees' onward movement from the first country of asylum in Africa toward further destinations has been a continuous concern for the UNHCR and the international community for at least the past ten years.[1] However, relatively little research has been done into the reasons for and dynamics of refugees' movements onward from their first country of asylum in Africa. Most of the literature is based on interviews with asylum seekers in Europe who were asked to recount their journeys, but there are two main difficulties with this approach.[2] First, it does not permit us to account for the many factors that underpin mobility and immobility, being based solely on the narratives of those who succeeded in moving. Second, it does not allow us to move beyond refugees' self-representations and to reconstruct the sociocultural milieus where decisions to move are taken. Also, the few studies conducted in transit countries—usually policy-oriented reports—do not clarify the moral, symbolic, and imaginative dimensions of migrants' choices. As a result, it is generally acknowledged that secondary movements are coping strategies to attain long-term durable solutions, given a paucity of prospects for protection and assistance in the first country of asylum. This is certainly true, but there is more to it.

No doubt, refugees have to face many challenges in the first safe country where they are given protection. Their freedom of movement and their rights to work and study are often strictly limited, which in turn limits their chances of long-term legal integration. Yet these structural limitations are not enough to explain why different refugee populations inhabiting the same structural and legal environment adopt different migratory attitudes. What differentiates the mobile ones from those who stay put? Is mobility just a question of access to social and economic resources, or does it also emerge from specific aspirations and moral obligations? How does the aspiration to live elsewhere become a concrete decision to move regardless of the risks? By confronting the desires and daily struggles of different groups of Eritreans in Ethiopia and Sudan, this chapter examines the roles of imagination, emotions, and shared moralities (i.e., ideas about what is moral and immoral, fair and unfair, desirable and undesirable) in relation to mobility and immobility in refugee settings.[3]

First, I compare mobile and immobile refugees whom I met in camps in northern Ethiopia. While accounting for the gap in socioeconomic resources that differentiate those who can move from those who cannot move, I also point to the role of different migratory aspirations. Not unlike my informants in Eritrea, those willing to undertake high-risk migration seemed to share a hierarchy of possible destinations, but others preferred to wait in refugee camps until they could return to their homeland. Second, I describe the daily challenges of urban refugees in Addis Ababa and Khartoum and show how emotional pressure to leave at all costs led many of my informants, even the most indecisive, to take the decision to move onward.

THE RUSH TO DEPARTURE

December was a month of preparation and departures in the camps. Many were waiting for the end of European winter. Several houses in the peripheral areas of the camps had been left deserted, and those refugees left behind were relocating toward the center of the settlement close to the hospital, schools, and places of entertainment. Reaching Khartoum in January–February was believed to be ideal for organizing the next step of the journey. Among my informants in the camp, several were negotiating with their relatives abroad to make sure they would support their journeys; others were asking around the camp to find the cheapest and most trusted middleman. At night big trucks destined to be loaded with migrants traversed the dusty roads of the Adi Harush and Mai Aini refugee camps.[4]

Shimelba, Mai Aini, Adi Harush, and Hitstats are the four main camps where Eritreans end up in Ethiopia after crossing the troubled, heavily militarized border (map 4). After a few months in Addis Ababa trying to get permission, ARRA, the government Agency for Refugees and Returnees Affairs, finally authorized me to visit these camps around the area of Shire. Juggling between my previously established informal contacts among Eritreans in the camps and the need to comply

FIGURE 6. Shimelba, the oldest Eritrean refugee camp in Ethiopia (photo by the author, 2013)

FIGURE 7. A barbershop in Hintsats camp (photo by the author, 2013)

with the formal requirements of ARRA (see Appendix), I spent a month observing, interviewing, and sharing some of the daily life of the refugees in the four camps.[5]

Located in an extremely hot, dry, and remote region, these camps were certainly challenging environments for settlement, but they were not necessarily worse off than the surrounding areas. Living conditions, infrastructure, and service could vary significantly among the camps, depending on the number of agencies active in the camp, humanitarian investments, and the date the camp had been established.[6] However, these camps, veritably big towns,[7] were usually relatively well served in terms of schooling and health status and health provisions and were blossoming with small business (informal banks, food stores, hairdressers) and recreational activities (cinemas, bars, and restaurants) established by refugees themselves. Safety was also not an issue there.[8] Yet the inhabitants of these camps, with the exception of those in Shimelba, strongly desired to move on to other destinations—mostly in Europe, the United States or Canada.[9]

The insufficiency of the rations, lack of monetary assistance, and the exhausting search for firewood were constant challenges there.[10] The crucial problem, however, was getting out of the camps and working. They had to seek permission to exit the camp, and employment was in any case limited and mostly irregular.[11] Many engaged in different livelihood activities, such as breeding animals, farming the land, working as daily laborers in the camp surroundings, setting up small businesses, and serving humanitarian organizations as interpreters, community workers, or teachers. However, what they earned only covered basic subsistence and did not allow them to help their families back home; nor did it provide them with the means to construct a viable future for themselves and their children outside the camp.

"What is the difference between dying slowly here in camps," said Jacob, a twenty-six-year-old engineering graduate in Adi Harush. "Or dying while crossing the sea? If we have to die, it is better to do it trying to reach Europe rather than wasting time here far away from our homes and without the possibility of constructing a future!" As the camp population mostly consisted of young, entrepreneurial men,[12] sometimes with university-level educations, it is easy to understand how, in their eyes, a life in the camp was untenable.

Refugees there felt stuck in a condition of social liminality—unable to fulfil family obligations as well as cut off from a recognized social status among their peers, families, and the society at large. Jacob's association of a life in camp with a "slow death" reflects the concept of social death discussed in chapter 1 with respect to my informants who felt left behind in Eritrea. Not unlike them, my respondents in the camps perceived themselves as immobile in time and space, caught in a meaningless loop of daily activities and constraints, which did not allow them to help their families, become adults, and realize their dreams.

As local integration is restricted, and repatriation sounds to the majority like a remote and unappealing solution, most individuals in the camps strongly desire to be included in a resettlement program. But this option is only for a few. In 2013,

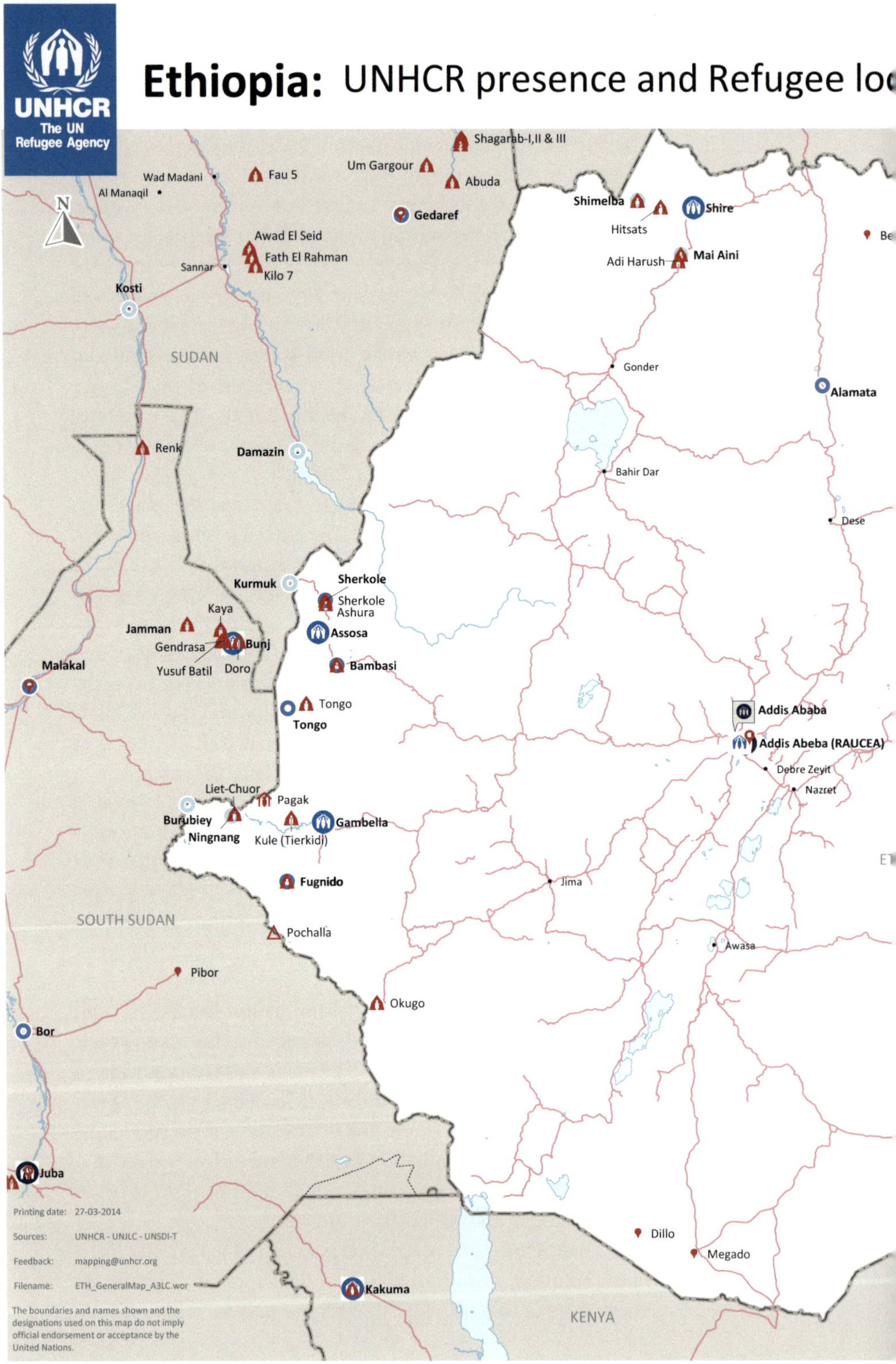

MAP 4. Refugee camps in Ethiopia (UNHCR 2014)

27 March 2014

Hodeidah

YEMEN

Red Sea

Dhamar

Rida

Ibb

Mayfa'ah

Al-Baida
Mayfar Hadjar

Bir Ali

Taiz

Ahwar

Assab

Al Kharaz

Zinjibar

Bab al Mandab

Aden

Gulf of Aden

DJIBOUTI

Obock

Bossaso

Aysaita

Djibouti

Hol-Hol
Ali-Addeh

Ali Sabieh

Berbera

SOMALIA

Aw-barre
Sheder

Dire Dawa

Hargeysa

Jijiga

Kebribeyah

Garoowe

Gaalkacyo

★	Capital
	UNHCR Regional Office
	UNHCR Country Office / National Office / Liaison Office
	UNHCR Sub-Office
○	UNHCR Field Office
	UNHCR Field Unit
△	Refugee settlement
▲	Refugee camp (* : New refugee location)
	Refugee centre
△	Refugee accomodation
●	Refugee location
○	Urban refugee location
•	Main town or village
—	Main road
	Coastline
	International boundary
	Undetermined boundary

Melkadida
Kobe

mayo

Hilaweyn

Buramino

Dollo Ado

Dollow

0   100.0

kilometres

Baydhaba

FIGURE 8. Cinema in Adi Harush camp (photo by the author, 2013)

FIGURE 9. Hintsats, the most recently established camp (photo by the author, 2013)

according to the UNHCR officers I interviewed in Shire, only 850 individuals were resettled—less than 1 percent of the Eritrean refugees in the country. This is in line with international resettlement rates.[13] Refugees are usually referred for resettlement only if they had been in the camp for over ten years or if they can be included in the category of especially vulnerable cases according to UNHCR guidelines.[14] Given these poor odds, many refugees were planning to resort to smugglers with the financial backing of relatives in the diaspora. Without their resources, migration to Europe is mostly unattainable.[15] Relatives' help is secured by transnational moral economies, which prescribe that those who are abroad support their left-behind kin. Migration is one of the main cases in which this support is required, and the determination of young Eritreans to move no matter the risks compels even unwilling helpers to comply with it. The availability of transnational family networks is thus crucial to understand who can and who cannot move from the first country of asylum. The large Eritrean diaspora explains why Eritreans have been able to migrate more than other refugee groups.

Many resided in camps only for the time needed to organize their trips to Libya. Almost all of the respondents in the small survey (of twenty-six households) I conducted in Adi Harush to investigate secondary movement expressed a desire to migrate onward.[16] The others simply seemed too helpless to express an opinion at all. Those who mentioned the United States and Canada were usually men and women who hoped to get there through some kind of family reunification visa or resettlement. The ones who answered Europe—usually young single men set to depart soon—mainly referred to Norway and Sweden as intended final destinations.[17] These were perceived as particularly favorable for refugees in terms of social assistance and prospects for employment. Southern European countries, like Italy, were never mentioned and nobody seemed to consider a life anywhere in Ethiopia, even outside the camp, as a possible long-term solution.

Although most people I met seemed to aim to move on as soon as possible, strategies could also differ depending on the gender of my interviewees. Female-headed households often included more than one family, as women tended to assist each other in childcare and to share the few resources they had. These women had often given birth either shortly before or shortly after arriving in the camp. They were usually waiting for reunification with their husbands who had left the camp trying to reach Europe. It was a common strategy among refugee families to diversify migration options.[18]

Not unlike my young informants in Eritrea, the young refugees whom I interviewed in camps shared a hierarchical vision of the world. Their desires to move to some countries instead of others mirrored their classification of places and their inhabitants along a ladder of legal stability, developmental achievements, moral worth, and socioeconomic prospects. Rather than seeing them in the context of a generalized "culture of migration," we can better understand their aspirations by referring to the idea of cosmologies of destinations, which allows us to consider the specific imaginaries and moral prescriptions attached to different destinations. The desire for mobility did not target the "West" in general, but rather specific locations within it.

Onward migration was an omnipresent topic of discussion and a pervasive practice in the camps. The households of young male refugees in particular seemed characterized by a continually shifting population. In Abraha's hut, for example, everyone wanted to leave soon. One of my refugee friends in Addis Ababa had given me Abraha's phone number and asked him to take care of me during my stay. After a tour of the camp facilities, he took me to his mud house. His housemates were four men in their late twenties and early thirties, coming from Segeneiti, a Catholic town in southern Eritrea. One of them was lying in the bed trembling with high fever due to malaria—which was endemic in the camps—but the other three spent some time chatting with me.

Mascio was around thirty years old. He had been in Sudan before and then tried to reach Israel, but on the border he was caught by Egyptian police and imprisoned for four months before being sent to Ethiopia. When I met him, he told me that he was tired of waiting in the camp: after a year and seven months there, it was time for him to try his luck again. This time he wanted to reach Europe. Jeremy, the other housemate, had a sister and a brother in Norway. He was waiting for them to send him money to cross the Mediterranean, and in the meantime he was breeding a small family of goats, which kept peeking through the front door. Abraha had relatives abroad, too: a brother in Canada who was going to sponsor him and a sister who had just moved from Italy to Switzerland in search for better opportunities. After being in the camp for over a year, Abraha did not seem willing to wait longer for his siblings to take action. A few months later I discovered that he had started his journey to Norway through Sudan. The stories of Mascio, Jeremy, and Abraha mirrored a widespread determination to move regardless of the risks. Often this determination emerged from a deeply felt obligation to left-behind kin who were waiting for their economic support.

Movements out of the camp were continual, but this does not mean that many individuals had not been in the camps for very long time. In Shimelba, the oldest Eritrean camp in Ethiopia, I met men and women who had been living there for over ten years, hoping to be resettled for lack of alternatives. Also in Adi Harush I met many refugees who had been there since the establishment of the camp in 2010. Of the 26 households I interviewed, three said they could not go anywhere, because they did not have relatives abroad to pay for their journey. Their livelihood strategies in the camp were evidently different from those who were not planning to stay long. They strove to be self-reliant. One of them, for example, was raising chickens to sell to the local market to support his young wife and baby; another family had set up a tea shop in the camp. Many of them were from poor rural areas in southern Eritrea, not far from the Ethiopian border. It is likely that their journeys to Ethiopia had not been very expensive.

This brings back the issue of forced immobility. Lacking resources, longtime residents in camps, the most deprived of all, could not even afford to live in Addis Ababa. They had no other choice but to hope that a resettlement officer would consider their cases. Having been obliged to flee Eritrea, they were now obliged to stay in Ethiopia, forming "trapped populations."[19] However, not everybody had been obliged to remain. Some had chosen to do so.

THOSE WHO CHOOSE TO STAY: THE CASE OF THE KUNAMAS

Most scholars emphasize how legal constraints, deprivation, and limited social resources lead to immobility among refugee and migrant populations. However, even in the most extreme situations, such as those of refugees in camps, one should not simply assume that everyone would like to migrate on. Sometimes, immobility can be a choice, reflecting personal aspirations and communal moral values. In the context of Eritrean migration, the Kunama ethnic minority from Shimelba is a significant counterpart to those who would do anything to move on.

In 2006, the United States offered to resettle around 6,000 Eritreans from Shimelba. The Kunama ethnic minority was the target group. Ethnically perse-cuted in Eritrea,[20] they closely fit the definition of refugees according to the 1951 Geneva Convention. However, something completely unforeseen happened: more than half of the Kunamas—2,800 out of 4,000—refused to be resettled, declar-ing that they preferred to stay in the camp, waiting to go home as soon as Eritrea became a peaceful place again. Eritreans from other ethnic backgrounds—mostly Tigrinya, the largest ethnic group in Eritrea—started to be resettled instead. When I reached the camp in December 2013, the population of the camp (about six thou-sand) consisted mainly of Kunamas who had refused resettlement, recent arriv-als, and a small number of Tigrinyas whose resettlement cases had been rejected or delayed.

I was quite puzzled when I found out about the rate of refusals among the Kunama refugees. Hitherto I had only met Eritreans—mostly Christian Tigrin-yas—who were trying their best to get out of Ethiopia and in the absence of a resettlement case or a family visa, they were ready to embark on dangerous border crossings. Why, then, did Kunamas refuse the opportunity to be resettled? My encounters with refugees, NGO workers, and UNHCR officers in Shimelba helped me to figure out some of the main factors behind this unprecedented response.

My Kunama translator for the occasion was Noah, the twenty-six-year-old son of Bartholomeus, an evangelical preacher.[21] His religious activity as well as his refusal to give up his land to Tigrinya settlers had made him and his family a target of Eritrean authorities. Noah's mother was the only member of the family who had stayed back home, and Noah and his brother were both in the camp waiting for resettlement. They, unlike other Kunamas, believed that resettlement to the United States was the best option. This had put them in conflict with other members of the community who discouraged resettlement. Their huts had been set on fire more than once, and the father always secretly traveled from Shire, Shimelba, and Addis Ababa so as not to become an easy target or endanger his family.

Among those who opposed Kunamas' resettlement in the camp, there was the Democratic Movement for the Liberation of Eritrean Kunamas (DMLEK), an opposition front active in Shimelba since the early 2000s. DMLEK had depended on the population of the camp for taxes and recruits, and group resettlement was a serious threat to its existence. Its militants had therefore spread the rumor that those going to the United States would be badly treated and sold as slaves. To reinforce the fear of America, the 1970s TV series *Roots*—narrating the misadventures of Kunta Kinte, an African slave in America—was screened in the camp. Moreover, Kjetil Tronvoll and Daniel Mekonnen, who were present in the camp in 2008, reported on DMLEK's recurrent threats.[22]

DMLEK was evidently not alone in fiercely opposing the Kunamas' resettlement, however. While doing my fieldwork in Shimelba, I was secretively informed by some of my informants that I should be careful about inquiring too deeply into the resettlement issues. According to them, some local officers were selling the identities of Kunama refugees accepted for resettlement to Ethiopian nationals.

Aside from the above pressures, other sources reported that Kunamas were scared of resettlement because of their unfamiliarity with urban living. The department responsible for cultural training in the resettlement program since 2007, noted that many Kunamas were "not familiar with most modern amenities, they have a fear of the apartments in which they'll live in the United States. Most specifically, they have a fear of fires in these apartments." Last, but not least, many of the Kunamas had left loved ones in Eritrea, and going to the United States would put an insurmountable distance between them. Resettlement was perceived as treason to their family members and community traditions. Old people were usually more determined in their decision to stay, and their younger relatives did not want to leave them behind.

Nana, an old Kunama lady whom I met in Shimelba, told me she had no interest in going to the United States, shaking her head. She and her family came from Bimbinna, a conglomerate of villages on the southern side of the Gash River. They had fled to Ethiopia in 2000 because of the war, she said, but her sisters had stayed behind. She was receiving remittances from her two sons in the United States, but she was not interested in going there. Many other Kunamas repeatedly said they did not want to resettle because part of their family was still in Eritrea. This was

FIGURE 10. Kunama refugees threshing teff (*Eragrostis abyssinica*) in Shimelba camp (photo by the author, 2013)

especially the case for those who reached Ethiopia in 2000 and had since then started to rebuild their lives in the camp.[23]

Older Kunamas' attitudes to migration were embedded in a completely different cosmology of destinations to that of the refugees I had met before. The United States was not considered an attractive place, but rather a place to be scared of, precisely because of its modernity and distance from the cultural and material world with which Kunamas were familiar. The return to the homeland, on the other hand, was portrayed as the only desirable way ahead. The homeland was the repository of positive values, and return there was felt as a moral obligation.

Besides having less historical exposure to international migration in comparison with the urbanized Tigrinya population, Kunamas tended to have a stronger relationship with the land, like most indigenous people around the world.[24] As the Kunama scholar Alexander Naty has showed, Kunamas' religious and cultural life is rooted in the landscape of southwestern Eritrea.[25] Without falling into unnecessary cultural reifications or wanting to fix people's identity in a specific place, it seems undeniable that the strong relationship between people and their land is also crucial in analyzing their aspirations to migrate elsewhere.[26]

Just as the Hutus studied by Liisa Malkki in Tanzanian refugee camps rejected local integration to preserve their long-term dream of returning to Burundi,[27] Kunamas also refused resettlement in order not to give up their imagined future at home. Not unlike the Hutus, they felt that migration would contribute to the loss of their "identity," the bundle of memories, practices, and relationships that connected them with the natural landscape and social fabric of their homeland. However, things had started changing for them too.

SONS AGAINST FATHERS: EMERGING GENERATIONAL DIVIDES

Although most Kunamas had refused to resettle in 2008, I quickly realized while in the camp that many had changed their minds. Those Kunamas who were only children at the time of the group resettlement proposal were now young men and women eager to move to the United States in spite of their parents' opinions. However, resettlement is a family process, and these generational differences were generating many tensions within families. Often young Kunamas remained stuck in the camp because their cases had been frozen because one of their parents having refused the resettlement in the first place.

A tall, shy-looking young boy sat down close to me while I was interviewing a group of Kunama men. I did not even notice him until Noah said, "Why don't you talk to him? His story is interesting; you should listen to him." Jambo lived in a poor hut with his three sisters, his aunt, her boyfriend, and her children. Jambo's mother had died, and he did not have a good relationship with his father, so the aunt had taken care of him since childhood. She came to greet us holding and nursing her baby. We sat in front of the hut, and Jambo started telling me how eager he was to go to the United States. The problem was that his aunt and his father had refused resettlement at first and their family case had been archived as a rejection. Even though Jambo was now nineteen, his case was linked with his father's case, who was still determined not to leave the camp.

Jambo's story was not an exception in the camp; rather it was the instance of a common conundrum, which the UNHCR resettlement unit had a hard time solving. In UNHCR's perspective, family unity is a principle to be protected—the opportunity for resettlement should not become the cause of family disintegration. For this reason, the group resettlement in 2008 was organized through family cases. However, the refusal to resettle as well as different positions inside the nuclear family had not been anticipated in UNHCR operations, and even now, many cases remain frozen.

Aside from their practical—and tragic—implications, Kunamas' shifting attitudes to resettlement can be interpreted as an instance of how migration progressively comes to be seen as an appropriate livelihood strategy in a community with little previous experience of it. Due both to exposure to processes of cultural circulation and progressive estrangement from the homeland, young Kunamas were gradually developing a preference for migrating on rather than waiting for an unlikely return back home. The feedback of the pioneers who accepted the reset-

FIGURE 11. Resettlement board in Shimelba (photo by the author, 2013)

tlement, the impact of their remittances in the lives of those left in the camp, and the wider exposure of the young generations to Western lifestyles had inevitably transformed the projects of many. Instead of going back to a home that they have almost forgotten or never even seen, most young Kunamas are now searching for a home elsewhere. Unlike their Tigrinya counterparts, however, those Kunamas I encountered were not ready to pursue migration at all costs.

I often asked those among the Kunamas who were interested in migration if they had ever thought about reaching Europe irregularly. Their usual reaction was a bewildered look, as if I had asked something ridiculous. "It is illegal, we cannot do it," one of them told me. Another man in his thirties, who had been telling me how desperate he was to leave the camp, said: "It is very dangerous! Don't you know that people die in these journeys?" These answers were surprising to me, since for the other Eritreans, illicit migration was almost a given. No matter the dangers or the legal implications, other Eritrean refugees living in similar conditions as the Kunamas in Shimelba were ready to run all risks to reach Europe. Irregular—undocumented—onward migration[28] was common, almost the norm in all the camps, with the exception of Shimelba. What determined such a difference between these groups?

Part of the answer lies in the different structure of opportunities available to Kunamas. While Tigrinyas had a well-established network of relatives abroad to support their journeys, and a large number of friends and acquaintances along the way to Europe, Kunamas' family and ethnic networks were less developed in the diaspora.[29] Moreover, only a few Kunamas had the financial means to move forward by themselves, and they were not familiar with the idea of doing so. It seemed that, in spite of the emergence of a new desire to migrate among the younger generations, mobility at all costs had not (yet) become the norm for them, unlike for other Eritreans I had previously met. Perhaps mobility based on a cosmology of destinations may emerge as a second phase after the diffusion of a more general culture of migration. While in the latter, mobility is a widespread orientation, it is not yet perceived as a moral duty. My research in urban areas of the Ethiopian and Sudanese capitals aimed at exploring the normative aspect of mobility among those who are determined to leave at all costs.

SEEKING WAYS OUT FROM ADDIS ABABA AND KHARTOUM

Refugees in Ethiopia and Sudan—the main recipient countries up today—officially have no freedom of movement or right to work outside the camps, but there are large urban refugee populations in both Addis Ababa and Khartoum.[30] According to official UNHCR statistics, there were 3,500 Eritreans in Addis Ababa in 2014.[31] Roughly 2,500 participated in the Ethiopian government "out-of-camp" scheme, many of them students at Ethiopian universities.[32] Besides these registered urban refugees, there were also many other Eritrean refugees living in the city. Some, after six months in the camp, could obtain permission to stay in Addis to follow up on their visa application, while others had short-term permission to visit their relatives. Many simply stayed in the city without permission.[33]

The situation in Khartoum, the Sudanese capital, is similar. Since the late 1970s, Khartoum has hosted a substantial population of both Ethiopians and Eritreans (around 33,000 in 1981 according to Ahmed Karadawi).[34] According to official UNHCR statistics, there were around 20,000 Eritrean refugees in Khartoum in 2014.[35] The actual number is probably much higher, considering the number of individuals who do not register with UNHCR or the Sudanese government's Commissioner of Refugees (COR).[36] A continuous flow of people leave Sudanese camps to settle in the city on their own—either to work or to look for migration opportunities. Unlike Ethiopia, Sudan does not have any out-of-camp policy and the only refugees allowed to live outside the camp are those who are vulnerable and included in the UNHCR protection program. All the others who live in the city usually have no legal right to reside there.

Although in Khartoum as well as in Addis Ababa I interviewed a wide variety of stakeholders, ranging from diplomatic officers to United Nations High Commissioner for Refugees and the International Organisation of Migration workers, I spent most of my time hanging out with Eritreans in different settings of the two cities. My first contact in Addis Ababa was with an Eritrean nun I had known since my first visit in the country in 2011. Originally from the village of

Mai Nefas, Sister Kudussan had been living in Addis Ababa for over twenty years. Unable to return home because of wars and diplomatic tension, she was stuck in a country she had had been brought up to hate. She managed a convent and its associated breeding farm on the periphery of the city. When I went to meet her, I soon realized that her convent had become a meeting point for young, usually Catholic, refugees from Mai Nefas and the surrounding villages. Many of them were waiting for their family reunification visas so as to be reunited with their husbands or wives. The convent thus became one of the main places where I could meet young refugees and participate with them in religious festivities or simple coffee ceremonies.

In parallel, I used to hang out with a group of Eritrean students from the University of Addis Ababa. Most of them in their late twenties or early thirties saw few prospects of remaining in the country. Their Ethiopian degree was in fact not enough to allow them access to the regular labor market. Among them was Adonay, a twenty-eight-year-old philosophy student, whose story I tell later.

In January—after my research in the camps—I moved to Mebrat Haile, one of the neighborhoods most inhabited by Eritreans in Addis, with Violetta, who had been a practicing physician in Eritrea before escaping with her uncle, Gaim, to Ethiopia. Overwhelmed by the work conditions, Violetta had managed to convince her uncle, who was a soldier in the border area, to escape. She was hoping to get a sponsor visa from a relative in Canada. When I met her in November, she was twenty-seven and living with her uncle in a one-room flat in Mebrat Haile. Her uncle was soon to leave for Khartoum, however, and she was happy to share the rent with me for a few months. Violetta became not just my flat mate but a valuable informant and a friend. Smart and fluent in English, Violetta was my translator in several occasions (see Appendix).

Our neighborhood was filled with Eritrean refugees. Many of them just managed small internet points or pool rooms; others were just living there waiting for the opportunity to move on. Our time was marked by house visits to our neighbors and friends. Many people I knew lived there: Alazar's family had recently moved there, other friends and relatives of those I had met in Eritrea and Italy were also staying there. Even members of some of the families I had met in Adi Harush waved to me on the streets.

In March, many of my informants from Eritrea and Ethiopia moved to Khartoum, and I decided to follow them. For example, Hagos, the spokesman for the group of Eritrean refugees at Sister Kudussan's convent, moved with his cousin to Aljiraf, a neighborhood in Khartoum traditionally populated by Eritreans. Lwam had left and reached Sudan in that period, and Violetta's uncle was there working as a *badjaj* (three-wheel taxi) driver. However, not all of them seemed keen to meet me again. Lwam did not contact me and I did not manage to meet Violetta's uncle, despite my efforts to do so. I believe that the reason why they avoided meeting me was not per-

FIGURE 12. Mebrat Haile: an Eritrean neighborhood in Addis Ababa (photo by the author, 2014)

sonal antipathy, but rather the fear that I might somehow disturb their plans to move on. Lwam, for example, contacted me only when she had safely reached Germany. Maybe they thought that, being in touch with their families, I might reveal their plan to leave the country to their relatives and make them worry. Maybe they believed that I would have tried to persuade them not to undertake that journey.

In Khartoum, I lived with Maria, a twenty-eight-year-old Eritrean and her eight-year-old child, Anna, in a house shared with other four Eritrean families in the Jabah area in March–April 2014. Violetta had explained to Maria that I was a researcher, asking if she could help me to settle in the city. She guaranteed that I was a decent flatmate with no special expectations and that I could help with the house expenses, so Maria generously accepted me. Maria had lived for several years in Addis Ababa before recently moving to Khartoum. As she told me, one of the main reasons she had left Ethiopia was because Anna's father was cheating on her. Her departure to Khartoum, however, was only thought as a temporary step on the path to further destinations. I spent most of my time with Maria, her neighbors and friends from Asmara.

Along with Eritreans, in both cities I had friends among the locals who helped me with the practicalities of life in a new country. I often tended to mix my Eritrean and local networks while going out in the evening or spending some leisure time together. This was for me a natural way of dealing with people who were close to me, but often these interactions gave rise to conflicts that I did not at first anticipate. The interactions between refugees and locals that I created with my presence in the field, however, allowed me to grasp some of deep-rooted mistrust and prejudices that separate Eritrean refugees from Sudanese and Ethiopians.

Although Khartoum and Addis Ababa present different challenges and opportunities for Eritrean refugees, in both places I found a constant desire to move on among my informants. As I show in the following section, this desire to move onwards is certainly the result of both the limited access to the local labor market, and the need to attain some kind of legal existential stability. However, the drive to migrate further also emerges from deep-rooted moral obligations toward left-behind family members and the imaginaries surrounding destination countries. These are continually reproduced in the relatively segregated places inhabited by Eritrean refugees in these two cities and generate a sort of collective effervescence, which provides fertile ground for embarking on dangerous border crossings.

ROUND-UPS AND THE RISK OF DEPENDENCY: CONTINUITY OF LIFE STRUGGLES BEFORE AND AFTER EXILE

After a three-hour Sunday mass, Maria and I found ourselves in the middle of a police round-up. We were just coming out of the Catholic Church of St. Peter and Paul in the center of Khartoum. Suddenly, the crowd started to get agitated. "There are policemen ready to take us when we exit the church," murmured an old woman with eyes full of fear. "They have already taken someone." Maria started to become nervous. "I cannot come to church anymore. It is too dangerous . . . now what do we do?" Some refugees were organizing a *hamjad*—a minivan—to pick them up at the entrance of the church. I went out to look for a *hamjad* to avoid the risk of Maria and Anna being arrested, and we got home safely.

In Khartoum, police round-ups are common and especially feared by refugees. Those who are apprehended without papers—but sometimes also those who have papers—are incarcerated, usually blackmailed in exchange for money and, sometimes, returned to camps. Eritreans call these round-ups *geffa,* the same word used to identify the round-ups in Eritrea to catch draft-dodgers. The need to run from police and authorities is one main element of continuity in the lives of Eritreans before and after their migration.

Round-ups were certainly among the top reasons why life in Sudan was considered unsafe and undesirable by my informants. They often told me of run-ins with Sudanese police and their attempts to pass unnoticed in order not to be harassed. "To be unnoticed" mainly entailed for men not to wander alone at night in unknown places, not to drink too much, and to follow the Muslim dress code (long sleeves and long trousers). For women, it meant wearing a long, black *jellabiah* (traditional Muslim dress) and head scarf as local women do.

Police controls were less common in Addis Ababa. However, while I was there in November 2013, my informants told me that the Ethiopian police were knocking on doors in Mebrat Haile to check refugees' permissions to be out of the camp. These controls were probably a consequence of rioting in the Tigray camps a few weeks before.[37] And even so, living an "unnoticed life" was easier for Eritreans in Ethiopia. Not only is Tigrinya spoken in Ethiopia, but Tigrinya Eritreans resemble most Ethiopian highlanders (Amharas, Tigriyans, and Oromos) and have both their religion and cultural elements such as food and traditional clothing in common with them.

Besides avoiding authorities, the biggest problem for those living in cities was dependence on relatives abroad. Once they leave the camp, refugees are usually not entitled to any assistance. UNHCR and other humanitarian organizations provide only limited support to a small number of refugees considered to be in special need. Thus, many Eritreans I met had to rely on their relatives' help for their daily living expenses. This was especially true in Addis Ababa, where finding work was harder. For example, Violetta had an uncle in Denmark paying her rent and sending her some money every two months. Likewise, Alazar's family received regular support from Minia's sons in Israel and Canada. My informants who were students at Addis Ababa University would have not been able to survive without the assistance of some relatives abroad, even if they received a small allowance and did not have to pay for tuition and accommodation.

Protracted dependence on relatives abroad was perceived as shameful, especially by young men, who acquire a status depending on their ability to provide for others. Like those young Eritreans stuck back home, the young refugees I met in Addis Ababa and Khartoum felt caught in a condition of socioeconomic, generational, and existential immobility.

Obtaining work in Ethiopia was generally deemed hard among refugees. Government control was tight and employers often asked for ID cards before hiring. Eritreans who could speak Amharic, or who had relatives or other connections in Addis Ababa, were more successful in finding work. Self-employment was tolerated and internet cafes and pool rooms managed by Eritreans kept popping up in Mebrat Haile during the months I spent there.

Although Khartoum was probably considered less safe, the job market seemed more accessible for refugees there. In Sudan, it was usual to find Eritreans employed as waiters, cleaners, and cooks. Many of them managed restaurants and other businesses in the name of a Sudanese national in the area of Jiref and Aldeim—historical Habesha neighborhoods in Khartoum. Some of Maria's neighbors worked in factories and workshops, while others owned rickshaws or minivans used as taxis. The Eritrean women I met—Maria too, for a short period—were employed as domestic workers.[38]

In spite of the challenging environment, these instances of informal integration and, at times, successful businesses illustrate that alternatives to onward mobility do exist. However, even those among my informants who seemed to do okay in Addis and Khartoum felt obliged to embark on life-threatening journeys to reach Europe rather than investing more in their present lives there.

Families back home were worried if their sons and daughters were in Ethiopia or Sudan. The refugees themselves perceive themselves in transit and those relatives abroad—like my informants in Italy—felt the pressure of helping them get to Europe or other developed countries. I used to insist with my closest Eritrean friends, like Maria and Adonay, that life in Addis Ababa and Khartoum was not so bad after all. Even if the challenges were many, I thought that it was worth looking for an informal job and starting a new life there, since options for leaving the country were either too risky or not accessible, but they believed that there had been no point in leaving Eritrea only to end up staying in Ethiopia or Sudan.

IMAGINING THE FIRST WORLD FROM A MALL IN KHARTOUM

Anna, Maria's eight-year-old daughter, had been impatient the whole day. Her mother was at work and I had been left to take care of her. "When is mom coming back?" Anna kept asking me. "Are we going to Afra?" Afra was a huge modern mall, not far from Khartoum international airport. Anna had never been there and probably had no idea of what it was, but from the way it had been presented to her, it sounded like a good place. During the day she had been boasting with the other children in the compound, "I am getting ready to go to Afra today . . . Milena and I will go there in the afternoon. You don't know what Afra is? Really?!!? Ahaha!" The other small children looked at her with their mouths open in admiration.

Afra was an oasis in the desert. The building, sheathed in shiny black glass, resembled an Arabic royal palace built of pinkish stone and surrounded by palms and fountains. Inside, vivid signs touted expensive shops selling international luxury goods. To pass from one floor to the other, we had to use the big escalators. It was Maria's first time on the escalator. "Anna *nei*—come! Give me your hand! Milena hold me, please!" Maria pleaded in a frightened voice. Our common friend, Michael, led us to a kind of pizza hut for dinner. We all ordered food, but Anna was too excited to eat; she wanted to go and play in the recreation room that she could see on the corner. After the pizza we ran around after Anna in the recreation room, full of trampolines and big inflatable balloons. "It's the first time I've seen Anna so happy," Maria said.

When we finally managed to drag Anna out, night had fallen on the city and the bright colors of the mall lights hid Khartoum's poverty. Maria exclaimed jokingly: "Oh! This is Italy, not Sudan! Afra is Italy and we have been to Italy today!" Michael then cynically pointed out the poor surroundings of the mall: "but all around us is still Sudan . . . "

Maria's ingenuous image of Italy—I believe she mentioned it more than another European country only for the sake of pleasing me—cannot certainly be generalized. Imaginaries are intrinsically and above all personal representations, although they also reflect collective views of reality.[39] In this case, Maria's association of the mall with Italy reflected an imaginary widely extant among many of my informants in Ethiopia and Sudan. Similar to what has been documented in African and other contexts, the mall, as the prototypical symbol of consumption, has come to represent modernity as a complex bundle of political and social freedom, technological advancement, and happiness.[40] In Maria's cosmology, the mall was a crucial feature of life in Europe, and she saw it as being somehow out of place in Sudan, a country which she despised for its lack of freedom, its dirtiness, its religious distance, and poverty.

Once home, while braiding Anna's hair before going to sleep, Maria energetically told her: "Anna, pray to our beloved sweet Jesus Christ, pray that one day you, Milena and I can all go to Italy . . . always pray, never forget it, ok? Good girl!" But there was never enough money, and Maria was also scared of the risks along the journey. However, the thought of providing a better future for Anna tormented her day and night. Her exhausting search for a way ahead, however, emerged not only from a desire for modernity, but also from a social milieu characterized by high levels of self-segregation, and socioeconomic and cultural homogeneity.

STICKING TOGETHER . . .

All of the dwelling arrangements I visited, whether in Addis Ababa or Khartoum, mirrored Eritreans' perception of being in transit, and their need to consolidate and build up their social resources by living together with their compatriots. Urban refugees tend to concentrate in the same neighborhoods and share accommodation among themselves. However, the areas inhabited by my informants were not ghettos: they were not especially destitute neighborhoods, and they were populated by refugees and locals alike. For example, Mebrat Haile, where I used to live in a one-room flat with Violetta, was a lower-middle-class neighborhood. It covered a whole valley with huge grey condominiums, which, by local standards, are modern, desirable accommodation. Most Eritrean refugees I met lived there, along with Ethiopians. Several groups of four or five shared a one-room flat with a single toilet, while others stayed in cheaper accommodation in other areas.

In Khartoum, the neighborhood where I lived with Maria and her child was mostly inhabited by Sudanese (but we also had several Eritrean neighbors) and was not particularly deprived. Other Eritreans lived in the traditional Habesha area of Aldaim or around Aljiraf and Al-Shafa, where there had been Eritrean

FIGURE 13. Typical Eritrean accommodation in Khartoum (photo by the author, 2014)

schools for refugee children since the 1980s and there were now recreational centers. Although our neighbors were mainly locals, our compound was exclusively inhabited by Eritrean refugees. A couple who worked in a soap factory by day and made sandals at night lived in front of Maria and Anna's one-room apartment. Istifanos, the husband, had managed to collect enough money to reach Sweden in June, while his wife waited for him to send her the reunification visa. Thirty-year-old Jennah and her two children lived behind us, waiting for reunification visas to join the father in Sweden. In front of Jennah lived an old woman with her silent sixteen-year-old nephew, who moved to Libya in less than a month. Finally, next to Istifanos's room, there was Haile's extended family. Most of them were waiting for family reunification visas to join their partners in Canada. and the others were looking for options to follow them.

Other refugee houses that I visited in the city were also socioeconomically and ethnically homogeneous. These enclaves were not only emerging from the need to support each other in a challenging environment. They were also the result of mistrust between Eritreans and local populations. Interethnic relations between Eritreans, Sudanese, and Ethiopians are embedded in a decades-long history of power imbalances, religious diversity, and political and national conflicts. It is crucial to gain insights into the stereotypes that characterize those relations in order to understand Eritrean views on Sudan and Ethiopia and why they do not represent viable destinations.

. . . WHILE DISTRUSTING OTHERS

Many of the Eritrean refugees I met all throughout my fieldwork depicted Ethiopians as lazy, cowardly, and uneducated, often referring to them as *Agame*, people from northern Ethiopia who used to work as low-status laborers in Eritrea in the past.[41] These stereotypes were created in opposition to self-representations of Eritreans as loyal, hard-working, brave, and educated. In issues concerning refugee procedures and associated complications, Ethiopians were often described as corrupt, envious of Eritreans and of the possibility of their being resettled elsewhere. Although commonalities with Ethiopian highlanders are acknowledged, as denoted by the self-denomination Habesha,[42] the social distance between the two groups seems wide. This becomes evident when looking at the perception of a suitable marriage: for many, having a daughter marry an Ethiopian would be a great misfortune. This is a concern especially because, in Tigrinya patrilineal society, children will take the name, the nationality, and their ethnic belonging from the paternal lineage.

Conversely, Eritreans were mostly depicted as conceited and arrogant by Ethiopians, who treated them with a paternalistic attitude. Violetta often had to endure comments from my Ethiopian friends, who, while intending to show their solidarity to her as an Eritrean sister, somehow insulted her pride. One of the first things they would say after they discovered she was Eritrean, was: "Oh you are our sister; Eritreans and Ethiopians are the same people, it is just because of dirty politics that we are separated and your people are suffering." Although this was meant to be friendly, it did not sound quite that way to Violetta, proud as she was, like most Eritreans, of the struggle for independence.

While Ethiopian and Eritrean identities are constructed as opposed,[43] yet united by a set of recognized physical and cultural commonalities, Eritrean and Sudanese people were seen as incommensurably different. Even before getting to Sudan, my Eritrean friends told me never to trust Sudanese. When I got to Sudan, I discovered that Sudanese often represented the reification of all evils in my informants' eyes. Maria, for example, thought that Sudan was filthy and that Sudanese people were not trustworthy. She hated the lack of freedom in the country, symbolized by the requirement to wear the veil and the long black Muslim dress.

These negative beliefs translated into Maria's daily practices. She invariably looked for an Eritrean taxi driver, saying: "Let's get a Habesha one. I don't like Sudanese." Maria said it was very easy to distinguish Sudanese from Habesha: according to her, the latter were cute and slim, while the former were fat with ugly faces. However, this categorization was clearly unrealistic. Once, one of my Sudanese friends, Ismael, a twenty-six-year-old graduate from Khartoum University, took me home. He was tall and slim, with a clean and kind face. Maria happily approached him in Tigrinya: "Are you Habesh?" Ismael replied in Arabic: "No, I am from here." Maria was very surprised to realize that Sudanese were not so different from Habesha in the end, but she kept disapproving of my friendship with Ismael anyway.[44]

In turn, as I realized during several conversations with taxi drivers, shopkeepers, students, and guides, Habesh were also seen rather negatively by many Sudanese. My sponsor in Sudan, a businessman in his thirties, bluntly expressed his doubts about me living with Eritreans instead of renting a hotel room: "Habesh people do not have prestige; they are not intelligent. We, the Sudanese, feel they are inferior to us. Why do you want to live with them?"

Some of the stereotypes characterizing Eritreans' interactions with locals in Sudan and Ethiopia are remarkably postcolonial. This is evident in the continuous comparison between the "cleanliness" and beauty of Asmara with the "dirtiness" of Addis Ababa and Khartoum.[45] Although partly resulting from colonial discourse, the complexity of interethnic relationships between Eritreans, Sudanese, and Ethiopians also emerges from precolonial conflicts and recent social history. Reciprocal fears, mistrust, and negative judgments cannot be understood without considering the thirty years of war against Ethiopian rulers, the forced displacements of thousand families from Ethiopia in 1998–99, and the difficulties historically experienced by Eritreans in Sudan.[46] Religious interpretations (such as the veto on Muslim women marrying Christian men) and other culturally shaped gender attitudes can be added to explanations based on social and economic stratifications.[47]

The above considerations are necessarily simplifications of a much more nuanced and larger range of attitudes marking interethnic relations in both countries. However, they provide a rough idea of widespread prejudices, which may increase an already existing segregation of urban refugees, while strengthening their self-identification as a group in transit. Living together with little or negative interaction with local populations reinforces Eritreans' feeling of being there only temporarily, while longing for other destinations. Within this sociocultural and legal context, it is not surprising that an emotional status comparable to what Émile Durkheim called a "collective effervescence" emerges in periods when structural opportunities for (irregular) mobility open up.

In *The Elementary Forms of Religious Life* (1912), Durkheim describes the collective feelings generated in the rituals of Australian Aborigines and argues that through this "collective effervescence," societal moral order as well as individual belonging to it was renewed and reinforced.[48] The mobility practices as well as the mobility-related discourse continually reproduced in the shared dwelling places of my informants were strengthening the moral and eschatological order implicit in their cosmology of destinations.

SPRING FEVER IN ADDIS ABABA . . .

"Egi bahari tsobok [now the sea is fine]" and "Egi serghie tsobok [now the road is good]" were common statements in the conversation among my friends and neighbors in Mebrat Haile. As the European winter was finishing and spring was at the door, the neighborhood was effervescent in anticipation of the departure of many of its inhabitants. These statements were not simply words in the air, but declarations of intent. Between February and March, more than half of the people I knew had left Mebrat Haile to go to Sudan and from there, crossed over to Libya and then to Europe. Even many of my friends in Eritrea, such as Lwam and Valentina, moved in that period to go to Sudan (Lwam arrived in Italy soon afterward).

March is the right month, according to popular wisdom there, to start the journey from Sudan to Libya. The Sahara desert is not too hot and the waters of the Mediterranean Sea will be calmer by April than during the winter. Many people I used to hang out with called me from Sudan to give me their news; others just disappeared, and I found out about their departure only long afterward. The ones who had remained wondered if they had made the right choice, or simply kept trying to get enough money to follow their companions to Sudan.

In the evenings, the internet cafés were still full of young people, but conversations and interlocutors had changed. Since I started living in Mebrat Haile, Violetta and I used to spend long hours in Amanuel's internet café trying to connect with our families or simply listening to Amanuel—the twenty-nine-year-old Eritrean manager—playing *krar,* a traditional lyre. Before March, I noticed those sitting close to me chatting with their families and friends in Eritrea through Yahoo messenger and Facebook or video-calling their relatives or partners in Europe or the United States. In March, conversations were more often with friends who had left Mebrat Haile and reached Sudan: "Temesgen hawey, denhando? Sudan Kemmei? [Temesgen my brother, how are you? How is Sudan?]" A group of young boys from the neighborhood gathered in Amanuel's internet point to talk to their friend in Khartoum and kept joking with him on skype: "Now you have to speak Arabic, bro, how are you managing?"

In that period Violetta and I often went to our favorite juice shop. Once, while we were waiting for our juices, a young Eritrean man started to talk to Violetta. "Are you one of us?" he said in Tigrinya. "Yes, I am," answered Violetta with a smile. "How did you know?" "I can see it from your face. You are an *Asmarina* [a positive term to define someone who grew up in Asmara]!" The two started chatting. Dani was twenty-seven and also from Asmara. "I am leaving to Libya soon, but I am scared," he said quietly, and then more resolutely continued. "I don't want to go, but I have no choice. I have no process [i.e. visa application] here,[49] unless your *ferengi* friend marries me"—giving me a sarcastic look. "One of my brothers is in Switzerland, the other has just made it to Norway . . . I have to go." Not only the fear of the risky journey, but also the anxiety of being left behind in the run for Europe was clear in Dani's words.

In that period, even those Eritrean refugees who had told me that they did not want to take risks to get to Europe became convinced that the moment was right. Amanuel, the internet point manager, for example, had told me about his plan to join some of his friends in Angola, but one evening in late February, coming back from a night out, I overheard him saying to Violetta in Tigrinya: "Now the sea is calm. I have decided to go to Europe. I am planning to leave in a few weeks." He explained that all his flat mates had already left. He reached Norway two months later.

Even Adonay, the philosophy student at Addis Ababa University, changed his mind around then. Since I had met him, he had been asking for my help to get a scholarship to a European university, but never seemed really to have Europe as his goal. "Have you heard what happened in Lampedusa last October?" he would say. "No, no, the risks are too high . . . that is not for me." Then his plans abruptly changed in March. One night I received a message from him: "Milena! I will depart for Sudan tomorrow. I will keep in touch with you."

I was amazed; the week before, we had proofread one of his last essays before his master's thesis and he seemed determined to finish his degree in Ethiopia. Why had he changed his mind? Worried about losing the opportunity at least to say goodbye, I phoned him, asking, "What happened, Adonay?" "Sorry, Milena—he replied—These journeys are very risky, I did not want to tell you. But nowadays these journeys can be profitable; the way through Libya is open and there is good rate of success."

We decided to meet in the Italian-built neighborhood of Piazza a few days later. Adonay looked worried in his tidy but worn-out button-down shirt. While we were sipping coffee from the terrace of a café, he kept touching his head and was nervously laughing while explaining to me about the uncle who was supposed to pay for his journey.

"But why, Adonay, did you change your mind? You said it was too dangerous!" I asked him. "I have been a burden for my family—he responded—At this age I should be able to provide for myself. At least. Yeah, yeah, it is not good, to become so miserable. I have been waiting here for very long, now it's time to risk. If I die, I will die, that's it."

The difficulties in finding jobs, shame at not being an independent man, and the desire to migrate to a more suitable destination had been the ingredients of Adonay's life for a while, but they had now become unbearable. Whereas all his friends, classmates at university and relatives were moving on, Adonay's prospects had not changed. Immersed in the emotional atmosphere of anxiety and departure characterizing Eritreans' dwelling spaces in those months, Adonay's carefulness about risks turned into determination to migrate at all costs. However, his plans were never realized. His uncle was not ready to pay, but instead promised to help him establish some kind of business in Addis. Unfortunately, the uncle died a few months later, leaving Adonay without support—either to migrate or to start a new life in Ethiopia.

. . . AND IN KHARTOUM

When I moved from Addis to Khartoum at the end of March, I found that even there, Eritrean refugees seemed to be affected by "the fever of leaving." Maria's place was a buzz of continuous coming and going of Eritrean refugees, especially on Sundays. Maria would sit in front of her small stove and start preparing coffee while kindly entertaining her guests. No matter what the topic started as, it would not take long before all conversations shifted to the usual question: "*Nski process allo*?"—Do you have a process?

Some of Maria's guests were lucky: they had managed to apply for a sponsor visa to Canada thanks to the help of some relatives there; others had found a husband or a wife somewhere who could grant them a reunification visa. Everyone was going to leave soon. Even those who did not have money for the smugglers were determined to leave. Rahel, one of Maria's guests, told us that she and her husband did not have money, but were planning to ask the smugglers to take them to Libya and from there, one call here, one call there, and with God's help, someone would pay. "After all," Rahel said. "Libya is closer to Europe than Khartoum, isn't it?"

The coffee ceremony in Maria's house was somehow a collective ritual in which mobility-related norms were reproduced and the longing for onward migration was elicited.[50] This could also eventually lead to attempting irregular migration or simply to frustration at the inability to move, as in Maria's case.

"I would really like to go to Libya," Maria sighed after a phone call announcing that a friend and her baby had made it to Italy. "But I am too scared for Anna and I do not have money. People told me that if you do not have money, the smugglers rape you. I heard of one girl who has been raped by five men!! But Europe would be good for Anna . . . I would like her to study in a college and to learn English well."

Although Maria's past has remained a mystery for me until now (at first she told me she had no close family members, but then I received a call from her brother in the United States) it was clear that she did not have relatives ready to pay for her journey—otherwise, I believe, she would have moved then. The meager salary from her cleaning job—which anyway did not last for long—did not allow for daily survival and the smugglers' fee to reach Libya. Out of the 500 Sudanese pounds a month (about €50), she paid 380 in rent, and the remaining money was barely enough for food—not even sufficient to send Anna to school. This brings us back to the conditions that produce immobility even in the presence of strong aspirations to migrate. Maria's case illustrates again how capabilities to move are stratified according to socioeconomic status, gender, and the ability to mobilize resources from one's own informal network of family and compatriots.[51] However, the availability of resources is not enough to make sense of refugees' determination to move on. Maria's aspirations to live in the First World and to provide a better future for Anna were continually reproduced by these social gatherings where all her guests talked about how and when to go.

"The road is great now," Seare, one of our usual guests, used to repeat confidently. "Nowadays there are no problems at all! You should go Maria! Don't be scared! Anna is big now . . . there are a lot of women who are still breast-feeding, but are already crossing the sea! Italians patrol the sea with helicopters, and ships come to fetch the refugees in the middle of the sea."[52]

"Yes," Maria muttered. "But we have no money." At this point the conversation would often turn to the role I could possibly play as Maria's helper.

Visitors would ask if I could provide her with a legal invitation to come to Italy or if I could pay for her journey across the Mediterranean. Sometimes they would ask Maria in Tigrinya, while on other occasions guests were more direct. Seare was extremely insistent. "What can you do for them? Take Anna with you then Maria will come by boat. I know one friend who can help us. If you pay the money then everything will be ok. Why are you scared? Now there is no problem!"

Although I told Seare that I did not agree with the journey, he kept insisting until I lost my temper and told him I was not ready under any circumstance to pay for such a risky trip. But these encounters left me wondering what my role as researcher was and what ethical principle I should have applied at that time (see Appendix). After these visits, Maria was often troubled. One time, she could not sleep and we stayed up for a while, chatting. "Milena, I am always thinking . . . where will Anna and I go?" she said. "How will we manage? My God . . . all our neighbors have some kind of process or some money, but I do not have anything. I always think I must be honest—if I am honest God will like it and He will open the way for me and for Anna. But I think too much, so sometimes, I start cleaning the room, I clean and clean and then I feel better." Most of the time I felt powerless in the face of all her difficulties and suffering. I told Maria that I was going to help her to send Anna to school, but her expectations were much higher.

After my departure from Sudan, I kept in touch with her, as with most of my closest informants, and helped her send Anna to school. We decided together that Ethiopia would be an easier place to settle for them. They had Ethiopian passports, so Maria could work and Anna could peacefully go to school. I asked one of my Italian friends in Ethiopia to look for employment for Maria and soon thereafter, Maria found work as a cleaner in two Italian houses that provided a good income. They found a room close to Anna's school and for a few months everything seemed to proceed smoothly. Then I received a call from Maria saying that she wanted to leave again to go to Sudan. Life was hard in Addis, too. Her husband had come back home, but he was still behaving badly, and Maria could not bear him. After a month, I received her call from Sudan. She said she wanted to go to Libya and take Anna with her. She wanted me to pay. I refused, saying that the situation in Libya was too dangerous. Our conversation left us both disappointed. I am sure she thought I was a stingy, ungrateful Western woman, and I thought she was a careless Habesha woman. Then, the news reached Maria that a boat with seven hundred people on board had sunk in the Mediterranean (April 20, 2015), which slowed down her plans to cross over to Europe. However, her restlessness has not ceased, even now. After that, she decided to go back to Eritrea—apparently it was safe for her to do so. Then, a few months later, she went back to Sudan. The last time I talked to her, she was asking me for help to move to Ethiopia again.

Maria's frustrated desire for mobility points to the strength of collective imaginaries, moral attitudes, and communal emotional energy surrounding the search for a new home among refugees in transit. Although the availability of money and the capacity to mobilize it through one's own networks is crucial to understand who moves and who does not, the determination to move at all costs reflects the power of shared moral expectations associated with migration and the widespread belief that these cannot be met in countries like Sudan and Ethiopia. Moralities, imaginaries, and emotions are not only relevant for interpreting the flow of migration from Ethiopia and Sudan, but also—and arguably even more so—in analyzing secondary movements within Europe.

3

An Endless Journey

*Transnational and Peer Pressure in
Onward Migration in Europe*

The previous chapter examined Eritrean refugees' desire to move on from their first country of asylum after escaping from their homeland. That desire did not disappear after they arrived in their first European country, in this case, Italy.[1] In spite of easy access to legal protection,[2] well-established Eritrean communities, and long-standing historical linkages, most Eritreans do not want to settle there. Instead, they repeatedly gambled on the possibility to seek asylum elsewhere.

Secondary refugee movement in Europe is pervasive, notwithstanding policies aimed at limiting it, such as the Dublin Regulation.[3] According to official figures, over 34,000 Eritreans landed on the Italian coast in 2014, but only 450 sought asylum there[4]. Most, if not apprehended by the authorities upon arrival, try to avoid the identification procedure and travel on to other countries, preferably Scandinavian ones, such as Norway and Sweden. This chapter adopts a transnational approach in order to make sense of how and why such movement takes place in spite of the related risks. Jumping from my informants' everyday lives in Italy to their families' houses in Asmara, I illustrate how the feeling of an "unfinished journey" emerges from several factors, ranging from limited contact with previous generations of Eritrean migrants to poor integration into local society, from the influence of information from destination countries to the expectations of families back home.

My argument is that the secondary mobility of Eritrean refugees is neither simply an adaptive strategy to cope with the difficulties of everyday life nor just the outcome of social connections in other countries. Rather, it is also the product of a shared cosmology of destinations that prescribes both socioeconomic goals and the most suitable destinations. Italy is not a final destination, either for migrants or for their families back home, in this set of moral obligations and geographic imaginaries, which overcome legal obstacles and persist even where local integration beckons.

HIDE AND SEEK: ERITREANS MOVING THROUGH ITALY

Many of the refugees whom I met in Eritrea, in Ethiopian refugee camps, in Addis Ababa and Khartoum, called me during the summer of 2014 to tell me that they were transiting through Italy. Lwam managed to cross over from Libya and continued her journey to Germany. Amanuel, the *krar* player who had managed the internet point in my neighborhood in Addis Ababa arrived in Sicily in August and proceeded to Norway a week later. Jacob, the resolute young engineer I met in Adi Harush, called me from Rome in June after almost a month in Libya to ask for help to continue his journey to Denmark. Seare, the promoter of the Mediterranean crossing at Maria's place in Khartoum, also called me from Milan before moving on to Denmark. Having known Lwam, Amanuel, Jacob, and Seare before, I was aware that Italy had never been their intended destination.

It was relatively easy for some of my informants to move on from Italy. Some of them simply bought a train ticket to Switzerland, Germany, or beyond. Others hired *passeurs* so as to cross without being caught and risking the registration of their biometric information—especially fingerprints—in the shared European database EURODAC, which would undermine their asylum application in other European countries. Invisibility is crucial for a smooth passage.[5]

Most of the Eritreans with whom I did my research in Italy between 2012 and 2013 arrived before 2009 and had not been able to escape the identification procedure.[6] Although this had made it hard for them to be granted asylum elsewhere in Europe, it did not prevent them from trying. Since their fingerprints had been recorded, some of my informants went so far as to burn them off chemically. Others left their Italian documents with their friends and moved to northern European countries, hoping that their fingerprints would not be found and that their cases would be considered differently by the authorities. Most of them were deported to Italy, but some managed to have their applications accepted after repeated attempts.[7]

These repeated attempts to seek asylum outside Italy were puzzling to me. I certainly knew that starting a new life was not easy in Italy given the little institutional support provided to refugees; however, I also thought that easy access to legal protection and well-established Eritrean communities in the country could function as magnets for newcomers. In light of the poor prospect of success, cost in time (two to three years on average), and dangers involved,[8] attempting to reach northern Europe did not seem worthwhile to me, but my informants thought differently. Eritrean migration through Italy provides an interesting point of departure for revisiting the debate on secondary mobility in Europe.

WELFARE DISPARITIES, ESTABLISHED NETWORKS AND ADAPTATION: REFUGEES' SECONDARY MOBILITY IN EUROPE

In spite of the efforts to homogenize the European asylum system (CEAS) deep-rooted disparities across welfare regimes play a crucial role in stratifying refugee reception. Asylum seekers and refugees in Italy receive little institutional support, whereas in northern European countries they receive stipends, housing, and other forms of assistance.[9]

The Italian reception system is widely stratified and varied. Several systems have been implemented to address asylum flows since 2000, with shifting balances in the roles of local and central authorities, civil society, and private actors.[10] This has produced extremely diverse reception conditions according to the period, the region, and the actors involved. Although regional differences in the assistance of refugees are not negligible and services provided can significantly vary from case to case, in general terms, the Italian reception system has hardly been effective in guiding asylum seekers and refugees through their local integration process.[11]

Most studies on secondary mobility have thus considered secondary movements as adaptive strategies to cope with economic, legal, and social restrictions that make life hard in the first country of emigration.[12] However, when applied to the Eritrean case, these interpretations fall short. Eritreans are determined to move through Italy even before having experienced the challenges—or the opportunities—of living there. They are resolute as regards seeking asylum elsewhere in spite of significant risks.

Other common explanations of refugees' secondary mobility in Europe argue for the relevance of historical and social connections in directing asylum seekers' destination choices.[13] Based on these accounts, asylum seekers would tend to go to countries—usually the ex-colonial metropole—with which they often share a common history, language, and cultural traits, and where they can often count on an already well-established community of compatriots. Even in this case, however, Eritreans seem an exception. In spite of colonial linkages to Italy and a historic Eritrean diaspora there, Eritreans generally do not want to remain in the country.[14]

In order to understand Eritreans' secondary movements, it is crucial to examine the transnational field of relationships in which refugees' everyday lives are embedded. Although relatively peripheral to refugee studies, the transnational approach has been crucial to understanding refugees' integration patterns, decision-making, aspirations, and movements.[15] Cindy Horst shows how the longing for onward mobility among Somalis living in Kenyan camps emerges from the continuous exchange of ideas, images, and money between refugees in developed countries and those in camps.[16] Khalid Koser and Charles Pinkerton highlight the role played by informal social networks in circulating information about possible destination countries and directing the choices of prospective asylum seekers.[17] Specifically with respect to the case of Eritreans seeking to reach Scandinavia, J.-P. Brekke and G. Brochmann argue that perceived inequalities between conditions in northern Europe and in Italy are only in part the result of objective disparities.[18] They also mirror information, images, and the aspirations of Eritreans in different locations.

Studies on transnationalism, however, consider the links between two sites; typically, the destination and the home country, or the home country and the expected areas of transit, or the area of transit and the preferred destination. Nevertheless, refugees participate in different transnational flows, which link them not only with compatriots who have reached their intended final destinations, but also with their families back home. On the one hand, they are often in contact by telephone, visits, and internet social networks with those kin and friends who have reached their final preferred destinations, usually a northern European country. On the other hand, Eritreans in Italy are linked to their families back home by a more or less implicit system of expectations concerning remittances, support for kin's prospective migration, and suitable countries of destinations. Such a trifold focus is of paramount importance to grasp Eritrean refugees' motivations to continue their journeys onward from Italy, as well as to understand their perception of "being stuck."

SPIES AND TRAITORS: HISTORICAL BACKGROUND AND GENERATIONAL DIVIDES AMONG THE DIASPORA

Eritreans have migrated to Italy since the 1960s. At first, this emigration mainly involved women employed as domestic workers by middle-class Italian families—who had often lived in Eritrea during the colonial era—in cities like Rome, Naples, and Milan.[19] In the late 1970s, however, many young men arrived, fleeing from violence and forced conscription in Eritrea. These often came to Italy with the intention of moving on to other countries that offered them better employment prospects and legal protection such as Germany, Canada, and the United States.[20]

Sociological literature from the 1980s describes numerous politically organized communities of Eritreans in Milan, Rome, Bologna, Bari, and Naples. In 1983, it was reported that in Milan there were some three thousand Eritreans with legal residence permits. Similarly, in Rome, it is reported that Eritreans numbered around three thousand in the early 1990s.[21] These numbers are likely inaccurate, however, given the difficulty in differentiating Ethiopians from Eritreans—they had the same nationality—and there were also numerous undocumented migrants.

Against this background, the literature on migrants' social networks might simplistically lead us to see the cohesive community of Eritreans in Italy as a major reason for refugee newcomers to stay in the country. However, the community in Italy, as much as elsewhere, is deeply divided.[22] Those who arrived before the 1990s are usually supporters of the former EPLF and current PFDJ government. Motivated by government propaganda, they see Eritreans who fled after independence as deserters and traitors.

During my field visits in Genoa, I met several Eritreans who had come to Italy in the 1970s. "These who come to Europe now are not refugees, but economic migrants!" Mrs. Gianna thundered from behind her desk in the local migration bureau when she heard what the subject of my research was. "They say that in Eritrea there is no freedom only because they want to attack the government! . . . They just do not want to work hard, but want to have a lot of money, a car . . . they see the pictures of their friends online, leaning on a Ferrari, but the Ferrari are not theirs! Only when they come here do they realize that the situation is very bad."

Mrs. Gianna's attitude to her young compatriots clearly reflected a pro government rhetoric that denied all the political aspects producing contemporary Eritrean migration, and in this, she was no exception among older Eritreans in Genoa. She introduced me to Rachele and her husband Giovanni, Eritreans of the older generation who had a small shop in one of the port alleys. I asked them if they knew any of those young Eritreans who had arrived in Genoa in the past five years. "I don't know them, Rachele replied. "I only see them passing through." Rachele and Michele also seemed to be convinced that there was no political reason to flee Eritrea, a political division that has hindered solidarity with recent Eritrean refugees. The older and the younger generations of Eritreans deeply distrusted each other. Mrs. Gianna's migration bureau was meant to be an important point of reference for immigrants and asylum seekers in the city, but the Eritrean refugees I met in Genoa were purposely avoiding it. "Mrs. Gianna and her friends are spies of the government," Brahnu, a twenty-seven-year-old refugee who had arrived in Italy in 2007, said. "We do not like to go to her office." My informants in Milan and Rome also routinely avoided contact with pro-government older Eritreans. As many of them owned Eritrean restaurants and the bars in the two cities, and the choice of where to have a meal could be complicated at times. Explaining why he did not want to take me to a specific restaurant in Milan, Gabriel said, "There are many things old Eritreans do not know . . . they have an old-fashioned mentality."

This does not mean that all connections between older and younger generations were severed. Not all older Eritreans were pro-government. Many were ex-guerrilla fighters in the ELF (the front antagonistic to the EPLF; see Introduction) and had been opposed to the current rulers right from the start. Older Eritreans in Italy are also often the ones who send money to help their kin migrate to Europe. Moreover, there were some local Eritrean organizations assisting young Eritreans At the beginning of my fieldwork, I tried to contact these associations in order to gain better access to the community, but I quickly realized that they were rarely a point of reference for recently arrived Eritreans. First, these associations were mostly engaged in transnational activities, rather than in providing services locally. Second, they had a more or less explicit political stance against the Eritrean government, and for this reason many newcomer refugees preferred not to have anything to do with them. As various scholars of Eritrea have highlighted, the exercise of "voice" has been significantly hindered by fear of government reprisals, as well as by the ongoing influence of the national unity and patriotism discourse.[23] Although some of the young Eritreans I met supported the recent opposition movement called Eritrean Youth for Social Change (EYSC), most tended to reject political engagement and to distrust everything associated with politics. Unlike in the 1980s, political parties now played a minor role in the lives of Eritrean refugees in Italy.[24] It is probably the generalized suspicion of all politicized forms of organized assistance that has led many newcomer refugees to organize among themselves to cope with the challenges of living in Italy, such as the lack of housing facilities.

LIVING AS SQUATTERS: BOTTOM-UP INTEGRATION OR SEGREGATION?

For those Eritreans who arrived before 2010, the general path was usually the following. During the assessment of their asylum application, they resided in a CARA (the Italian acronym for Centri di Accoglienza per Richiedenti Asilo, reception centers for asylum seekers), then they were pushed out without any assistance. The main system of assistance in place for refugees and asylum seekers since 2001, the Servizio centrale del Sistema di Protezione per Richiedenti Asilo e Rifugiati, or SPRAR, and its related regional projects could only host about 7,600 individuals in 2011, for example, when there were 37,000 asylum applications.[25]

Extreme poverty among refugee populations has been widely documented in the main Italian cities. The economic crisis, which has particularly hit those sectors where foreign workers are mostly employed,[26] has increased the difficulties for newcomers in finding employment. Moreover, due to limited institutional support in terms of housing, many refugees have found informal accommodation in squats, shantytowns, and overcrowded houses. In Genoa, my informants tended to share cheap flats in the area of Sampierdarena, an ex–working class neighborhood on the periphery of the city, today mostly inhabited by immigrants;[27] in Milan and Rome, many had started squatting in abandoned buildings. Looking at these housing arrangements is crucial to understanding the complex interaction between social segregation, forms of local integration, and transnationalism. It is in these

FIGURE 14. Collatina, the first squat inhabited exclusively by Eritreans and Ethiopians in Rome (photo by the author, 2012)

FIGURE 15. Ponte Mammolo, a now dismantled shantytown on the periphery of Rome (photo by the author, 2012)

contexts that Eritrean refugees exchange information about living conditions in other countries and reciprocally foster the desire to move on.

Along with the informal settlements—more or less shantytowns—that autonomously emerged at the periphery of the city, such as the village of Ponte Mammolo (fig. 8), organized squats have become one of the main housing strategies of recently arrived Eritreans in the city. These organized squats are the result of an interaction between refugees' housing necessities and the local movement for housing rights,[28] which has been active in the area for over fifty years.[29] Such an interaction has produced a wide range of different squats inhabited by Eritreans, characterized by different levels of ethnic concentration, socioeconomic integration, autonomy from the political movements and seclusion from the outside.

Four informal housing arrangements inhabited by Eritrean refugees—the shantytown of Ponte Mammolo and the squats of Collatina (fig. 7), Anagnina (fig. 9), and Metropolis (fig. 10)—became the focus of my observations in Rome between June and December 2012. At the time of my study, Collatina hosted around five hundred Eritreans and Ethiopians; Anagnina had around eight hundred inhabitants, mostly Somalis, Ethiopians, and Eritreans; a hundred Eritreans were living in Ponte Mammolo, along with migrants from eastern Europe; and some eighty people from all around the world lived at Metropolis. Although these places had infrastructural problems, they also had services such as running water and electricity, as well as shops, restaurants and cafes. Along with other neighborhoods of the city where Eritreans have traditionally been present—such as the area around the Termini railway station—the squats had become important meeting points.

In the beginning many of these squats were occupied by refugees with the help of left-wing groups of the local housing rights movement, but lately many squats have become independently managed by refugees, and some have been squatted at refugees' initiative, such as the building close to Termini Station.[30]

A combination of institutionalized marginality and instances of active citizenship,[31] these squats evolved into self-segregated areas mostly off-limits for the locals. For example, Collatina, the first squat (2004) exclusively managed by Eritrean refugees, had become inaccessible to Italians. A sign on the front door of the building stated: "Access to the building is not granted to people who do not live here." Unsurprisingly, the rule applied only to "outsiders" and not to fellow Eritreans, who could visit friends inside or use the internal shops and facilities (restaurants, barber shops, tailors, etc.). Similar to Collatina, entrance to the Termini squat was prohibited to "non-Habesha." When I visited Alazar, I had to sneak in without being noticed by the guard always standing at the door. According to my informants, these entry policies have been enforced by the organizing committee for fear of journalists' drawing the squats to the authorities' attention.

Squats like Anagnina and informal settlements like Ponte Mammolo were less strict in their entry policy but nonetheless very isolated and closed to the outside. While I was free to enter and exit Anagnina and Ponte Mammolo, people there

FIGURE 16. Anagnina, a Roman squat inhabited by over 800 people from the Horn of Africa (photo by the author, 2012)

FIGURE 17. Metropolis, a squat inhabited by both Italians and migrants (photo by the author, 2012)

would still look at me with suspicion if I was not accompanied by an insider. This closure to the outside is probably due to the irregularity of these settlements and the fear of being spied upon and reported to the authorities. However, this perpetual suspicion is also somehow typical of Eritreans, as a result of the extremely repressive political environment that they have experienced throughout history (see Appendix). In practical terms, the Eritreans' suspicion of strangers meant, not only that I had to make significant efforts to gain the trust of my informants, but also that I could not rely on a single informant to grant me access to different sites, even in the same city. Because it was such a segmented and divided community, I had to navigate different social networks to access different populations of Eritreans.

I was able to gain access to these places thanks to my long-term friendship with Alazar, his networks, and my previous contacts with Eritreans in Genoa. After having been given five years-refugee-status, Alazar left Italy in 2009. A few months later, I had a phone call from him. "Milli, how are you? I am in Norway! It is cold here," he said. The conversation did not last long, because my Tigrinya was too limited, as was Alazar's English. We spoke again on the phone a few times and then lost contact for a year. I then heard that he had been deported to Italy after Norwegian authorities discovered that his asylum case had already been processed and accepted there. When I started my research on Eritrean refugees in Italy in 2012, I found him living in the Anagnina squat in Rome and working as a skycap at Ciampino Airport for a few days a week. Alazar knew people and places and everyone knew him.

He introduced me to Senay, a childhood friend of his from Asmara, who put me up on an old sofa that reeked of alcohol in his one-room flat in Metropolis for most of the time I spent in Rome. Located in a particularly deprived and marginalized area of the capital, Metropolis was a mixed squat where Peruvians, Roma, Moroccans, Sudanese, Italians, and Eritreans were living together. Although life in the squat was marked by interethnic collaboration, the cohabitation was not always easy: I witnessed several violent fights between Peruvians and Roma during my stay there. Entry policy was very strict there as well, but at Senay's request, the committee, mainly led by an Italian left-wing organization called Blocchi Precari Metropolitani (Precarious Metropolitan Blocks), or BPM, temporarily accepted me. Nevertheless, at the entrance gate there was always a picket line to check who was going in and who was going out.

Although Alazar and Senay could grant me access to most squats and Eritrean gathering places in Rome, they were not familiar with the Eritreans living in the shantytown in the Ponte Mammolo area. Alazar would not even enter the messy accumulation of shelters comprising the settlement. In order to have a guide in that community, I had to call my Eritrean friends in Genoa, who put me in touch with Kibreab, a former sociology student at the University of Asmara. Like most inhabitants of Ponte Mammolo, he had a common background with my informants in Genoa: they all came from the same area in the south of the Eritrea.

Alazar, Senay, and Kibreab became my main informants in Rome. All three were nearly thirty, unmarried, living in unstable material conditions, and had come to Italy the hard way across the Mediterranean. They had all tried to move on from Italy, but had been sent back. Nonetheless, they were still planning the next move to try to circumvent the Dublin Regulation. At the time of writing, Alazar is the only one of the three left in Rome; Senay managed to obtain asylum in Sweden on his second attempt; Kibreab, after trying to obtain asylum in the Netherlands, gained entry to the United States by marrying an acquaintance living there. Each of them enabled me to enter a different informal settlement, peopled with different characters, and with its own rules and features. Alazar showed me the world of Anagnina squat, hosting me there for several nights and days; Senay welcomed me in his room in Metropolis for a few weeks; Kibreab guided me through the Ponte Mammolo shantytown.

These settlements were ethnically homogeneous and their population was characterized by low socioeconomic and cultural integration. With the exception of Collatina, which had almost become a permanent squat for Eritreans and Ethiopians who had regular jobs and had been living in Italy for a while, the population of the other squats was mainly jobless, or employed part-time in low-skilled temporary or seasonal jobs. My Eritrean informants living in Anagnina, for instance, were working as transporters in Ciampino airport or for global couriers such as TNT and SDA. Those living in Ponte Mammolo were unemployed or worked as fruit pickers in summer. Moreover, they spoke little Italian and did not have any contact with locals. They used to spend their free time in Eritrean bars in the area close to Termini Station or in the cafes and restaurants inside Anagnina or Collatina.

This systematic separation from the Italian society is important to examine how social expectations and desires concerning other destinations are reproduced. The levels of internal homogeneity and external segregation of Eritrean refugees in Italy are comparable to those of their counterparts I met in refugee camps or in Addis Ababa and Khartoum. Although the structural confinement of the camps is different from the complex socioeconomic processes that pushed Eritrean refugees together in these informal settlements, these settings share two remarkable commonalities: limited or no interactions with the local society, and a widespread suspicion and fear of locals, who are often identified as possible threats.[32]

FEELING AND BEING STUCK: PERCEPTIONS AND PRACTICES OF (IM)MOBILITY

The term "stuck" has often been used of asylum seekers and migrants settled in transit countries who would like to seek asylum elsewhere, but cannot.[33] "To be stuck in transit" conveys the idea of a status that should be temporary becoming permanent because of structural constraints on mobility. It also implies normalization of precariousness and uncertainty, at least for some categories of people.[34]

Although the idea of "being stuck" touches on migrants' limited access to geographic mobility, it is important to keep the two concepts separated. As Joris Schapendonk observes,[35] the perception of being stuck does not always correspond to a physical impossibility of moving. In his case study, migrants that got stuck in Morocco were very mobile in their daily practices. They moved camping arrangements to be prepared to escape from local authorities; they regularly crossed the Moroccan-Algerian border to work, and some of them even went back to their countries. Likewise, Eritreans in Italy felt stuck, but were highly mobile. In spite of being fingerprinted in Italy, they had tried more than once to seek asylum in other European countries; some of them had gone back to Africa to visit their families (in Eritrea, Ethiopia, Sudan) or/and to marry other Eritrean refugees in Ethiopia, Sudan, Angola, and elsewhere. After Alazar arrived in Italy in 2008, for example, he sought asylum first in Norway, and then in Sweden. When his fingerprints were found, he voluntarily came back to Italy. He then went to visit a friend in Angola, and in 2012, he went to Ethiopia for a month to get married. Such movements were common among Eritreans I met.

To be stuck in transit is thus not necessarily a physical condition. Rather, it points to an emotional and social condition, or to an existential perception of unsettledness. As Ghassan Hage observes, "a viable life presupposes a form of imaginary mobility, a sense that one is going somewhere."[36] When this sense of going somewhere is lost, individuals experience existential immobility—which he calls *stuckedness*. According to Hage, most voluntary migration stems from a willingness to react to this immobility. This is also the case for the many Eritrean refugees I met. Yet they felt stuck at all stages of their migration. My informants in Eritrea thought that their life was going nowhere due to the—as they perceived them—hopeless economic and political conditions of the country. Likewise, those Eritreans I encountered in Ethiopia and Sudan felt that they had no future there. Thus, the experience of existential immobility among my informants in Italy was a perpetuation of what I encountered before.

As mentioned in a previous chapter, structural obstacles to migration are only one of the various dimensions of their immobility. Their feeling of being stuck emerged from the social condition of dependency. In practice, my informants in Italy were still unable to provide for their families. They often felt trapped in that state of eternal adolescence which they had hoped to escape by leaving Eritrea. "I have been working in Italy for five years and I still cannot support my brother who is getting married in Eritrea, nor send money to my family," Ogbazgi muttered amid the strident noise of the Genoa railway station. We were waiting together for the train that was to take him to Switzerland, his final destination. He added, "This is not good—I am not a child anymore." His words exemplify the feelings of underachievement of many Eritreans in Italy. Their journeys cannot end until they have attained the status of adulthood.

Moreover, as often highlighted by those scholars who have studied migrants in transit,[37] the perception of being stuck in transit implies limited engagement in the country of residence, and a strong emotional orientation toward the desired country of destination. The Eritrean refugees I met were highly connected with other Eritreans in other countries and in the homeland, but did not show any intent to engage in the place where they lived. Not only were social and economic contacts within the Italian society limited, but also their intentions to get a job, to learn Italian, or to obtain regular housing were weak. For instance, when I asked Kibreab why he did not work harder on his Italian skills, he answered, "My mind is not settled. I cannot focus on studying. We have too many problems and our families back home are waiting for our support." Although it is undeniable that the Italian context was challenging in many senses, one may wonder if their pessimistic attitudes also contributed to their own marginality. The perception that it was possible to quite easily obtain everything they needed "somewhere close by" seemed to direct all their efforts toward the next attempt to seek asylum in another country, rather than toward trying to find their way in Italy.

WHAT PUSHES ERITREANS TO MOVE ONWARD?

Peer pressure . . .

Living in squats with compatriots at the margins of the receiving society and sharing the same ideas and desires about future migration are the two factors that underpin Eritrean refugees' attempts to move beyond Italy. Similar to what I have previously observed in refugee camps and in urban setting in Ethiopia and Sudan, dwelling in the same spaces may facilitate the emergence of a shared emotional atmosphere that is conducive to further migration, which I have called a state of *collective effervescence*.

Some of the informal settlements where I stayed in Rome, the houses I visited in Genoa, and also the public spaces usually frequented by Eritreans were crossroads of people coming and going. The ground floor and second floor of Anagnina, in particular, was known as a kind of informal center of assistance for Eritreans who have no other place to go and cannot be privately hosted by friends or relatives. Those in need were usually "Dubliners" (i.e., returnees to Italy from other European countries under the Dublin Regulation) or new arrivals. For instance in the summer of 2013, after I came back from my fieldwork in Eritrea, Anagnina was busier than usual: the main hall and the second floor were flooded with old mattresses on the floor where the new arrivals, transiting from Lampedusa to other European countries, were sleeping.

In Anagnina as well as in other places mainly inhabited by Eritrean refugees, new arrivals find not only accommodation and some practical help, but also some protection from the risk of meeting public officials who may force them to provide their fingerprints. In Metropolis, for instance, Senay hosted a young man who had not been fingerprinted yet and wanted to move on to Switzerland. Similarly, in the houses in Sampierdarena (Genoa) I visited, Eritrean women who had joined their husbands through family reunification procedures were waiting for the right moment to reach another European country and seek asylum there.

Likewise, Ponte Mammolo was a refuge for people in transit and for others who had been forced to return. Some had just arrived from reception centers in the south of Italy, and some others had recently been sent back from northern European countries. While I was walking in Ponte Mammolo with Kibreab, I saw many women with children and asked him if the kids were going to school. "No, they usually don't," Kibreab said. "They are in transit here, waiting to move on toward other countries where their fathers and uncles are."

While all these people were moving northward, those who were stuck in Italy were feeling left behind. Conversations about the pros and cons of living in different countries were continually going on in places like Anagnina. "Have you ever been in other countries in Europe?" Alazar's neighbor asked me in one of the many afternoons I spent chatting and listening to music with Alazar and his friends on Anagnina's first floor.

"Yes, I have been to France, for example," I answered.

"Oh! How is it?"

"It is a nice country . . . "

"And is it good for refugees?"

"I think it is more or less like Italy."

"Oh . . . I see. Northern European countries are better."

The hierarchy of destinations I observed in Eritrea, Ethiopia, and Sudan was evident in this conversation, too. Northern European countries were considered top destinations, while Italy was believed to be a good place to some extent—for the weather and because people were deemed friendlier—but with no socioeconomic opportunities. The United States, Canada, and Australia were also seen as top destinations. On the contrary, Greece and Spain were known for being undesirable and even unsafe countries. These widespread representations were also reproduced by the flow of information, images, and people coming back to Italy from those top destinations.

. . . information and images from the First World . . .

Despite their ethnic segregation, the Eritrean refugees whom I met in Italy were deeply embedded in transnational relationships with their kin, friends, and acquaintances in other countries. The transnational dimension of their daily lives is noticeable in their use of technology.[38] For example, Alazar used to receive many calls a day from his friends still in Sudan, from others who had reached northern Europe, from family members who worked in Israel, and still others in the United

States. Senay was more active on Facebook: he used to spend a long time looking at the pictures of his friends who lived in other countries and chatting online with them. Such a widespread flow of information and images elicits a feeling of disparity between the "unlucky" ones in Italy and the "lucky" ones who live elsewhere. It also produces of a sense of longing for further migration.

Information and images from the First World not only reach Eritrean refugees in Italy through technology. As most of them have attempted to seek asylum further north, they have directly experienced the differences of being an asylum seeker in Italy and in a Scandinavian country. Senay, for example, had tried to seek asylum in Sweden and often remembered his days as an asylum seeker there as a beautiful period of his life. "You see, Milena, I was fat at that time, because I was relaxed," he told me, while we were sitting in front of his Facebook pictures. "I had such a great time there," he added. "I met my old friends from Asmara, and you see what a house we had?! Not like the ugly squat where I live now."

"Dubliners" are not the only ones who come back to Italy. Whenever the Eritreans who have made it to the First World come back on vacation, they bring images and information that make their "stuck" friends want to leave. Social, cultural, and economic remittances play a key role, not only in places of intense out-migration, like Eritrea, but also in so-called transit areas, such as Italy. Once, I went with Alazar and Senay to meet a friend of theirs, Girmay, who had come from Switzerland for a few days' vacation. We sat in an Eritrean bar, not far from Termini Station, where Alazar, Senay, and Girmay and the bar owner gossiped for a whole afternoon, exchanging information about how to move from one place to another and sharing views about the lifestyles and living conditions in different countries.

Moreover, unmet family expectations concerning their migration path and economic support for their kin weighed like stones on their shoulders. While ethnographically exploring the disturbances in the flows of communication, gifts, and remittances between refugees in Italy and their families in Eritrea, the next sections illustrate the implications of these unmet expectations on practices and resilient aspirations of onward mobility.

. . . and expectations from Eritrea

Eritrean emigration is not perceived only as an individualistic search for better life prospects, but also as a strategy to ensure families' well-being through remittances. It is embedded in a web of economic, moral, and cultural expectations concerning the destination of the migration journey, the kind of life they should have in that country, and the kind of support refugees will provide for those who stay behind. Although many studies investigate the moral economy of migrants' remittances, kin obligations, and gift exchange in transnational families,[39] the influence of families on migration decisions has rarely been considered an important factor in refugees' movements.[40] However, kin-bound obligations and values directly impacted my informants' feelings of being stuck, as in Gabriel's case.

Gabriel arrived in Italy in 2007, when he was twenty-three. He stayed in a center for assistance of asylum seekers in Crotone in Calabria for a few months, the time necessary to be granted legal status. Then, like most other refugees in that period, he left on his own. He went to Rome, where he slept in the Anagnina squat for a while, and then moved to Milan, where a friend of his had told him that there were more work opportunities. He remembered the period in Anagnina as a horrible nightmare. "Everything was dirty and we were sleeping on the ground. I hate Rome." In Milan, too, until it was demolished, he lived in a squat—in Porta Romana, where he had a small shop. "I was doing good business there," he told me during our long strolls around the periphery of Milan. He found a job in Rho Fiere, an industrial area of Milan, and worked there for two years, but when I met him in the summer of 2012, he had lost the job and was involved in a legal dispute with his ex-employers.

Gabriel loved Milan, especially for its elegant shops, from which he liked to buy expensive clothes and shoes, which made him feel he had really reached the First World. Although he often complained about his compatriots, he spent most of his time in the Eritrean neighborhood around Porta Venezia, where he used to eat his lunch or drink beer. He felt at home there somehow. He kept on saying that he could have found a job whenever he wanted in Milan, because he knew people and was a hard-working man. However, his job hunt was continually delayed: he was undecided whether to stay in Italy or move on. "My family thinks Italy is not good for me," Gabriel used to tell me. "They want me to go to Germany, where we have some relatives . . . but I want to decide my life for myself."

At first I did not give much importance to this statement about his family's pressure to move on, but as soon as I entered Gabriel's family's house in Asmara in 2013, I realized that I had been wrong not to do so. After having let me through the door and into the living room, Ester sat down in front of me, briefly introduced herself, and welcomed me into the family. Then, only a few minutes into the conversation, she asked me why Gabriel did not move to Germany or a Scandinavian country. She was worried about her nephew and thought the situation in Italy was not good for him. I explained to her that Gabriel was not allowed to seek asylum in another European country, and that it was probably better for him to try his best to find a new job in Italy. However, she was not convinced. After a while, Yordanos, Ester's eldest daughter, came into the living room. "I know it is not easy," she said, "but we see other people who have settled down in other countries in Europe. Now they are doing well. We wish the same for him."

Gabriel's relatives were aware that life for refugees in Italy was hard. As I realized during my fieldwork in Eritrea, most families knew that. I was often asked: "How is the crisis going in Italy?"; "Is it true that people cannot find work there?" Aragay, one of our neighbors in Petrosia, told me, "Everyone knows that our guys in Italy are living in bad conditions, work is hard to find and people sleep in the street." This information was usually provided by those Eritreans who had managed to pass through Italy and were residing in other countries. Eritrean national television also used to broadcast news about refugees' hardships in Europe so as to discourage further illicit emigration from the country. However, the fact that refugees were facing hardships in Italy was not enough to exonerate them from blame. Believing that other countries in Europe could offer young Eritreans more opportunities, families often complained about the fact that their sons had not made enough of an effort to move to those "good countries."

Although families had general ideas about opportunities in different European countries, they seemed to ignore other important, but more specific aspects of migrants' lives abroad. In particular, they did not know about the Dublin Regulation and the problems that refugees had to face after being expelled back to Italy. Young Eritreans seemed better informed on these issues; for example, many of them knew about the importance of avoiding being fingerprinted in Italy in order to seek asylum in other northern European countries. Nonetheless, even among them, misinformation was far from rare.

Families' expectations about their children's onward mobility were not only rooted in the belief that Italy could not provide good conditions for settlement. They also mirrored the hope that migrant children would be able to support them. More specifically, support was expected in two domains: economic remittances for everyday survival in Eritrea and assistance to siblings who intended to migrate. This is crucial not only for understanding the pressure experienced by refugees abroad, but also to analyze the relational mechanisms that maintain the flow of refugees from Eritrea to Ethiopia, Sudan, Italy, and beyond. The fact remains that most of my Eritrean informants in Italy were not able to meet their families' expectations, since they were struggling simply to survive. This had significant implications for their family relationships and for the social status ascribed to them by their community of departure.

THE PRICE OF DISAPPOINTING FAMILIES

Gabriel's family members in Asmara, particularly his sister Lwam, were bitter about the fact that Gabriel had not remitted anything since his arrival in Europe. Although they knew life was hard in Italy, they still felt bad—especially because he did not send anything through me. "Not even a picture," Lwam said, saddened. "Life is hard in the village where my parents are. I hope one day I will be able to help my father." At that time, she was often thinking about migrating to make up for her brother's lack of success.

Lwam used to accompany me on visits to the families of my "Italian" informants. She often shared the feelings of frustration of the families for whom I had not brought gifts. She once commented to me upon leaving one home, "For people here, if someone migrates and cannot survive on his own, but still waits for money from relatives, it is like he is dead. It is already a shame to live with family here in Eritrea, but you can accept it. But if you go abroad and you have to ask others [for money], that is not life, it is death." Her words powerfully define the price that an emigrant may have to pay if he/she disappoints social expectations. The risk of "social death" feared by refugees I met in Ethiopian camps seemed to be even greater for those who had reached Italy but were not able to send remittances back home.

Not only families but also the community at large negatively judged refugees who did not help their families back home. That became clear to me when Lwam and I went to visit our neighbor Tegesti for a Sunday coffee. Tegesti was a smiling, prosperous woman in her fifties who often used to come to Ester's place for a chat and a cup of coffee. Her family had a clothes' kiosk at the market close to the *medeber* ("caravanserai" in Tigrinya). Her house—a construction of sheet metal, scraps of wood, and plastic tarps—was just one street behind the one where my hosts used to live. Tegesti invited us to sit on the terrace outside, while Aragay, her husband, was shaving, holding a small broken mirror with one hand and the razor with the other.

While we were drinking our coffee, Tegesti started speaking about her two sons abroad. They were apparently doing well in Angola, but had not yet started to send remittances to the family. One son had left three years before and started working in Khartoum as an electrician. All the money he earned there was spent to help the younger brother emigrate. After his brother joined him, they moved to Angola and started working in a supermarket. With four other children to support, Tegesti was hoping to receive some money soon: "We cannot survive here without their help! 100 euro a month is 5,000 nakfa here!"

Tegesti then asked me about Lwam's brother, Gabriel. I reported that he was fine, and she exclaimed wryly: "It is not enough if he's okay, because the family here is waiting for nakfa! Nakfa! Nakfa!" She rubbed her thumb and index finger together in the "money sign," looking into my eyes to be sure I got the point. Lwam laughed bitterly. She clearly felt embarrassed about her brother. Aragay mediated, saying that everyone knew how hard life was for refugees in Italy.

In order to avoid the social stigma associated with being in Europe but unable to help family members back home, Eritreans I met in Italy kept trying to move on to other European countries, deemed to be more generous. Until they succeed in that, however, they have a hard time dealing with their families back home. While mobile phones as well as other communication technologies have greatly facilitated transnational communications, they have also increased social control over migrants. Calls to and from family members and friends may become a burden for refugees, who feel overloaded with requests for money.[41] Avoidance of communication is one of the possible strategies to cope with overwhelming demands. Several of my informants had, in fact, stopped calling home. Senay had not called home for two years. Senay's lack of contact with his family was common among other Eritrean refugees I met in Italy. For instance, while I was in Asmara I met with Samhar, Kibreab's eldest sister. She told me that Kibreab rarely called them: "He says he is busy . . . I know that he does not call because things are not going well in Italy and he cannot help the family. Please, when you go back tell him that things are okay here. Just ask him to take care of himself."

In fact, Kibreab had been homeless and jobless for most of the previous four years. Back in Italy, I showed him the pictures of his family and gave him his sister's message. "I feel ashamed to call them and hear about all their problems without being able to send them anything," he told me bitterly. "I want to call when I can send some money. We have come here to help them . . . but now things are hard."

Kibreab's words show that contact avoidance is not only rooted in the intention to escape requests, but also in feelings of shame about what is recognized as an unfulfilled family obligation. Not much had changed in these young men's perceived social status since they had left Eritrea. Geographic mobility had not led to the expected social mobility. In Eritrea they could not reach adulthood because of compulsory national service, and in Italy they were still children who could not support their relatives, or please them with eye-catching gifts.

GIFTS AND COSMOLOGIES

Before leaving Italy, I had asked my Eritrean friends if they wanted me to take some gifts to their families, and some of them filled my luggage with pasta, olive oil, clothes, electric razors, phones, shoes, and pictures. Others did not answer my question, but still gave me the contact details of their families, whom I then visited. Others just avoided me for the whole time that preceded my departure. I noticed that those who sent gifts were the ones with a more stable emotional and economic situation. They were also the ones who had kept more in touch with their families.

Brahnu, a thirty-year-old who lived in Genoa, asked me to take some gifts to his family in Decamhare. Although he was still struggling in many senses, Brahnu was better off than many other Eritrean refugees in Italy. He had a job as a waiter in a catering business and carved traditional music instruments to sell over the internet to musicians around Europe. When I told him I was going to Eritrea, he gave me a bag full of things for his family: shoes for his mother, religious posters, family pictures, a razor for his brother, and a camera—the latter two items being needed for a business scheme he had thought up for his brother and cousins. When I went to Brahnu's family to deliver the gifts, his mother told me that her son had always been very mature and clever. Brahnu called his mother that day. and they all praised him for his generosity.

I gathered that Brahnu kept in touch regularly with his family, sometimes sent them money, and was ready to help his brother to leave the country. His gifts were certainly appreciated for their economic value, but they were primarily symbols of an ongoing relationship between him and his family. Brahnu's family also filled my bag with gifts for him and his daughter: a traditional dress for the girl, traditional baskets, homemade *shiro* (traditional legume flour), and *berbere* (a local spice mix).

This system of gift-exchange tends to parallel the flow of remittances, but is still distinguishable from it. Some scholars frame gifts as another kind of material remittance,[42] but gifts among my Eritrean informants and their families are better analyzed by looking at the example of the *kula* ring in the Trobriand archipelago described by Bronisław Malinowski.[43] The exchange of products involved in the *kula* ring—such as necklaces and bracelets made of shells—did not have a direct economic value, but was crucial to reaffirm trust, which underpinned trade relationships among the different islands. In a similar vein, the gifts sent by my refugee friends to their families were not as important for their economic value as for their symbolic value: they were symbols of an ongoing relationship that included economic remittances and practical support for other members of the family to migrate.

This is also the reason why, in other cases, my informants avoided sending gifts. Gifts had no meaning when the relationship between the family and refugee had been interrupted by the impossibility of the refugees fulfilling their perceived obligations. For Senay, Gabriel, and Kibreab, it would have been ridiculous to send gifts if in reality there was no real possibility of providing material help to their families. Moreover, their families did not make an effort to send gifts back to them, except for a few packets of homemade *shiro* or some pictures.

Even though the value of transnational gifts was mostly symbolic, they still had to fulfil some requirements. Things coming from Europe should be new, advanced, or the latest model. Family members often expect high-quality products, consistent with the "modernity" associated with life in the First World. Anything less than that may be criticized, and the sender may be judged selfish and not generous.

Alazar's family, for example, was very critical of the gifts he sent them. On my first visit to their place in Asmara, I brought them pasta, soap, olive oil and some second-hand clothes that Alazar had given me at Termini Station before my departure. I then met them again in Addis Ababa, after they had all fled the country and were trying to find a way to move on to Europe or Canada. Robel and Lula—Alazar's younger brother and sister—had crossed the southern border between Eritrea and Ethiopia on foot. After three months in a camp, they managed to get permission to leave. Alazar's mother Minia and her husband went to Khartoum by bus and then by plane to Addis Ababa, and they all started to live together again in one of the big condominiums in Mebrat Haile, just a few blocks away from my own flat. Alazar had also given me some gifts for them on this visit, such as a second-hand computer, a pair of brand-name sneakers, a second-hand mobile phone, and several cheap items of clothing.

During one of my visits to them, Lula told me with a disgusted expression that the gifts sent by Alazar were not nice. "The problem is that Alazar does not like to share his money with others. All the clothes he sent are not good. I hate them. I don't like anything there. I don't even like skirts, I've never worn them. He sent so many . . . Look! All the stuff he sent is still in the suitcase!" Robel agreed, snickering, and complained about the laptop: "You see, it only works when plugged in!"

Minia, on the other hand, was more defensive about "her" Alazar, but she was trying to understand from me what kind of life Alazar was leading. She did not know much about her son's living conditions: she was not aware that he had a job, she did not know where he was living, and could not understand the hardships he faced. Then Lula started praising Gaim, their other brother: "Gaim is really generous. I would like to become a medical doctor. I want to become a perfect person. Especially since I met Gaim. . . . He could not study when he was a child, but he's done so many things for me, making me study. I feel I want to be perfect for him."

Gaim had earned a lot of money working in Israel and had just managed to move to Canada with a fake Ethiopian passport. He had paid for everyone's flight from Eritrea and was trying to get his siblings out of Ethiopia whatever it took. Alazar for his part could not see the point in helping everyone migrate to Europe, when life is so hard there too. The way he saw it, it would have been better for them to settle in Ethiopia and start a small business there. When he came to the railway station to give me the gifts for his family, he showed me the nice pair of brand-name sneakers that he had bought for Robel. "This costs 90 euros! I never [would have] bought this for myself. . . . They asked [for] so many things, but they do not realize that with a salary of 800 euros, it is hard to survive here. They ask, ask, ask, because I am in Europe. But I let them ask," he said, laughing.

By comparing the gifts from Alazar with those from his brother, the left-behind kin were reproducing the cosmology of destinations that frames Italy as a country of transit and Canada as a top destination. An interesting parallel can be drawn here with Ivan V. Small's findings on transnational gift exchanges in Vietnam and their impact of the spatial imagination of remittance receivers.[44] According to Small, in the eyes of those who receive them, remittances and gifts represent not only the intentionality of the overseas giver, but also the world he inhabits. Using Small's interpretation, the gap in the recipient's valuation between the gifts received from Alazar and those received from Gaim represented the gap between the two worlds they inhabit: Italy, where Eritreans were still struggling, and Canada, a modern, First World country that offers a "good life."

To a certain extent, we could also say that people are valued according to the place they have managed to reach. Alazar was seen as unsuccessful compared to Gaim, who had managed to reach Canada. The help that Alazar was giving to the family was also devalued by the comparison with the support that Gaim had been giving to the family. His gifts were considered insignificant compared with the ones sent by Gaim. Even the migration support that Alazar had managed to arrange for Lula was not comparable with what Gaim could do for them from Canada. In fact, Alazar had arranged a fake marriage for his sister and was trying his best to find another one for Robel, but, as Minia happily exclaimed, "Now that Gaim is in Canada, he will send visas for everyone!" Things were obviously not as easy as Minia thought, but her words illustrate the widespread system of values, images, and expectations related to migration and specific destinations.

4

Moralities of Border Crossing

*Inside the World of Smuggling and
Transnational Marriages*

Among Eritreans, the use of smugglers' services and transnational marriages to cross tight international borders is systemic. Whereas policy makers, international organizations and the media generally sanction these illicit migration practices as despicable and exploitative,[1] this chapter highlights the underlying sense of justice, fairness and solidarity underpinning them. From an emic point of view, smuggling and transnational marriages are mostly seen as expressions of solidarity and legitimate economic transactions.

The analysis of migrants' views of these covert and unauthorized practices seeks to illustrate what authors like Nicholas De Genova, Sandro Mezzadra and John Pickles call migrants' struggles over borders and the political order these borders protect.[2] Without being explicitly oppositional and political, these views implicitly and practically unsettle dominant politics of migration. They show refugees' awareness of the aleatory nature of today's borders and the lack of legitimacy that bureaucratic bans on visas have in their eyes, leading to their refusal to be subject to them.

Some scholars have recently pointed out that migrants' moral understanding of borders is crucial to analyzing unauthorized migration. Drawing on the studies of legal noncompliance, Emily Ryo argues that Mexican unauthorized crossings to the United States is rooted in migrants' norms and values that do not recognize legal authorities establishing and enforcing border controls as legitimate.[3] As she illustrates by analyzing data from two surveys conducted in Mexico, the perceived unfairness among Mexicans of U.S. border regulations is associated with the decision to breach them. The lack of legitimacy of U.S. border enforcement, she suggests, is rooted in the long history of political, social, and economic interdependence between the United States and Mexico and the relatively recent targeting of Mexican migrants in U.S. policies and procedural justice.

Underlying conceptions of fairness and justice are also crucial to understanding refugees' deceit in institutional settings. Cheating, lying, and noncooperation have commonly been reported in refugee camps, reception centers, and other refugee facilities.[4] Struggling to survive in an institutional environment shaped by the patronage of different service providers, those in camps have to find their way through lies, deception, and trickery. As argued by Gaim Kibreab, these emerge from a gap between refugees' ethical views, which make them accountable to their community and families, rather than to those managing the structures or allocating aid.[5]

Likewise, emic moralities[6] are crucial to make sense of migrant smuggling and transnational marriages. By analyzing the protagonists' point of views, I show that these activities should not only be considered as risky, deleterious enterprises to which refugees passively submit. They are instead collective tactics put in place to achieve what my informants believe is their right to mobility. The focus on illicit practices is thus not a voyeuristic investigation aimed at reinforcing the image of the reckless, untrustworthy migrant. Its objective is to uncover their—more or less implicit—radical political dimension. By this, I do not mean to downplay their contradictory and problematic aspects.[7] Rapes, torture, and death are extremely common among those who are smuggled across borders. Likewise, power imbalances and abuse can at times underpin transnational marriages. These instances are, however, the inevitable implications of the lack of alternatives for legal and safe migration, not the root causes of migrants' suffering.

WHOSE FAULT? PERCEPTIONS OF MORAL AND NATIONAL BORDERS

"Miss Milena, first of all, may I ask you the purpose of your stay?" Hagos asked me in English in front of a group of twelve other Eritrean refugees who had gathered at Sister Kudussan's place to talk to me about the change of visa policy at the Italian embassy in Addis Ababa. That was one of the main concerns for Eritreans at the time of my fieldwork in Ethiopia (2013–14). In fact, a recent change in procedure at the Italian consulate had made family reunification processes with partners in Europe significantly more difficult. Hagos, a thirty-year-old refugee and his fellows from Mai Nefas, a village in Eritrea, had apparently seen in me a possibility to reverse this worrying tendency.

"I am here to conduct my research on Eritrean refugees for my PhD," I replied. Hagos seemed satisfied with my answer and continued:

"Miss Milena, we appreciate you very much because you came here to listen to our stories. So I prepared a few points for you. Point 1: We have been forced to escape from our country because of the lack of freedom, such as the freedom of expression. If someone says something he will be taken to prison and none will hear of him for long time. We have to do national service for long time. Can you comment on this, Miss Milena?"

"I am aware of the problems in your country," I said. Yonas, another Eritrean refugee, translated this into Tigrinya for the other participants.

"Point 2: Here in Ethiopia we face many difficulties because we don't have opportunities for study and work. Ethiopians are our enemies and do not want us to go to Europe and the United States. They took away our rights and shoot us when we express our opinion. We have no freedom here. Can you comment on this?"

I responded that I knew that they had no rights to work in Ethiopia, but that they should also consider concessions by the Ethiopian government, such as permission to attend university and the then recent "out-of-camp" policy, allowing Eritreans with family connections in Ethiopia or who could prove to be able to support themselves to reside outside camps.[8]

" . . . very few opportunities to study," Hagos replied, smiling. "Third point: Recently a boat full of our people sank in Lampedusa.[9] I personally think that the first responsible for this tragedy is the government of Eritrea; secondly I think the one responsible is the embassy of Italy in Ethiopia, because many people had a process[10] with Italy but their visas had been rejected by the embassy. Can you comment on this?"

I replied that I could not judge other people's work and that the consulate had its own ways to check the plausibility of marriages.

"How can the embassy know which marriages are real and which ones are false?!"

I explained to them that the consulate staff cross-checked the data and the information refugees provided about their partners. At that point, the atmosphere heated up. Dbab, a woman in her fifties, shook her head; Candle, a young woman on my right, exclaimed that the problem was the Ethiopian translator at the embassy. Hagos added "those . . . they don't want us to go to Europe." Georgis reported that the previous week, twenty-eight Eritreans had applied for reunification, but only two had been accepted—"But the marriages were true! I know it!" he said. Hagos continued: "Fourth point: because of colonization, I think that Italy has the obligation to receive and welcome Eritreans. Thank you for listening Miss Milena."

Saying that I could not change the laws on asylum and the regulations on international migration, I tried to address their doubts about visa proceedings and rights of asylum seekers. But my answers did not bring solutions to their problems, and most of them left the room unsatisfied. Yonas, the twenty-two-year-old translator for the occasion, smiled bitterly while walking out of the door and murmured,

"I do not need any process. My legs will be my process." He intended to cross the desert and the Mediterranean in the next months with the help of smugglers.

Yonas's statement powerfully exemplifies the determination of many Eritrean refugees to vindicate what they perceive as their rights through actions. Faced with all those bureaucratic and legal mechanisms—such as visa requirements and international asylum regulations—which immobilize them in a geographic, social, and political condition of marginality, my informants' attempts to circumvent borders can be seen as resistance practices expressing their right to escape.[11] The practice of unauthorized border crossing to Europe was not negatively sanctioned by the groups of Eritreans I met; rather, it was considered to be the "only possible alternative" to an unfair social and geographic immobility in Africa. Likewise, circumventing consular regulations for the purpose of obtaining visas was not perceived as an immoral act, because embassies and what they represent were not recognized as legitimate authorities.

Hagos's hierarchy of blame for recent migrant fatalities illustrates the extent to which refugees' perspectives differ from the predominant conceptions of history, rights, and responsibilities implicit in the public discourse on unauthorized migration. Faced with the death of their compatriots at sea, he and the other refugees apportioned blame firstly to the Eritrean government, which was compelling them to leave the country, and secondly to the international community, specifically Italy, which did not permit refugees to move freely to Europe and to other developed countries. Ethiopians were also pointed out as enemies, obstructing Eritreans' path to freedom. Although perceptions about smugglers were not univocal among refugees I met, as illustrated later, smugglers were not even mentioned among those possibly responsible for migrants' deaths. Nor were the migrants themselves blamed for their attempts to cross the border illicitly. This perspective completely overturns common interpretations of unauthorized migration in international public discourse.[12]

In the United States as well as in European policy and media discourse, smugglers are typically considered those mostly accountable for migrants' suffering. The European Agenda on Migration, adopted by the European Commission in 2015, identified the fight against migrant smuggling as a priority. Smugglers are targeted "to prevent the exploitation of migrants by criminal networks and reduce incentives to irregular migration."[13] However, as many commentators have argued, the availability of smuggling services is not among the "incentives to irregular migration." Rather, these emerge from the deterioration of conditions and limited long-term prospects in transit countries. Whereas authorities tend to emphasize smugglers' violence toward their customers, authors like David Spener have highlighted instead the structural violence of nation-state borders, which create a sort of global apartheid.[14] Smuggling, in this perspective, as a mechanism that facilitates "autonomous migration" in violation of state regulations, is a resistance practice.

Hagos's claims were in that period materializing in organized protests – the ones he referred to in his speech against the symbols of the international asylum regime and Western nations. Just a month before I arrived in Ethiopia (October 2013), a large protest had taken place in the camps in the north of the country.[15] During a mourning ceremony for the victims of the Lampedusa accident, refugees voiced their anger at a system that, in their eyes, did not provide them any prospects beyond risking their lives at sea. The main claim was that the Lampedusa tragedy had been the consequence of insufficient resettlement quotas from the camps. Peaceful demonstrations were held, but smaller groups of young refugees also threw stones at local bureaus. Significantly, the most violent acts targeted the symbols of the current asylum regime, such as UNHCR offices and services, as several of my informants who were present at the events confirmed.

My informants' claims, however, were far from being the coherent product of a mature political consciousness. Revolutionary and reactionary aspects were ambivalently present in their claims. While protesting against the injustice of the international asylum system, Hagos evoked Italy's historical colonial role to challenge current restrictive visa policies, saying, "because of colonization, I think that Italy has the obligation to receive and welcome Eritreans."[16] Such postcolonial claims were common among Eritreans across my research sites.

Taking into consideration this shared moral framework is key to overcome simplistic understandings of illicit practices surrounding border-crossing. The analysis of the specific moral, social and economic contexts in which they are embedded reveals blurred boundaries between refugees and smugglers, victims and exploiters, marriages of convenience and those established on the basis of love, tradition, or solidarity. Drawing from my ethnographic interviews with a variety of informants throughout my fieldwork and participant observation among refugees and smugglers in Ethiopia and Sudan, the next sections examine the social and moral roots of smuggling and transnational marriages in the context of Eritrean migration.

EXPLORING THE SOCIAL AND MORAL WORLD OF ERITREAN UNAUTHORIZED MIGRATION

Human smuggling has received widespread attention by policy makers and scholars over the past twenty years.[17] Mostly analyzed concurrently with trafficking, smuggling has often been described for its exploitative character. However, an increasing number of ethnographic studies point to a very different aspect of smuggling. Researchers working on the U.S.-Mexico border have illustrated how *coyotaje*—the smuggling of immigrants into the United States—is socioeconomically and morally embedded in migrants' communities.[18] Other scholars working with Somalis, Afghanis, Syrians have illustrated how smuggling activities are often framed as acts of solidarity in communities affected by protracted displacement.[19] Tekalign Ayalew Megiste, in particular, talks about smuggling as system of "protection from below" from below in the context of Eritrean migration. Smuggling, he argues, emerges as a sort of community knowledge historically developed through contextual experience and transnational exchanges of information, "that allows those in transit to be guarded from criminal organizations, environmental challenges, and restrictive migration regimes, but also from the trap that asylum conditions—including refugee camps—have become."[20] My ethnographic investigation similarly shows how smuggling is deeply embedded in its history and society.

DISGUISED AS SHEPHERDS: A LONG HISTORY OF BORDER CROSSING

Clandestine border crossing has long been a necessity in the region. History books, private chronicles from the 1970s–80s,[21] and oral narrations of first-generation refugees show that many mechanisms of the contemporary smuggling process have been in place for a long time. Escaping the purges of the Derg in the 1980s, Eritreans would disguise themselves as shepherds to avoid patrols. Many of them used local guides—equivalent to contemporary pilots—who requested a payment according to the relationship with the smuggled individual: relatives would not have to pay, while others might pay up to 600 Ethiopian birr—equivalent to about U.S.$300. Violence, rapes, and kidnappings were also common.

The chronicles of the time testify to the long-standing existence of an elaborated professional and economic system developed around people smuggling.[22] Then, as today, this system involved a wide variety of individuals who enabled the unauthorized passage of Eritreans from one country to another. This multiplicity of characters, roles, and activities is hardly reducible to the mainstream categories of the international debate. During my research I heard several terms used for the "professionals" of the migration business. The commonest were *pilots, delelti,* and *semserti.* It became clear that words like "smugglers" and "traffickers" did not make much sense in the context I was studying. Looking at the internal differentiation of the smuggling business in Eritrean migration shows, not only how misleading it is to use the word "smuggler" to identify all these different figures, but that these practices are embedded in Eritrean society and in refugees' social milieu.

PILOTS: THE GUIDES

"Pilot" is the word used by Eritrean refugees to refer to the "guide" who actually accompanies escapees walking through the border in return for payment. In the literature on Mexico-U.S. border crossing, these guides are called "coyotes."[23] This role is especially important in the crossing between Eritrea and Ethiopia or Eritrea and Sudan, which is mostly done on foot. However, not everyone I met had crossed the border with the help of a professional pilot. Many of the refugees I interviewed told me that their getaway was possible because they had been moved to a military post or to a teaching job in some areas close to the Sudanese or Ethiopian border. From there some of them knew the way or had friends who helped them.

According to the refugees and brokers I interviewed, professional pilots are Eritreans highly familiar with the border region. Ex-militaries and shepherds are also suited for this role due to their physical resilience. In fact, they are generally well trained to walk for long hours at night to avoid soldiers.[24]

It was surprising to discover that aside from a few who lived in border communities and managed to work as guides without being noticed by authorities, the majority of pilots did not live in Eritrea. As I was told in several instances, many of them were Eritrean refugees in Sudanese and Ethiopian camps. They used to go and collect people in Eritrea and then take them across the border. Others had two passports and could freely enter Eritrea and Sudan.

I never had the chance to formally meet a pilot, but my informants spoke about them in almost legendary terms. The disregard of the dangers, their physical resilience and knowledge of the territory make pilots objects of respect and admiration as well as fear and hatred when things do not go smoothly as wished. Petros, a twenty-four-year-old theology student who had recently fled from Eritrea to Ethiopia, said, "They [pilots] are heroes to me! They grant us a way out from Eritrea in spite of huge risks!" However, on other occasions I was told that pilots would not hesitate to abandon slow walkers to the soldiers' mercy if they had to.

While pilots are crucial in the first part of the journey from Eritrea to neighboring countries, drivers become more important in the second and third parts of the journey when people are driven from Sudanese or Ethiopian camps to Khartoum and from there through the Sahara desert in Libya. In Libya, pilots and drivers are replaced by boatmen. As I have been told, while pilots and drivers in the first part of the journey were usually Eritreans, drivers and boatmen in Ethiopia, Sudan, and Libya were of different nationalities: drivers in Ethiopia were usually Ethiopians, and in Sudan, Sudanese; boatmen in Libya were sometimes Tunisians, but in many other cases they were chosen from among the Eritrean refugees themselves.[25] People with some nautical experience or mechanical skills are sometimes allowed or asked to steer the boat in exchange for a discount or free passage. These details, however, are continually changing, along with the geopolitical fluctuations surrounding migration corridors. Since my informants passed through Libya, the situation in the country has worsened dramatically, and the conditions of the smuggling business have completely changed. As I was told by several research participants in 2015 and 2016, Eritrean middlemen who controlled the passage through Libya had to interrupt their operations due to the violence in the country, as well as Libyan and Italian police interventions targeting them.[26] The seeming lack of well-established Eritrean brokers in Libya and the shift of the control in the smuggling business to Libyan militias and Touba Bedouin may be among the main reasons for the radical deterioration of the conditions of migrants who want to traverse Libya and a huge increase in the risk of being kidnapped and tortured. If smuggling is, as Tekalign Ayalew Mengiste argued, a system of "protection from below," anti-smuggling actions risk to further increase migrants' vulnerability in already extremely unstable and violent contexts.

HAWALAS: THE MONEY-TRANSFER AGENTS

Transactions of money between smugglers, refugees, and relatives abroad paying for the journey usually take place through informal circuits. The financial agents of this informal money-transfer system are called *hawalas*. The system works as follows: the refugee's relative, who usually lives in Europe or the United States, pays a local hawala in cash; this hawala in Europe has contact with another hawala in Eritrea, Sudan, Ethiopia, or Libya, who pays the money to the smuggler who has provided the service. The two hawalas will each charge a commission for this service, settling with each other later.

This practice is centuries old and well known—albeit by different names—not only in Eritrea, but in the whole Horn of Africa, the Middle East, and South and East Asia.[27] These informal financial systems are based on the transfer of the debt from one person to another and can work only if there is trust between agents and between them and the customers. The hawala system originates in contexts where there is no institutional banking or when a formal financial service is not convenient.[28]

In the case of Eritreans, hawalas are typically individuals who have a shop, or are involved in some kind of trade in Eritrea or elsewhere. To have a shop allows the hawala to settle the debt via a trade transaction, so hawalas usually come from the Eritrean lower middle class, or from more resourceful families who have trading licenses and good contacts with government officials to ensure a smooth business.

These systems of money transfer have increasingly become the target of Western governments' controls because of alleged implications in funding terrorism, but the greater part of their business consists of migrants' remittances.[29] With regard to the Somali *xawilaad,* Anna Lindley argues that "their services have served to sustain local livelihoods and alleviate suffering."[30] Likewise, the hawala system in Eritrea not only enables payment to smugglers, but is also used to sustain families at home in times of crisis. However, hawalas are not only targeted by Western governments. In 2015, the Eritrean government enacted a series of financial interventions that severely affected the business of hawalas, as well as the positive impact of remittances and the purchasing power of locals.[31] This may have also indirectly influenced the possibilities of relatives abroad financing journeys out of the country and led, along with other factors, to the decrease in Eritrean arrivals in Europe in recent years.

THE UNIVERSE OF BROKERS

Eritreans in Ethiopia referred to brokers mostly as *delelti,* while those I met in Sudan mostly called them *semserti.*[32] Both words refer to specialists in unauthorized migration who are able to provide a wide range of services, from fake papers, like national ID cards and passports, to business marriages and border crossings. Different *semserti* are specialized in different services, depending on their contacts with local authorities, pilots, drivers, and military officers. Their job mostly consists of "connecting" demand with supply—customers with pilots and drivers— and they are usually the ones who make the highest profit. They are often responsible for organizing the logistics of the journey, such as travel arrangements and the provision of food and shelter during stops.[33]

However, in every transaction there can be more than one middleman. Let's imagine that Rachel, a fictional Eritrean girl, wants to find a way to escape from the country. She personally does not know a pilot or a *semsari,* so she would usually ask someone who has already escaped the country to put her in touch with a trusted pilot. Her hypothetical friend, Simon, who lives in Addis Ababa, does not have direct contact with the pilot, but he knows a middleman. Simon finds out that the price to cross the border is U.S.$1,000. Depending on Simon's will to help Rachel or to make some money out of her request, he may or may not add U.S.$500 for facilitating the transaction. Likewise, the middleman whom Simon had contacted may not be in direct contact of the pilot, but, as a ring in the chain of transactions, he may charge some money on top of the initial price set for the pilot to accompany Rachel across the border. The less direct and longer the chain of people that connects the customer and the pilot, the more expensive the trip is.

This gives an idea of the ramifications of the smuggling business within some sectors of the Eritrean population and shows that clear-cut distinctions between refugees and middlemen, and even between victims and exploiters, often make little sense in this context. Most middlemen are refugees themselves, who may have been involved occasionally in helping someone to get out of the country with a big, little, or no compensation in exchange. However there were degrees of professionalism and expertise within the universe of middlemen. Some do it sporadically or in their free time, others do it full time, like Tsegay and Michael, whom I met, respectively, in Addis Ababa and Khartoum.

Tsegay, a church boy . . .

To meet someone directly involved in the smuggling business became crucial for me in order to understand the inside mechanisms of the migration industry, which was moving thousands of Eritrean refugees across the border. However, it was not easy to get to know one of them. When I asked my informants and friends in Addis Ababa, all of them told me that it was impossible: smugglers would be too scared to talk to me. Public attention was at the time focused on secondary movements of Eritrean refugees from the camps in Tigray to Sudan, and the Ethiopian police were known to be strict with anyone involved in the smuggling business. Adonay tried asking a classmate of his who was working as a middleman on the side. He refused and even got angry at Adonay for mentioning his existence to me. Temesghen, my neighbor in Mebrat, also discouraged me from searching, exclaiming: "They do not want to share their *injera* [flat bread typical of the Eritrean and Ethiopian culinary tradition]."

However, one day in February, Stephanos, one of the young theology students I met through Sister Kudussan, called me to say that his "friend" had agreed to talk to me. Surrounded by excavation works in Mexico Square, Violetta (my interpreter at the time) and I met for the first time with "the smuggler" Tsegay. Contrary to all conventional images of smugglers as cruel villains, Tsegay was a smiling man in his late twenties with a clean, kind face and a funny trotting gait, wearing a checked shirt and a black leather jacket. He invited us for a pizza in a nearby restaurant and told us his story.

Originally from a small village close to the Catholic town of Segeneiti, Tsegay, the third of ten brothers, had been raised in Asmara. After school, he was sent to Assab as a soldier but fled in 2008 through the Danakil desert. He began his activities as *delalai* simply because he needed money. His uncle in the Emirates was not financially supporting him, and finding work was not easy in Addis at the time. He wondered what people desired the most, and found that the answer was easy: "to leave." Together with a former comrade from Assab, he started the business in 2010, about three years before I met him.

In the beginning, his business was mainly based on crossing from Eritrea into Ethiopia. In my understanding, this period of his activities overlapped with his stay in May Aini camp, where as an ex-soldier, he had little difficulty getting pilots to trust him; then, a year before I met him—probably when he had made some money and could move to Addis Ababa—he expanded the range of services he offered. When I interviewed him, he could organize the trip from Ethiopia to direct Sudan or to Libya, provide passports or residence permits in Ethiopia, and arrange business marriages.

Tsegay told us that getting into the business had not been hard. Competition, as he said, was fair. He claimed he had not received any threats from other competing brokers. His job mainly consisted of putting customers in contact with people offering the services they required: staff in the Ethiopian Ministerial Office of Nationality for an Ethiopian passport, a driver for a journey to Sudan, a guide for the escape from Eritrea. Although some collaborations with these other agents were stable, none was set in stone, and they could be changed or canceled if opportunities and conditions changed.

Tsegay planned to work as a *delalai* just until he could get enough money together to leave the country himself. The year before, he had had to pay for his brother to get to Sweden, and this had delayed him, but, he said, "In a year, I should be all right." He dreamt of reaching England—in his view a country of opportunities for those like him who wanted to pursue further education.

When the interview came to an end, Tsegay nodded his head and invited his two friends who had quietly been sitting at a nearby table to join us. Violetta was at ease chatting with those guys. They were all *wodat Asmara,* "Asmara boys," smart talkers, full of jokes and stories. They laughed a lot together, while I tried to catch the main sense of the conversation in Tigrinya. Violetta suddenly remembered that she had seen Tsegay before: "Oh, you were in that comedy at the Catholic Church of Saint Paul [in Addis Ababa]! You were very good and sang with a loud and clear voice in the choir!" Yes, that had been him. He attended that church regularly. After that, Tsegay and his friends became regular visitors at Violetta's and my place, but he was not the only *delalai* I met. After moving to Khartoum, I happened to run into another broker.

. . . and Michael, "a schoolboy"

It was an ordinary Sunday in Khartoum. It had been a few days since I had started living with Maria and her eight-year-old child, Anna. That day, after going to the market, Maria took me to the house of her friend Seifu, a thirty-two-year-old Eritrean woman who had been Maria's neighbor in Asmara. Seifu was sharing the place with other two Eritrean ladies and three young Eritrean men. All of them were waiting for a family visa or for the right moment to move to better destinations. Seifu had been in Khartoum for three years and was waiting for a reunification visa with her husband (a "business" one, as I later understood) who had moved to Sweden.

We were sitting in Seifu's living room chatting with her housemates when Michael and two Somali men walked in the door. Michael was an old friend of the household. Seifu, Maria, and their housemates had all grown up in the same neighborhood in Asmara. Short and thin with shiny curly hair, tidy clothes and a pair of glasses, Michael hardly seemed twenty, like someone fresh from school.

Michael barely said hi to me, but he kept glancing in my direction while Mohammed, his talkative Somali partner, was telling me how he and Michael had become friends during a holiday together. I found myself unable to believe his story entirely, and when Michael and his friends offered us a lift home, I asked Michael, "What do you do in Khartoum?" He ignored me, but the driver answered: "We sell cars." Before dropping us off, Michael asked for my telephone number, and not long afterward, he called me, saying: "I think we have an appointment. We'll be there in thirty minutes." I was surprised, since we had not fixed any appointment, but the prospect of meeting up with Michael also felt promising.

From that meeting on, until I left Sudan, Michael opened up a whole world for me. On that first night out, he revealed to me that he was a *semsari* and took me to one of the bars frequented by people smugglers in the city. Michael and his business became one of my main interests, but hanging out with him was not always easy. Although I used to meet up with him together with Maria, Anna, Seifu, and other friends on social occasions such as Easter celebration or Sunday coffees, we could not speak about his work in the presence of others, since he wished to keep it secret. He was otherwise available only during working hours, which, for him, meant nighttime. But even then, he was often unwilling to answer my questions, saying: "Not now Milena, I am trying to relax, please." He knew that I was a researcher and that I was interested in his job, but it seemed hard for him to see me as a professional; for him I was more of an entertaining companion. Planning was almost impossible with him. Sometimes he would give me an appointment only to cancel, saying, "Sorry Milena . . . *sra allo* [I had to work]"; at other times, he would just call me in the middle of the night to tell me: "We are coming. Get ready."

I managed to have significant conversations with him in unconventional environments, such as his house before he was too drunk or high to understand what I was asking; in noisy bars full of *semserti;* in romantic luxurious restaurants, interrupted by the continuous phone calls of his assistants; in the warehouse where migrants transiting to Libya were temporarily staying, while Michael and the guardians were drinking whisky and dancing to loud pop and Tigrinya music

KILLERS AND *SEMSERTI:* RESPONSIBILITY AND ACCOUNTABILITY IN THE SMUGGLING BUSINESS

While driving around Khartoum Talata, Michael pointed out at some flashy Middle Eastern restaurants at the side of a popular road we were passing. "These are the shops of the killers. They sell our people like beasts. I am a *semsari,* but I have humanity."

The "killers" in Michael's terms were what international conventions call traffickers, that is to say, criminals who exploit other human beings, usually in the sex industry, slave labor business, and body organs market.[34] They are usually distinguishable from smugglers because they get hold of their victims by force, whereas smugglers' services are usually sought by the migrant. Although separately defined in international protocols, authors have often analyzed them as contiguous businesses. Many, in fact, have highlighted that migrants' experiences defy easy categorization, since smuggled migrants may be coerced, punished, and held hostage at many points along the way.[35]

Although smuggled migrants may end up being trafficked, smugglers and traffickers usually have divergent interests.[36] While smugglers want their customers to be highly satisfied with their services, because their profits depend on their reliability and good reputation, traffickers prey on their victims and do not care about their popularity. In the context of Eritrean migration, the Rashaida ethnic group and other Bedouin groups are especially infamous for the kidnapping of refugees who tried to cross the Sinai Desert from Egypt to reach Israel.[37] Many kidnappings have also been reported from the area of Kassala in eastern Sudan.

These "killers" took their victims to bases in the Sinai and tortured them so that their screams would convince their families abroad to pay a ransom, which could amount to U.S.$50,000. According to several reports, from four thousand to thirty thousand Eritreans were trafficked in the Sinai from 2009 to 2013, for ransoms totaling U.S.$600 million.[38] According to Michael, the owners of those restaurants in Khartoum were related to the traffickers and were using the restaurant to launder the money they made from the kidnappings. Once I asked Michael if he had ever sold people to the Rashaida: "No, no, never! You know, one month ago in a village outside Khartoum, there was a truck full of Eritrean refugees from Ethiopia. The Rashaida came. They were armed with guns and wanted to kidnap them. My assistants had guns too and protected the refugees. Only one died in the shooting. I care for my customers . . . Ah and do you remember the other day when I told you that I was busy? It was because a truck of people from Ethiopia had been caught by the Ethiopian police. I paid money from my own pocket to free them!"

For Michael it was very important to mark his distance from the killers and to state his "humanity," despite the irregularity of his business. He also tended to stress that he was taking responsibility for the smuggled refugees. Tsegay similarly said that one of his duties was to look after his customers: "I take responsibility for the people I send." Were the two smugglers I encountered examples of "good" *semserti* or were these claims just good business?

Tsegay's and Michael's attention to their customers, their claim of "being responsible for them" can be interpreted as part of their ethical code or an expression of empathy with the refugees, but also as a marketing strategy. Tsegay did not have difficulties admitting that "to take responsibility" was necessary for the success of his business: "If someone I send dies, I lose customers," he stated bluntly. As both smugglers explained to me, the success of their activities was mainly based on word-of-mouth reputation: the death or imprisonment of some customers would mean that next refugees would choose another *delalai* over them.

Semserti, in any case, are the ones held responsible by other refugees and their families if something goes wrong. For this reason, collaboration with trustworthy partners (pilots, drivers, other *semserti*) and the control over the whole smuggling process were crucial in Michael's and Tsegay's business. Partnerships in business were mainly based on personal knowledge and national belonging. Tsegay preferred first of all to collaborate with Eritreans he had known for long time, then, on a scale of decreasing trust, he could work with Eritreans in general, Ethiopians and with other nationalities, only if they had no other available contacts. Eritreans were the most trustworthy, not only because of national solidarity, but because they were accountable for their deeds. With a somehow disturbing clarity Tsegay reminded me that the business of smuggling people could get serious: "It is easy to track an Eritrean and his family if something goes wrong." For this reason, Tsegay usually required one of his Eritrean collaborators to accompany drivers of other nationalities and ensure that things went as planned.

Without denying that violence can be an integral part of smuggling, especially when things go wrong, the above ethnographic insights illustrate that it is crucial for scholars to carefully consider that smugglers and traffickers are the same people: they instead belong to competing markets.

A LOT OF MONEY AND HOW TO SPEND IT:
A MORALITY OF SHARING

Owing to the covert nature and shifting conditions of the business, it is difficult to give a realistic estimate of the overall amount of money circulating around the smuggling of migrants, but in 2017, the International Organization for Migration (IOM) estimated around U.S.$10 billion annually.[39] In particular, it is calculated that the routes from West, East and North Africa to Europe, and South America to North America generate approximately USD 6.75 billion a year.

Against this background, Michael's was only one of many small enterprises that thrive. He was indeed able to earn a lot of money; during the five weeks I was in Khartoum alone, he received sixty Somalis from Shagarab and thirty Eritreans from Ethiopian camps. If, as he claimed, he earned around U.S.$1,000 for each person he sent to Libya, he would have grossed around $90,000 in one month. He was also getting money from people who were crossing from Eritrea to Sudan and those who paid to be driven from Ethiopia to Khartoum. Certainly, Michael's profit might dramatically decrease if his customers were apprehended by the police or kidnapped along the way.

Michael's earnings as a smuggler also had positive implications for those around him. Young men hanging out at Seifu's house often ran small errands for Michael in exchange for some money. Michael was extremely generous with his friends: he bought new furniture for Seifu's house, gave money to Maria and Anna whenever he saw them, bought a big ram for Easter, and treated everyone—including me—to a night of dancing on one of the many barges on the Nile River in Khartoum. His generosity was almost excessive; I often felt I was experiencing some kind of potlatch.[40]

However, not all smugglers are so wealthy. Earnings depend on the popularity of the smuggler, the number of customers available, and the competition. For example, Tsegay told me that his earnings were not so great, probably because he had only recently started out in the business. His income fluctuated strongly, depending on the season. In a good month—usually from January to September—he could earn up to 12,000 birr (U.S.$550), but in some months, there simply was not enough demand for his services.

LIKE SURGEONS?

Both Tsegay and Michael held anti-government political views. In their opinion, the government is the cause of all the suffering Eritreans face. Tsegay supported a recent political movement called Eritrean Youth for Social Change, which promises to unite all Eritreans in a single front of liberation from the dictatorship of Isaias Afwerki, the independent nation's first, and thus far only, president. Michael's political views were more ambivalent, but he often declared: "I hate those below [in] the government. Isaias is a hero, I love what he represents and his history, but those below him are all corrupt."[41]

Both Tsegay and Michael thought that I, as researcher, had an important role to play in witnessing and denouncing the suffering of their people. It was because of his political views that Tsegay agreed to talk to me. He appreciated the fact that someone was interested and would publicize the hard conditions under which Eritreans lived. Michael similarly often praised me for having made the effort to go to Sudan to see with my own eyes what Eritreans were going through (see Appendix).

Tsegay and Michael regarded smuggling refugees as a "remedy" for the tragic situation of their people, rather than an extension of it.[42] When I asked Tsegay how he thought of his role as a *delalai,* he replied: "You know, in life good things go together with bad things. Even a doctor has to do things that imply a high risk and sometimes the death of his patients. For example, when a doctor takes his patient into the operating theater, he has to ponder possible risks and positive outcomes of the operation. Similarly, I have chosen to look at the positive outcomes of my work: my customers will benefit greatly from the surgery [I perform]." Tsegay and Michael presented themselves as providing the means to quench people's thirst for a better life and freedom of movement.

Nevertheless, Tsegay and Michael were not completely comfortable with their job, which they tended to keep secret from their loved ones. When I asked Tsegay if his family in Asmara knew about his job, he smiled, embarrassed, and said: "No, I do not think they would appreciate it." Similarly, Michael wanted to keep his job secret from even his closest friends in Khartoum. The first time Michael told me about his other life as a smuggler, he cautioned: "Don't tell Maria, Samson, and the others about my job, okay? They are like my family here; I do not want them to be involved." His generosity could be interpreted as a way of addressing his sense of guilt about the way he earned his money. Although he sometimes boasted about his wealth, he was not proud of his activities. The first time he confessed to me what he did, sitting in the bar that night, he whispered: "All these people are not good . . . I am not good either." Likewise, their customers have contradictory moral views of *semserti.*

CUSTOMERS' VIEWS ON BROKERS: HEROES OR VILLAINS?

Although news media and international organizations characterize people smugglers as profiteers and exploiters, studies show that they are often highly respected in their communities, sometimes even considered philanthropists.[43] In other reports, their business does not bear a particular moral connotation and is perceived as something ordinary.[44]

The refugees I met sometimes showed disapproval of smugglers, and sometimes admiration for them and appreciation of their services. When I asked Adonay in Addis Ababa what his view on smugglers was, he answered: "It is not ethical; people are sold from one person to another and they risk their lives." During my fieldwork in Ethiopian refugee camps, Jacob, a twenty-six-year-old engineer resolved to move to Europe, thought likewise. "They are exploiters," he said. "They just want to make money out of people's misery!" Nevertheless, he was determined to use their services before long, and when I pointed out what I saw as a bit of hypocrisy, he replied, "We have no other choice." Isaias, another older Eritrean refugee, who was present during my conversation with Jacob, had a different view: "Smugglers are not exploiters," he said. "They just give people what they ask of them. Some are very generous; they take people even if they do not have enough money to pay them . . . so many times I saw people begging them to put them on the truck during the night!"

I often got negative answers when I asked other refugees directly about smugglers. Positive comments were more common when an opinion was not solicited. Maria and I once visited her friend Gerre in a nearby neighborhood of Khartoum. Like the other Eritreans I met in Khartoum, he was living in a compound he shared with fellow Eritreans. One of his neighbors was a *semsari*. As we were leaving, Gerre said of his *semsari* neighbor: "He is an *honest* one. All the people he sends to Europe get safely to their destination." Gerre's moral assessment of his neighbor was not concerned with the latter's breaking international laws on smuggling; it was based on the reliability of the services provided.

Refugees' answers to my direct questions were regularly influenced by what they thought I wanted to hear. Since I was a white European woman doing research on refugees and smuggling, my informants probably imagined that I endorsed the general humanitarian discourse that portrays smugglers as criminals and refugees as victims. This relational mechanism, I believe, should also be considered when researchers conduct their interviews with refugees in the destination country. Without underestimating the amount of suffering they often experience during their journeys, it should also be considered that refugees may change their attitudes to smugglers once they arrive at the destination because of the labeling process typically produced in asylum procedures and reception: the more the smuggler was labeled as a criminal, the more the refugee could play the role of the suffering victim. Performing victimhood can be crucial for recognition of refugee status upon arriving at one's destination.[45]

Luckily, most of my informants whom I met again after the journey did not have especially bad experiences with their brokers. The sea crossing and long periods of custody while waiting to embark were physically exhausting, they said, and the food provided was bad, but they did not seem to blame all this on their *semserti* in particular. The unstable political conditions in Libya, the risk of being caught by police or militias or being attacked by Libyans were responsible. Trust of and loyalty to the smuggler remain strong even after they arrive at their destination. Senay, my host in the Roman squat, told me how he had felt protected the entire time until he had crossed the sea by the *semsari* who helped him in Libya. He was deeply thankful to him and ready to reciprocate the favor anytime.

Occasionally, the Eritreans I interviewed modified their declared attitude to smugglers after I clarified my neutrality on the topic. Once I was chatting about smuggling with Gebreyesus, a talented twenty-eight-year-old novel writer who was among Maria's friends in Khartoum. When I asked him what he thought about smugglers, he said that that profession was deeply "unethical," being against international law, but later when I expressed my doubts about the moral condemnation of smugglers, he said: "In a sense, smugglers could be compared to those individuals who helped black people during slavery moving from the South to the North in the United States and today are considered heroes. . . . Who knows? Maybe one day smugglers will be considered heroes, too, because they helped people find freedom."

Comments I heard about *semserti* were not limited to the ethical/unethical nature of the occupation. Gebreyesus, for example, found *semserti* generally quite ridiculous: "They are so arrogant . . . always with their phones, talking about money . . . but they don't think about the consequences of their actions." Maria, my host in Khartoum, was more concerned about the long-term prospects of the profession. In fact, although Michael was very concerned about keeping his work secret to his close friends, Maria suspected it: "Michael has so much money . . . he spends it here and there . . . I think he is in the smuggling business . . . but it is not good for him . . . now he may have a lot of money, but one day he may lose everything. I tried to tell him the other day to be careful, but he is too young, he won't listen."

In sum, perceptions of smugglers among Eritrean refugees are mixed: sometimes, they are depicted as champions of generosity, but hated if customers feel cheated. However, the moral judgment generally does not concern the nature of the activity, but the quality of the service and the way it has been provided. Unauthorized border crossing is not negatively sanctioned, nor are the actions of those who enable it. As a matter of fact, refugees' dreams of moving elsewhere could not be realized without the assistance of these experts.

Aside from unauthorized border crossing, Eritrean refugees have other ways to overcome what they see as the unjustified obstacles to mobility. One of the main alternatives to being smuggled across the desert and the sea is to arrange a marriage with somebody living abroad.

ANOTHER WAY OUT: TRANSNATIONAL MARRIAGES

Transnational marriages can involve partners of different nationalities, but most typically they are contracted compatriots either at home or living in desirable destination countries. Although such marriages are often organized and paid for with the sole purpose of emigrating out of Eritrea, Ethiopia, or Sudan, many others emerge out of a "cultural logic of desire."[46] On the one hand, the desires and romantic dreams of those who feel stuck in Eritrea, Ethiopia, or Sudan are projected onto charming expatriates; on the other hand, those who have reached Europe—mostly men—seek to start a family and plan their future with their first childhood love or a girl recommended to them by their families. These unions are variously the result of geopolitical power imbalances, gender obligations, personal desires, and solidarity.

From a gender perspective, for Eritrean men I met in Italy, as also observed among other groups of migrants, transnational marriages were a way to abide by traditional values, meet kin, and settle down with a "trusted person."[47] As described in previous chapters, the achievement of manhood by establishing one's own family is one of the reasons why many young men have left Eritrea. For their part, Eritrean girls are usually happy to marry compatriots living in Europe. As described in the first chapter, *beles,* migrants, are favored by many young women in search of their soul mates because migrants and the world they represent are positively valued in Eritrean society and because of the opportunities related to a marriage with a person living outside Eritrea. Even families bless these unions, thinking that a *beles* would offer better prospects to their daughters. Arranged marriages, which are often seen as sites of female subordination and distress, may instead be considered sites of agency. In fact, Eritrean women actively pursue their migratory aspirations through them using their family and ethnic networks. However, it would be wrong to think that they favor these marriages only for pragmatic convenience.

Tangled with instrumental motivations and cultural logics of desire, transnational marriages are also solidarity mechanisms in a context where migration represents the main channel for personal realization, socioeconomic mobility and families' survival.[48] Exchange of favors among members of the same community and traditional family arrangements commonly underpin transnational marriages.

Before moving forward, it is important to briefly distinguish among the different categories of marriages to which I refer in this chapter. According to the European Council, a marriage of convenience is understood to refer to a marriage contracted for the sole purpose of enabling the person concerned to enter or reside in a member state.[49] Marriages of convenience are not necessarily "business marriages," as my informants would call them. The latter imply that someone who wants to move to Europe or elsewhere would pay someone who is already there to marry him/her. Marriages of convenience and business marriages are different from arranged marriages, which are typically organized by families or among the partners even if there is no prior intimate relationship between the future couple. This kind of union is not in any way illegal—it simply reflects a different idea of marriage, family, and love. Marriages of convenience, arranged, and love marriages are much more intertwined in the perspectives of my informants than in bureaucratic categorizations.

When I arrived in Addis Ababa in October 2013, I met many young Eritrean women and men waiting for spousal visas. To my surprise, most of them were engaged in a reunification processes involving a partner in Italy. This had started to be a concern for the Italian consulate in Addis Ababa, which thought there was something strange behind the increase in Eritreans' applications for reunification visas. The complex moral entanglements of these marriages were at odds with the moral assumptions of the consulate's staff.

BUREAUCRATIC ENCOUNTERS: THE ITALIAN CONSULATE AND THE REFUGEES IN ADDIS ABABA

"We see many of them in our visa section," an Italian consular official told me in 2013. "We have up to forty Eritreans a day. Since 2011, it has become a mass phenomenon. We believe these are all fake marriages. We cross-check the data, call the supposed husband or supposed wife and check that they know the person that is applying for visa. Sometimes we find an age gap [that is] too big. For example, sometimes the guy has left the country when the woman was still a child and it is plausible that they had a sentimental relationship. Sometimes it is clear that they never met." The position of this official is based mostly on the cultural assumption that love and intimacy are sine qua non conditions for a real marital relationship.[50] Marriages that do not correspond to this normative ideal are thus put under special scrutiny in the context of bureaucratic procedures for family reunification visas.[51] Federica Infantino found that arranged marriages, holiday flings, couples who had met in cyberspace, and those with a considerable age gap were all often subject to visa restrictions at European consulates in Morocco.[52] As the notion of "marriage of convenience" is hard to defend in legal terms, much discretion is left to the individual officials, with the result that these bureaucratic practices are often used to filter out not only illicit but also regular migration.[53]

These observations are pertinent in analyzing the position of the Italian consulate in Addis Ababa. The diplomatic officer cited above, for example, saw marriages between partners with a big age gap as likely to be "fake." The fact that partners had not known each other long before the marriage was also a reason to doubt that there had been a sentimental relationship before the marriage. However, as in many other non-Western societies, a sentimental relationship is not a precondition for marriage in Eritrean society.[54] It is still widely accepted that men marry younger women, and that marriages are arranged by the families of the spouses. When I told the Italian official this, she replied:

"Yes, but they come to Europe and they have to respect European regulations on marital matters. Anyway, the ones that come to apply for visa certainly are not political refugees . . . these are not like those who land in Lampedusa. These are young girls, 17–18 years old, with fancy polished nails, that don't even know what politics is . . . it is certain that by now Eritreans know how to cheat the system. . . . There are criminal networks behind these marriages, just as they are behind the secondary movements to Sudan. These young boys and girls would not know how to find the contacts, the houses to rent in Addis, the documents to organize the journey and the marriage."

The position of the Italian consular official well represents a mix of common misconceptions about marital regulations, criminal networks, and the way real refugees should look. She assumed that arranged marriages were against European regulations—even though at most they could be against European moral views about the right marital motivations. She also equated, or at least related, the traditional practices of arranged marriages and marriages of convenience with the operations of criminal networks. Although "business marriages" may be arranged by a middleman, this does not mean that a whole criminal network lies behind the union.[55] Finally, the attractive young girls, nicely dressed and wearing nail polish, who regularly came to apply for reunification visas, did not correspond with the official's mental image of political refugees. "These are not like the ones who arrive in Lampedusa," she said, implying that the ones on Lampedusa were real refugees. Apparently, those in Addis Ababa were not desperate enough.

It should be noted that the interview took place only two months after the Lampedusa tragedy in October 2013, in which over 360 Eritreans died. At the time, no doubt partly owing to the pronouncements of the pope, the prevailing discourse and general atmosphere in Italy tended to see all boat people as desperate refugees seeking safety, whereas at other times, such as the period following the "Arab Spring" of 2011, the public debate was rather dominated by the perception of an invasion of boat people.[56] Although it was mostly correct to say that most girls who had escaped the country even before going to Sa'wa probably knew little of politics, it is also true that their political stance was irrelevant to their applications for family reunification visas. The Italian consular official was not responsible for assessing the legitimacy of Eritreans' refugee statuses, nor was that relevant to the procedure of family reunification. Instead, the "fake refugees" argument was used by the official as proof that these applicants did not deserve entry visas.[57]

The change in Italian visa policy was a big topic of discussion among Eritreans and source of concern for many of them. As an Italian citizen, I became the target of their complaints, as shown in the remarks of Hagos and the other Eritrean refugees I met with at Sister Kudussan's place, quoted earlier in this chapter. Once, a thirty-two-year-old Eritrean refugee named Simon, who was living in Italy, insisted on talking to me about this, even when I told him I could not influence any of the decisions made by the visa officers. He had come to Addis to get married and found the situation at the Italian consulate very worrying: "How can they pretend to know which is a real marriage and which is not?" he said angrily. "For example, I met my wife on Facebook when I was in Switzerland. Her cousin was with me there and she gave me my wife's contact info. Then I came here to marry her. This is my life! How can they see in my heart?! In Italy it is hard to find girlfriends and we cannot go back to my country to get married; that is why we came to Ethiopia."

Eritreans usually migrate in their twenties or thirties when they are still single. Thus, it is no wonder that once they have reached their destination, they also aspire to get married and form a new family. These are aspirations which men carry with them from the time they leave Eritrea, where the obligation to do national service hindered their ability to become traditional breadwinners. Almost all my informants in Italy (who were mostly men) got married during the five-year span of my research, and many of these unions were not arranged for economic purposes. Often, getting married with someone in Ethiopia and Sudan was also a strategy to pursue their own social and geographic upward mobility or to help a fellow Eritrean stuck back home or in transit.

These marriages usually involve Eritreans living in Sudan and Ethiopia for a number of reasons. First, it is especially difficult to find a partner in Europe, since there are usually far fewer young Eritrean women in Europe than men. Second, their still limited integration in Europe makes relationships with natives harder to establish. To this, we may want to add common endogamous preferences among Eritreans. Transnational marriages are a solution to all these problems.

The disappointment of Eritrean refugees was rooted in their previously held assumptions about the generosity of the Italian visa section. There had been rumors that the Italian consulate was liberal in issuing family reunification visas. As I was able to confirm through informal interviews with visa officers from the Norwegian, Swedish, and Swiss consulates in 2014, family visas were in fact harder to obtain there. Usually, only couples who had children and could prove it by a DNA test stood a chance of being reunited with their partners.[58] The less stringent procedure of the Italian consulate might have been one of the reasons behind the numerous applications received by the visa section at that time. More important, this increase may simply have corresponded to the rising number of Eritreans who sought asylum in Italy in those years and wanted to reunite with their previous partners. However, not all these unions were necessarily genuine.

FAKE MARRIAGES?

Although the approach of the Italian consulate to the issue of family reunification visas was based partly on wrong assumptions, some of my informants' claims of innocence were also hard to believe. Since 2009, I had heard of "business marriages"—that is how Eritreans refer to marriages that have been paid for—and throughout my fieldwork in Rome and Genoa, I met many Eritrean refugees who had gone back to Addis Ababa and Khartoum to get married. Some of them did it with the sincere purpose of settling down, but many were paid to do so, or did it as a favor to relatives or friends.

False marriages were common in the squats I visited in Rome. Alazar's room-mate in Anagnina, Ibrahim, showed me photographs of himself with his bride in Sudan—standard shots taken in front of the city hall with the witnesses of the marriage and a few individual ones of the groom and the bride in cheap (Western or *habesha*) ceremonial dress. "Is this a real marriage?" I asked Ibrahim. "Yes, yes," he said, and Alazar exploded in a big, revealing guffaw. In September 2013, after his second asylum application had been refused in Sweden, Alazar traveled to Addis Ababa for his own wedding. When he came back he showed me the pictures, say-ing: "Look how elegant I was in this suit! *Konjo naw?* Beautiful, right?" This mar-riage was an exchange of favors among families in need. In a few months' time, the reunification documents would have been sent to Ethiopia, and Alazar's "wife" would then be able to enter Italy without being fingerprinted by the consulate and continue her journey to seek asylum in other northern European countries. More-over, the woman Alazar married had a sister in Sweden, who married Alazar's brother in Sudan to get him a visa to enter the Schengen Zone.

As I learned from Alazar and several other informants, the prices for a bogus marriage in 2013–14 varied from 13,000 to 17,000 euros, depending on the country of residence of the spouse.[59] For example, a marriage with someone in Italy would usu-ally cost 13,000 euros; a marriage with someone in Norway was worth 16,000 euros; but marriages with a Canadian resident usually cost around 17,000 euros. Although the prices were quite stable, they were not fixed and depended on the reciprocal arrangement or on the commission asked by the middleman organizing the deal.

Sometimes, individuals who trusted me had no difficulty confessing it; others pretended that their marriage was real until their cases had already been rejected at the consulate and they had moved on to other places. For example, Hagos, the speaker for the group of refugees at Sister Kudussan's house, told me that his mar-riage was fraudulent only when I met him again in Khartoum. He had paid for his marriage in Italy, and as things did not work out with the visa, he was waiting to get his money back.

Pursued by those who have been systematically excluded by all other means of regular mobility, even business marriages can be seen in some instances as collec-tively organized practices of resistance to a system that does not serve refugees in any meaningful way. Certainly, only refugees who have the necessary family and economic resources can afford them. Others with more limited means may fall back on cheaper but riskier smugglers' services. Still others, of course, are obliged to stay.

I also received many "marriage proposals." At times, the romantic attention I received may have been sincere, but it could also be interpreted as mirroring a specific political economy of desires and values. As a white, middle-class, relatively young woman with a European passport, I was likely to be seen as a sort of exotic object of desire. However, on other occasions, it was impossible to misinterpret the intentions behind marriage proposals. Robel, Alazar's brother, advised me,

"You are not married, right? You could earn a lot of money if you wanted to." Other times, these proposals were simple requests for help. A young Eritrean man repeatedly asked me if I could help him to reach Europe by marrying him. Sister Kudussan also suggested that I could marry one of her relatives—as an act of Christian charity.

As the above instances illustrate, business marriages were not perceived as negative, immoral practices. Rather, they were mostly normalized as simple business transactions or exchanges of favors among families in need. Sometimes, they were even regarded as expressions of generosity and solidarity among members of the same community in crisis. Although business marriages could also involve reciprocal exploitation among refugees, they were mostly seen as a legitimate way to escape the geographic, social, and gender immobility forced onto them.

LOVE, CONVENIENCE, AND TRADITION

As has been noted, Eritrean refugees are rarely happy to settle down in Italy, but owing to the Dublin Regulation, they often get stuck there. They may then believe that by getting married to someone in Sudan or in Ethiopia, or by reuniting with wives from those countries, they will be able to pursue their initial intentions to obtain asylum in northern Europe. Since family reunification visas did not at that time require them to be fingerprinted by the Italian consulate,[60] once the reunified partner was in Italy, he/she would immediately move to another European country and apply for asylum there. The refugee, usually a man, who had applied for family reunification from Italy, would then join his partner in the chosen European destination. Thus, transnational marriages both make it possible to move on to one's desired destination and partially fulfill kin expectations related to manhood. This is illustrated by the case of Ogbazgi, whom I met in January 2011.

On a flight from Rome to Addis in 2011, I met two friendly young Eritrean men, Ogbazgi and Kibrom, who had been living in Italy for three years. Ogbazgi was working in a greenhouse in Sicily, and Kibrom was a builder in Sampierdarena, Genoa. They were going to Addis Ababa to marry two Eritrean girls from their villages in the southern highland region. During our chats, Kibrom kept teasing Ogbazgi, saying that his future bride was almost a stranger to him. Ogbazgi denied this, but other Eritrean friends had already told me about "business marriages," and I thought Ogbazgi's was one of them. However, I realized later that Ogbazgi's case was different.

Ogbazgi and Kibrom invited me to their weddings a few weeks later. The two young women were originally from the same village as the two young men. They had both crossed the border illicitly with the specific intention of marrying their childhood friends. The families had given their blessings. After a few days, Kibrom and Ogbazgi returned to Italy, and their wives applied for visas. In less than a year, the two young brides arrived in Italy and then moved to Switzerland to seek asylum and settle there. Ogbazgi and Kibrom followed them there soon after. I met Ogbazgi again on his way from Genoa to Geneva in summer 2012. He told me that he was going to miss Italy, but at the same time, he was looking forward to a better life in Switzerland with his wife. He had initially had a few problems legalizing his position there, but after the birth of the first child, he was granted legal residence in Switzerland and could stay with his family. Ogbazgi and Abeba have had their second child and have more or less adapted to their new life in Switzerland.

Ogbazgi's case illustrates how family obligations, mobility strategies, convenience, and love can all play a part in transnational marriages. Ogbazgi's marriage was to some extent arranged. The two partners had not really seen each other for a long time, but as they described it to me, they had been best friends as children. Their families were from the same village and agreed that their union would suit both parties. When I spoke to Abeba, his young bride, she seemed happy with their wedding and looked forward to her new life in Europe. By marrying her, Ogbazgi was also pursuing his aspirations to move on from Italy, while forming his own family and achieving an important step into adulthood. Although unconventional from a Western perspective, their marriage cannot be considered fake or one of convenience. Traditional family expectations about marriage and adulthood, the desire to leave Eritrea, the aspiration to settle down with a trusted partner known by the family, feelings of love, care, and solidarity are all valid and even crucial ingredients of marriages across borders among Eritreans.

This brings us back to the morality underpinning border-crossing practices. My earlier account of the world of smugglers and transnational marriages illustrates the gap between legal borders and the moral boundaries of those who cross them. The lack of compliance to border regulations among my informants reveals different perceptions of fairness, rights, and responsibility, which have their point of reference in the community. Although they may involve contradictions, transnational marriages are collectively organized, socially embedded tactics to circumvent what is perceived as an unfair regime of immobility.

Entrapped

Making Sense of High-Risk Migration through Gambling

Legal channels of geographic mobility are progressively diminishing, and a significant number of migrants try to overcome national borders in unauthorized ways. However, unauthorized migration often implies high risks. International media often report on the incredible journeys of those trying to reach Australia, Italy, Greece, or Spain in makeshift boats or on the death of migrants trying to cross the Mexico-U.S. border through the desert. Most of these attempts are commonly explained by referring to migrants' desperation.[1] However, this interpretation can only partially make sense of the motivations of those embarking on these risky ventures. Eritreans' trajectories, as described throughout this book, show that their movements cannot be reduced to simple mechanical reactions to danger. The space for choice, although often severely constrained, was evident in my informants' tortuous and fragmented journeys across borders. If a choice exists, how do refugees weigh the risk of staying versus the risk of leaving?

After a review of the main available explanations of high-risk migration,[2] I propose to examine refugees' decisions through the concept of entrapment, as developed in gambling studies. This idea is crucial, I argue, to understand the emic perception of mobility and immobility, because it introduces cognitive cogency to mobility choices in the presence of significant obstacles. My informants' heartfelt obligation to move on is not only the combined result of limited long-term prospects in different countries of arrival and the set of expectations, desires, and moral prescriptions—the cosmologies of destinations—they shared with their peers and families. This obligation is strenghtened by the sequential character of their stepwise migration. The concept of entrapment enables me to show how the duty to move ahead becomes more and more compelling because of the accumulating emotional and social costs of migrants' journeys.

Although it reconstructs in detail what is at stake for my informants at each step of their journey, this chapter is not meant to be a rationalistic cost-benefit analysis. Rather, it is an attempt to grasp the feelings, the values, the perceptions of those who keep migrating no matter the risks. To make sense of their journeys, it is crucial to acknowledge that each move is substantially related to and engendered by previous ones. This is not simply because they are all part of a personal, moral, and social set of expectations about migration and its goals. It is also because high-risk migrants, not unlike gamblers, are betting in a game of risk that becomes almost impossible to leave. I am in no way suggesting by this analogy that my informants' conduct is comparable to that of compulsive players. Gamblers and refugees are different in a number of aspects, ranging from the risks at stake to the conditions they face. However, they have one crucial characteristic in common: they make not only one, but many sequential risky choices. I argue that this serial aspect, widely ignored in the literature on high-risk migration, is key to making sense of migrants' determination to move on in spite of mounting losses.

THE DEBATE ON HIGH-RISK MIGRATION: TAKING STOCK AND A WAY FORWARD

One of the main explanations of high-risk migration rests on the assumption that individuals would avoid life-threatening journeys if they knew how dangerous they were. The issue is then enabling access to reliable information. Awareness campaigns organized in the last pen years by the International Organization for Migration in areas characterized by intense emigration have tried to sensitize prospective migrants to the dangers of unauthorized migration. However, even when information is available, migrants may avoid it or discredit it as irrelevant to their case, some scholars argue.[3] Maria Hernández-Carretero, for instance, found that many of her Senegalese informants who were determined to attempt to cross to the Canary Islands expressly rejected information about the difficulties of the journey and just focused on the possibilities of enjoying a better life in Europe.[4] The point is, then, not only to disseminate the information, but to make it convincing. It has also been pointed out that migrants may not find the source trustworthy.[5] Most notably, international organizations and national authorities are not deemed credible, inasmuch as they are seen as representing less the interests of the migrants than of those who want to stop unauthorized migration.

A second trend of explanations concerns the relativistic perception of risk. Whereas the public debate and risk analysts have assumed that risks are objective and absolute facts, social scientists have often pointed out that the definition of risk itself depends on social and cultural criteria.[6] Therefore, perceptions of risks cannot be categorized as biased or unbiased, irrational or rational, lay or expert views, but should be analyzed against the relevant social and cultural background. Migration scholars have also used this approach to make sense of high-risk migration.[7] As these authors claim, potential migrants may be aware of the dangers involved in unauthorized border crossing, while still perceiving them as "acceptable." But how can life-threatening risks become acceptable?

Whenever a large number of individuals from the same place engage in high-risk migration, a "culture of acceptance" may emerge. Building on Paul Slovic's risk theory,[8] Lynnaire Sheridan's work on the Mexico-U.S. border illustrates how common and familiar dangers may be less worrying than those seen as rare, but memorable. She shows that migration risks not only become normalized, but may also become desirable, as a sort of rite of passage to adulthood.[9] This is not specific to Mexico, but has been widely documented as happening in other areas of extensive long-term, widespread emigration.[10]

Life-threatening risks associated with migration may become acceptable when the risk of staying is perceived as even higher than the one of leaving. Whenever somebody lives in conditions of severe personal distress, socioeconomic vulnerability, with a lack of reasonable alternatives and even absence of future prospects, even high risks can be reframed as opportunities. According to Madeleine Hayenhjelm, those risks are radically distinguishable from those related to lifestyle, or large-scale technological or societal risks, and could thereby be defined as *risks from vulnerability*.[11] In contexts such as the ones from which unauthorized migrants originate, marked by socioeconomic stagnation and by intense emigration, geographic immobility is often equated with "social death."[12]

The risks that Eritreans run when they flee their country can thus also be classified as "risks from vulnerability." Their context of choice is typically characterized by poor outset conditions, by limited reasonable alternatives, and by the hope that running the risk will bring a positive change to their lives. As described in chapter 1, the everyday life of many young people in Eritrea is severely constrained by government (such as by compulsory indefinite national service) and economic deprivation, while the flow of images and information from the outside world conveys the idea that a better life is achievable elsewhere. Unable to realize their most basic aspirations regarding freedom, work, and study, as well as their hopes of having a family, young women and especially young men are often stuck in a condition of social liminality.

Although the above considerations about the culture of acceptance and the relative value of risk are useful for analyzing my informants' attitudes to border crossings, they also have a limit: they imply that migrants just move from the origin to the destination, and that the migration decision is made at one single point. On the contrary, the cases of Eritreans and many other refugees and migrants show that migration is rather a stepwise process.[13] Decisions to engage in dangerous

FIGURE 18. Young Eritreans in Hintsats camp (photo by the author, 2013)

journeys are made all along the way: when Eritreans decide to flee their country, when they continue their journey from the first safe African country to Libya, when they search for ways to reach Italy, and, once again, when they try to move on to northern Europe. Although their agency is significantly constrained, in every lap of their journey there is a choice to be made between the risks/opportunities to stay put and the risks/opportunities to move on.[14] It is crucial, I argue, to consider these moments of decision, not in isolation, but as parts of a sequential, cumulative process, in which previous choices influence subsequent ones. In order to examine such a process, I suggest a frame of analysis drawn from the study of gambling behavior. However, before moving on to that, let me draw on the ethnographic material I collected in Ethiopian camps to show why assuming Eritreans' limited access to reliable information explains their risk-taking behavior is mistaken.

ONWARD . . . NO MATTER THE RISK

My informants across four countries were usually well aware of the potential dangers of their journeys. Eritrean refugees in Italy knew the risks involved in seeking asylum in northern Europe after having been identified in Italy, and my informants in Eritrea knew the consequences of being caught fleeing the country, but this did not stop them from repeatedly attempting to do so. After having been imprisoned for over a year after a failed getaway, for example, Paolos, Johanna's brother, mentioned in chapter 1, tried to escape twice more, and, when I met him, he was resolved to do so yet again. Likewise, those I met in Ethiopia and Sudan were resolute in their determination to reach Europe no matter the perils.

When I asked refugees in Adi Harush camp in Ethiopia if they were aware of the dangers awaiting them on the way to Europe, I always received the same answer: "Yes, we know." The tragic 2013 Lampedusa sinking was still fresh in the minds of the camp inhabitants: some of the people who died there had lived with them in Adi Harush, and others had been friends of theirs in Eritrea. Their knowledge of the risks wasn't necessarily secondhand either. Some of those I met had already experienced failed journeys. Still, they were ready to try their luck again.

While conducting my small survey on migration aspirations in the camp, Jeremiah, my interpreter, and I entered a little mud hut with a low ceiling and colored posters of Bollywood actors on the walls. Welcomed by the smoke of coal and the smell of roasted coffee beans, we sat inside facing a small crowd of young men waiting to drink their coffee. Saleh and Mukhtar, two young men in their late twenties, were our hosts. They had been in the camp for a year and eight months respectively. I started asking everyone my usual questions about their plans for the future, but they were usually received with a sarcastic smile. Sure, they all wanted to move on from the camp soon. Saleh liked Canada, but was not sure how to reach it; Mukhtar was planning to go to Germany. The others did not say where they wished to go.

"We just want to get away from here," one of them said.

"I understand," I replied. "But are you aware of the risks that you could face on your way?"

"Yes, we are," he answered, and hugging the man on his right, said by way of explanation, "He come from Sinai." The Sinai desert, as I reported before, is probably the most horrific site of Eritrean migrants' suffering. Those who survive it tell horrific stories of kidnappings and torture and show scars on their bodies as proof.[15]

The man who had been to Sinai was called Bere. He had escaped from Sa'wa in 2010 with some of his companions and reached Shegarab camp. He wanted to get to Israel, but things did not go as planned. While he was trying to reach Israel with the help of smugglers, he was sold to a Bedouin Rashaida criminal gang in the Sinai and imprisoned there for two months until his family in Eritrea paid a ransom of U.S.$2,500 (125,000 nakfa) Released by the traffickers at the border with Israel, he was caught by the Egyptian police and beaten so badly that he had to be hospitalized for a week. Then, he was taken to prison in a nearby Egyptian town, where he stayed for four months before being returned to the camp in Ethiopia in September 2010.

Overwhelmed by Bere's misfortunes, I stammered: "I am so sorry . . . maybe now the UNHCR will consider you for some kind of resettlement process." But Bere promptly replied: "I have no process. I stayed here three years and now it is time to leave. There is no future for us here, and our families are waiting for us. God will be with me."

The perceived lack of future, the need to migrate for the family's sake, and seemingly fatalistic acceptance of God's will were not new to me.[16] I encountered them whenever I talked to Eritreans about their aspirations to migrate. However, I was surprised to hear such determination from somebody who had already gone through so much suffering. And Bere was not an isolated case. In Mai Ayni, Adi Harush, and Addis Ababa, I met ten refugees who had undergone similar experiences in the Sinai and Egyptian prisons. Some of their stories were so brutal that my interpreters could hardly keep translating. In spite of all that, six of them were ready to move again after resting for a while.

Bere's instance blatantly points to the inadequacy of blaming the decision to engage in high-risk migration on lack of information about risks. This determination to move on seems to indicate that the dangers of the journeys, even the most fearful ones, have become normalized as part of a sort of subculture of risk. Is it possible that, as Lynnaire Sheridan has argued in the context of Mexico-U.S.[17] border crossings, my Eritrean informants had come to accept the risks as an ordinary—perhaps even a necessary—part of their migration experience?

GET RICH OR DIE TRYING

I met 40-year-old Jeremiah the day after my arrival in Adi Hurush camp. Jeremiah had a house to himself in zone 1, the nicest area of the camp. He had been granted such privileged accommodation because he was HIV-positive, had had TB for a long time, and was cyclically sick. He coughed the entire afternoon while talking to me about his life before and after becoming a refugee. Jeremiah had read a lot and was interested in politics, religion—he was an evangelical Christian—and music. He kept quoting the Bible, Dan Connell's investigative journalism,[18] and songs by Tracy Chapman and 50 Cent.

Jeremiah had led a very adventurous life: he was born to an Eritrean father and an Ethiopian mother in Addis Ababa, moved to Eritrea after independence, and became an important manager of Assab Port. After revealing and denouncing corruption in the administration of the port, he became unpopular among political cadres and had to flee the country. Then he lived in Uganda, South Sudan, Kenya, and Ethiopia, continually trying to reach the First World in any way possible—by resettlement process, study visa, fake papers, transnational marriage, or smugglers—all in vain. Finally, sick and tired, he had somehow "retired" to the camp, where he was able to get some free medical care (although limited) for his condition.

"I was one of them once," Jeremiah said, referring to those young refugees who were doing their best to leave the camp to reach Europe or other developed countries. "I would have done anything to get there. . . . Indeed I tried everything . . . but now I am tired, my time is finished. I am out of the game." Then he tried to explain the mentality of the young refugees on the move: "Do you know 50 Cent?

The title of one of his albums is *Get Rich or Die Tryin'*. Do you know it? We have a similar expression in Tigrinya, "Wey keb, wey geb." It means "Either you rise or you fall." That is what they think. They know about the danger of Sinai, they know about the danger of Lampedusa, but they see their friends who made it to Europe; they see their neighbors leaving from the camp and reaching Sweden or Norway. They cannot wait here; they want to have the life they see on TV. They will not stop until they do." After all his experience, Jeremiah was advising Yohannes, his young friend and brother in faith, not to follow the flow of those who were chasing after success. "I told him to get married here in the camp and start a family while he is here. In the camp he can slowly develop his artistic skills [Yohannes was a very gifted painter] and wait for some opportunities in Addis Ababa or in other countries."

Jeremiah's remarks indicate how Eritrean migration is embedded in a complex set of collective images, societal expectations, and personal desire to be part of the imagined outside world. This is also what I have tried to highlight throughout this book, using the concept of "cosmologies of destinations." Moreover, Jeremiah's account underlines the role of peers in reciprocally reinforcing motivations to migrate, as well as the imitation mechanism among travelling partners, kin, and acquaintances as crucial in the decision to do so. Jeremiah's words illustrate the mentality of a sort of subculture of migration in which risks are elaborated through cultural categories, normalized and accepted as inevitable. Trained in the military, often accustomed to challenging environments and even to punishments, many Eritreans may have developed a sort of acquaintance with risk. Moreover, as I illustrated in previous chapters, the practice of unauthorized border crossing belongs to the history of the Eritrean people and is today a pervasive practice, involving thousands of them every month. However, even if Eritreans are used to even the most extreme risks, they are still scared by them—and for good reason.

Many of my informants in Ethiopia and Sudan were fearful about their prospective border crossings. In Addis Ababa, Adonay was extremely scared when he thought his departure to Libya was approaching. He could not concentrate on his studies thinking about the journey and was extremely emotional during our conversations. When I met Hagos (spokesman for a small community of southern Eritreans in Addis Ababa) again in Khartoum, he told me that considering the favorable conditions provided by Italy's Mare Nostrum ("Our Sea") operation,[19] his brother was pushing him to go to Libya. But Hagos was hesitant and frightened. Dani, a freshly arrived refugee in Addis Ababa, told Violetta and me before moving on: "I am terrified . . . I don't want to go, I know all the risks, it is so dangerous, but I have to go, I have no choice. I don't have any process here." These instances suggest that the decision to engage in difficult journeys is not so much the result of an increased tolerance of risk, but rather the consequence of feeling they have no reasonable alternative. Eritrean refugees felt "entrapped," caught in a condition that obliges them to keep moving onward, no matter the risks.

Trying to make sense of my informants' attitudes, I came across the scholarship on gambling. The concepts I found there—among them, entrapment—resounded with my informants' ways of framing their attempts as games of risk, chance, and fate. In referring to their migration attempts, they often defined them as lottery draws.[20]

REFUGEES AS GAMBLERS: A NEW APPROACH
TO MIGRATION TRAJECTORIES

What do Eritrean refugees' migratory practices and gambling have in common? Although this parallel is admittedly unusual, it has, I argue, the potential to uncover neglected aspects of contemporary forced migrants' complex and lengthy trajectories.

Gambling and high-risk multi-step migration share several characteristics. First, these two activities both involve chance, investment, risks, and opportunities. They are both games of chance in which individuals willingly risk money, time, energy, and personal security to win a prize or attain a goal. Second, my informants, like regular players, tend to bet more than once. They are serial riskers. Here, I am not trying to suggest that migrants' attempts to migrate are compulsive behavior. What I am interested in here is to show the common sequential feature of my informants' trajectories and gamblers' bets. Migration trajectories to Europe can entail several wagers. They risk once when escaping their country, twice when moving on to Libya, three times when they cross the sea to reach Italy and four times when they attempt to obtain asylum in northern Europe. This would apply to a successful, extremely lucky trajectory, but migration pathways are usually far from linear. Rather, they correspond to the "fragmented journeys" that Michael Collyer sees as a common feature of global migration systems.[21]

One's escape from Eritrea may be the last of a series of attempts. As described in chapter 1, many of my informants had tried to flee more than once and were sometimes severely punished for doing so. The passage from Ethiopia to Sudan and Libya often involves betting that their relatives will be able to pay for their journeys. As noted earlier, relatives were often reluctant to pay for these risky journeys; thus, many of my informants negotiated their passage to Libya with their middleman without telling their families. A phone call asking for payment for past (travel to Libya) and future (travel to Italy) services may catch relatives, often in the diaspora and unprepared and unable to pay, by surprise. Inability to pay can result in long periods of waiting in harsh conditions, and sometimes in deprivation and torture.[22] The sea journey across the Mediterranean is also likely to be the last of many failed tries.[23] Finally, attempts to seek asylum in northern Europe are usually repeated more than once when refugees are returned to Italy under the Dublin Regulation. My informants share a systematic tendency to take repeated risks with regular gamblers.

Yet high-risk migration and gambling differ on several crucial points. First of all, the conditions in which refugees and gamblers "bet" are drastically different. As already mentioned, the risks run by refugees could be defined as "risks from vulnerability," since they are characterized by poor outset conditions, lack of reasonable alternatives, and hope of a positive change. Refugees' ability to choose is thus limited, whereas gamblers' bets may be seen as an unconstrained leisure activity on the part of quite well-off individuals.[24]

Above all, the risks and rewards involved in gambling and in high-risk migration differ in quality. A gambler primarily risks money; a refugee primarily risks his/her life. What is at stake for migrants is the possibility of safety or a better life, whereas the expected reward of gamblers is eminently money. Compulsive gamblers can certainly reach the point of risking their social status, even their lives to some extent, at the final stages of their pathological compulsion to bet, but these are not the first stakes of the game. For many refugees—this is certainly the case of Eritreans—migration is instead a life-or-death game from the outset. Moreover, the numerous cases of Eritreans kidnapped in Sinai remind us that not only death, but also extreme physical suffering can result from a wrong step in high-risk migration journeys. No matter how relativistic perceptions of risks may be, it is undeniable that loss of life and physical suffering still have an ultimate value for human beings. Thus, even if refugees have arguably higher probabilities to succeed compared to gamblers,[25] they risk something that is incommensurably more valuable. Nonetheless, the parallel between gamblers and Eritrean refugees still has the potential to uncover some important mechanisms underpinning refugees' attitudes to risk.[26] The concept of entrapment is particularly interesting in making sense of why migrants take risks no matter the cost.

ENTRAPPED

The emotional condition experienced by Eritrean refugees once they have left their country can be associated with the feeling of *entrapment* typically documented among gamblers.[27] Entrapment defines the psychological condition of gamblers who feel obliged to continue betting both time and money owing to the perception that they have gone too far to give up. Individuals may feel compelled to bet repeatedly in order to win a higher stake and then repay previous debts. According to Jon Elster, entrapment could be caused by a high level of tolerance for risk developed after serial gambling and the thrill connected to it; however, it could also simply be analyzed as a causal mechanism whereby individuals continue betting in order to pay previously contracted debts.[28] This, as Elster suggests, can be considered a rational mechanism, since a possible disaster is preferable to a certain one. For instance, if an individual has already lost a lot of money and has to face major negative consequences as a result, he/she may keep betting the money left in the hope that it will enable the gambler recoup his/her losses.

The word "entrapment" is often used in migration studies, at times as a stronger synonym of being stuck, to highlight those structural process—legal, economic, and political—that immobilize migrants in a place or condition. Steff Jansen employs this term to describe the spatial immobility produced by bureaucratic paradoxes of visa regimes.[29] Guillermina Núñez and Josiah Heyman call enforcement at the Mexico-U.S. border "entrapment.[30] Although these analyses and the cases they describe largely overlap with the instances and processes of immobilization that I describe throughout this book. The notion of entrapment as drawn from gambling studies adds an important dimension to this debate. Entrapped individuals not only feel immobile, they also feel caught in a loop of actions from which there is no way out except "winning." The idea of entrapment thus is not only descriptive of a condition, it also implies a course of action. For Eritrean refugees to feel entrapped means that they feel obliged to keep trying to move on to their final destinations in spite of the risks and the losses. The idea of entrapment can, thus, play a crucial role not only in unfolding the manifold meanings of mobility and immobility, but also for the investigation of migration dynamics.

In order to leave Eritrea, many of my informants spent significant amounts of money—several thousand euros—usually borrowed from their family back home or from relatives abroad. This does not mean that refugees will be indebted at the end of their migration, as described for other immigrant groups,[31] but they are expected to start contributing to their families' incomes back home by sending remittances and helping other members of the family to leave the country. While they are in Ethiopia and Sudan, they nonetheless remain heavily dependent on their families, sometimes even for their daily survival. Even if they manage to get a job there, their salary is usually not enough to help their families back home; rather, it is barely sufficient for their own survival. As a result of their migration, then, they have worsened both their social status and their dependency on their families.

On their way out of the country, Eritreans have not only invested a lot of money. The journey has also cost them a lot in several other aspects—in a way they have lost their entire world, including their dear ones and their familiar life environments. While crossing the border, they endured significant physical challenges and risked being arrested by Eritrean police or dying. In Ethiopia or Sudan then they have faced hostile environments and accumulated stress partly connected to the past they left behind and partly to the future they have not yet reached. All these costs have been paid, not simply to escape conscription in Eritrea, but to win the prospect of a decent life for themselves and their families. This is deemed possible only outside Africa and beyond southern Europe. This socially defined goal is reciprocally strengthened and emotionally reproduced through moments of "collective effervescence" in their dwelling places. If the jackpot defined by the cosmology of destinations is not won, all the huge investments up till then become worthless. This is why the only perceived solution to solve their situation and to justify previously accumulated losses is to face risks even higher than those run to escape from Eritrea by moving on to Libya and then to Italy.

The condition of "entrapment" assumes many other meanings in the passage from Ethiopia/Sudan to Italy through Libya. First, entrapment is not only a psychological condition here, but a physical one, inasmuch as the journey to Europe entails several steps of forced immobility. As I explained earlier, migrants often willingly accept the possibility of being imprisoned by smugglers for the time needed for their kin to pay for the journey. These moments of forced immobility do not emerge from lack of agency. As argued by Noelle Brigden and Cetta Mainwaring in their analysis of migrants' journeys across the U.S.-Mexico and southern European borders,[32] these periods of involuntary immobility are strategic choices enacted by migrants in order to fulfil their migration project. It is at this point of the journey that the paradoxes and complexity resulting from the interplay between choice, aspirations, and constraints are mostly evident. Bound to the idea—and moral obligation—that there is no other alternative but moving on, migrants choose temporarily to give up their freedom to achieve their goals. By doing so, they force their relatives, mostly living abroad, to come up with the necessary resources for travel they often did not agree to. Entrapment here does not define only the physical experience of migrants and their psychological status, but also the condition of their families and kin, who are bound to finance journeys that may lead to the deaths of their loved ones. Once they have reached Italy, achieving socioeconomic integration remains very difficult.

Many Eritrean refugees in Italy face multiple challenges in integrating into the Italian labor market and starting to send remittances back home. Thus, their social status in their community of reference back home is arguably even lower than when they were in Africa. Although they have reached Europe, they are not able to help their families and prove their manhood. Even in Italy, then, Eritrean refugees are entrapped between mounting losses and the hope of achieving a better future by running more risks. Moving inside Europe, in their eyes, is simply one more step forward. They have already gone so far—not only in terms of distance from home but also in terms of money and time invested—that they simply cannot give up at this stage. Despite the legal residence they have gained, their lives in Italy are unexpectedly hard, while the lives of their friends who made it to Norway, Sweden and other northern European countries seem easy and comfortable.

In the case of secondary movements within Europe, refugees usually no longer risk their lives, but failed asylum applications generate psychological stress, a significant expenditure of time (two to three years on average), and, to a lesser extent, a loss of money. The psychological stress is owing to living in an unstable condition for long time—sometimes detained—without knowing the result of their bureaucratic process; and being obliged, after their return to Italy, to start their lives anew, such as obtaining legal papers again and finding accommodation and a job. However, most of the trauma is caused by the failure of their migratory plans, the same plans that pushed them out of their homeland and kept them moving on to Europe.

In a way, one might say that the power of their families' and their own cosmology is even stronger in the last step of the journey. In spite of safety and legal residence, individuals' aspirations and family expectations become more pressing. The feeling of being so close to the final destination, the First World, but not able to reach it, elicits even stronger desires to move on and led my informants to attempt again and again to seek asylum in northern Europe, in spite of the low odds of success. In fact, it should be noted that although the risks involved in failed asylum attempts are not perceived as particularly high, the odds of success in this last lap of the journey are dramatically lower than in previous crossings. If refugees' biometrics have been recorded in the European biometric database, EURODAC, the migration gamble becomes comparable to a lottery in which the odds of winning are extremely limited and investments are low.

This chapter has analyzed my previous ethnographic material through an analytical frame that can make sense of widespread, ongoing, and resilient migration in the face of huge obstacles. Drawing from the study of gamblers' behavior, I argue that refugees' commitment to keep migrating on progressively increases, in spite of mounting losses and high risk, mainly owing to the social and emotional condition called entrapment. To talk about entrapment here is another way of looking at immobility, not only as a structurally determined physical state, but also as an emotional condition, which is typically experienced by those migrants who repeatedly take risks in searching for their new homes. While summarizing the geographic, social, economic, generational, gender, and emotional dimensions of (im)mobility, the notion of entrapment points to the cognitive aspect of feeling stuck and its implications for migration dynamics, attitudes to risk, and resilience to mobility barriers.

Although the case of Eritrean migration is specific for a number of historical and political reasons, my informants' trajectories may be considered as exemplary of refugees' reactions more generally against the increasingly restrictive structure of opportunities they face. The idea of entrapment could potentially be applied to asylum migration dynamics on a larger scale. Through this framework, it is possible to better understand why a number of asylum seekers repeatedly run very high risks in order to reach developed countries, and why migration and asylum flows have not significantly decreased, despite increasingly tightened immigration policies. It is crucial to take into consideration here the cumulative stepwise character of their migration. Previous choices, the risks already run, and the strong personal and family investments all affect subsequent decisions, which, from an emic point of view, often become obliged choices.

Conclusion

What pushes thousands of young people to leave their homeland every month? What makes Eritrea—a country neither involved now in open war nor really at peace for almost two decades—the ninth refugee-producing nation worldwide? What leads Eritreans to migrate on after they have reached first countries of refuge in spite of the incredible dangers of doing so? This book has answered these questions by illustrating the power of transnational moralities, shared imagination, and emotions in the migration stories of my research participants and their families. Their struggles to evade detection, cross borders, and find a suitable home speak of the many paradoxes surrounding asylum regimes, migration management, and their implications in the contemporary world.

Against the common framing of refugee flows as emergencies or exceptional events, *The Big Gamble* has aimed to emphasize the "normality" of these movements.[1] This does not mean that the political and institutional conditions that produce and reproduce them should be accepted. Quite the opposite. Analyzing the systematic/normalized aspect of these migrations implies acknowledging how extremely critical circumstances have become ordinary owing to the unchanged political situation in countries of origin and the inability of asylum regimes to provide prospects for those in protracted displacement. Recognizing that high-risk mobility has become the norm and not the exception allows researchers to investigate not only how political and institutional factors influence the drivers of migration, but also how individuals, families, and communities organize to respond to chronic lack of prospects, both at home and in exile. In this way, it is possible to illuminate agency and the exercise of choice even among those conventionally defined by the lack of those.

In contexts where crisis has become ordinary, old-fashioned categories such as the binary distinction between voluntary and forced migrants make little sense. For people struggling every day with structural violence, lack of freedom, and deprivation, the desire to leave home is deeply intertwined with the need to do so. Mobility here is a choice, although extremely constrained; it is an aspiration socially cultivated to the point of becoming an expectation. Among communities with a global diaspora—the result itself of a decades of displacement—these expectations tend to be directed toward certain destinations, historically identified as providing better prospects for safety and stability.

One of the main implications of these considerations is that forced migration should not be the key notion in the debate on asylum rights and refugees. It should rather be replaced by analysis of how mobility and immobility are produced and reproduced at different stages of the migration process. This analysis should be focused on the moral, social, and emotional factors that enable and hinder aspirations to mobility and their realization. Although the idea of forced migration emerged as a conceptual tool more widely to embrace those circumstances—not necessarily mentioned in the Geneva Convention—that force people out of their country, its theoretical strength remains limited. The condition of "being forced" is still an overwhelming part of it. This implicitly excludes appreciation of the role of aspirations, imaginaries, and moralities in understanding why many leave their home country, and why they try to keep moving forward once they have reached a first, second, or even third safe haven.

This argument has implications for public discourse, since the moral—as well as legal—grounds for providing protection to asylum seekers should not be based on how helpless/choiceless/pushed they are. The right to seek protection should be separated from the assumption that the only deserving refugees are those who are exceptionally forced out of their countries by a sudden humanitarian crisis or an explosion of violence. Vulnerability does not equate with lack of choice and agency. In fact, in some cases extreme vulnerability may be the result of an active attempt to circumvent border enforcement. As Noelle Brigden and Ċetta Mainwaring highlight, "migrants temporarily surrender control at points during the journey, accepting momentary disempowerment to achieve larger strategic goals."[2] Prevailing discourses over refugee deservingness should not exclude an appreciation of refugees' agency and their capabilities.[3] This is crucial not only for understanding who can move and who has to stay put, but also to shift common visions of refugees as burdens to social welfare, rather than potential contributors to richer societies. Those who seek to improve refugees' living conditions and chances of protection should not try to impose the image of the deserving refugee as a choiceless victim, but rather to discard the binary logic opposing forced and voluntary migrants, deserving victims and bogus migrants. Due to the tragically ordinary dimension of its exodus, the Eritrean case is a point of departure from which to blur boundaries between forced and voluntary migrants, to reflect on the manifold meanings of immobility in migration journeys and the transnational social mechanisms reproducing refugee movements over time.

Migratory departures are an ordinary reality in Eritrea. Historically associated with the sacrifices of the war against Ethiopia, as well as with the crucial importance of remittances to the livelihood of those who stay behind, migration is a key ingredient in the symbolic and practical organization of Eritrean society. Nationalistic propaganda, intimate family histories, and locals' daily survival revolve around it. However, in an illiberal political atmosphere such as the Eritrean one, current emigration remains a covert and counterinstitutional enterprise, which is publicly condemned and severely punished. As in many other contexts characterized by chronic stagnation and structural violence in Africa, and not only there, escaping is seen by the young as a way to achieve freedom, economic stability, and the moral status associated with adulthood. Migration may be differently perceived by young men aiming to become family breadwinners and young women fleeing a suffocating patriarchy, but geographic mobility is generally viewed as a path to social recognition among their peers and respect from their families. Migration from Eritrea cannot be reduced to a reaction to danger. Rather, it is a long-term strategy to combat socioeconomic, political, and existential immobility, enable family survival, and pursue one's dreams.

Unlike that of forced migration, the concept of involuntary immobility, as elaborated in the work of Jørgen Carling and Stephen Lubkemann,[4] is crucial for making sense of current exodus from Eritrea. To leave a country where passports are not easily obtainable takes a lot of effort and resources. Those with enough contacts among high-ranking officials may be able to secure permission to exit. Others need money, contacts, physical strength, and courage to cross highly patrolled borders without authorization. This means that access to geographic mobility is highly stratified in Eritrea. Who can and who cannot move depends crucially on socioeconomic family status and the accessibility of transnational networks. Those who can pay more are also those who can travel more safely—by employing more experienced brokers, safer means of transport, or obtaining semi-legal papers—even if in unauthorized ways. Whereas a successful passage generally mirrors individuals' determination, as well as families' contacts, resources, and networks, immobility is the only option left for those who do not have the means or the capabilities to pursue their aspirations. All my informants' histories were extraordinarily telling about freedom to move on (conspicuous by its absence) or backward as a powerful factor of social stratification on a global scale.[5]

(Im)mobility, however, is much more than a physical experience that Eritreans, like many other migrants, face at every step of their fragmented migration trajectories.[6] Their sense of being stuck is telling of other forms of immobility. Most of them share a perception, as well as a very real condition, of *social* immobility, related to the lack of access to resources able to fulfil their basic social rights, as well as deep-rooted aspirations to modernity; and, in parallel, of *generational* immobility, pointing to the societal constraints on the transition to adulthood that they were expected to realize, and to which they aspired. Both forms of immobility are remarkably gendered in their manifestations. More fundamentally, the Eritrean youth I met—whether movers or stayers—were often exposed to a form of *temporal* immobility, inasmuch as their precarious conditions seemed to lock up their lives in an "extended present," with little scope for long-term projects, unless projected elsewhere; and indeed, of *existential* immobility, as highlighted by their ways of positioning themselves in socially widespread and legitimated cosmologies of destinations. Finally, there is another crucial aspect of immobility that I observed: the sense of entrapment that binds migrants to try again and again to reach their desired destination in spite of incredible dangers. Further research on the interplay between mobility and immobility, as enacted at all of the levels highlighted above, can contribute to advancing the understanding of contemporary migration at large, well beyond the conventional and hypostatical categories of refugees/forced migrants versus economic/voluntary migrants—and, for that matter, well beyond the Eritrean case.

Many concepts developed in the study of voluntary migration, such as aspirations, cultural imaginaries, and culture of migration, are valuable in the study of refugee flows too. All these notions emphasize the symbolic value of migration in societies marked by long-term outflows of people, but they do not directly connect these symbolic dimensions with the moralities underpinning migration motives and practices. This is why the notion of cosmologies of destinations is of added value here. Unlike previous notions, the idea of cosmologies of destinations specifically refers to the distinctive sets of norms and prescriptions associated with the right/wrong destination that have been stratified in decades of exodus from the country. The web of moral obligations connecting families back home, refugees in transit, and kin in the diaspora is key to accounting for the persistent desire to move on, to grasping the complex negotiations over journey payment, and to appreciating emic perceptions of borders and smugglers. In sum, drawn from the classic understanding of cosmologies as cognitive and moral ways of categorizing the world and orienting subjects' actions, this concept illustrates (1) how collective imaginaries of places entail moral views of what it means to reach them; (2) how deep-rooted images and moralities influence daily interactions between refugees and locals; and (3) how these moral and cognitive views shape further attempts to migrate.

From the outset of their migration and through subsequent steps, the young men and women whom I met pictured a hierarchy of worlds, the top level of which can be reached only through migration. Specific destinations, such as northern Europe, US, or Canada, are perceived by them as well as by their families, their peers and their enlarged networks as sites with better prospects in terms of security, work, and freedom. This collectively shared hierarchy is not simply an imaginary, but mirrors a moral understanding of the world, not unrelated to the amount and quality of remittances, that defined some places as suitable destinations and others as unsuitable. Thus, whereas Alazar's brother in Canada was perceived by his family as brilliant and successful, Alazar, who was still stuck in Italy, was subjected to their criticism.

My informants' trajectories across Ethiopia, Sudan, and Italy were determined not only by limited integration prospects and legal constraints, but also by transnationally reproduced family obligations, and common visions of the expected goal—and destination—of migration. Communication with compatriots around the world and with families back home feeds into what is perceived as the moral obligation to move on. On the one hand, information and images from those who had reached their final destinations elicit the desire to move there. On the other hand, the obligation to remit back home push those "in transit" to migrate no matter the risk. These considerations bear significant implications also for the study of secondary mobility, not only in Africa, but also within Europe, as I show in the case of Italy. The determination to migrate elsewhere, typically to northern European countries, in spite of repeated deportation back under the Dublin Regulation can only be understood by keeping in mind financial obligations to left-behind kin that cannot be met by people struggling with limited institutional assistance and poor labor market opportunities. Although the Eritrean case has its own historical, cultural, and legal specificities, it is likely that similar conclusions could be drawn about the motivations and the trajectories of migrants stuck in transit areas such as Ventimiglia, Calais, or Dunkirk.

Historically developed moral assumptions about places and their inhabitants significantly impacted the interaction between my informants and locals in different locations they inhabited after leaving Eritrea. Resulting from colonial legacies, historical conflicts, and long-term discrimination, a deep-rooted distrust of locals often influenced my informants' limited contacts with locals. While living together in camps or in shared housing in Addis Ababa and Khartoum, my informants nourished one another's feelings of being stuck. When a migration corridor opens, the urban and camp areas become "effervescent" with an emotional atmosphere that contagiously encourages even the undecided to depart. In a way, these forms of collective effervescence are the emotional manifestations of the shared worldviews and norms that constitute the cosmology of destinations. Similar mechanisms are visible in the areas where Eritrean refugees live in Italy.

Although most of the Eritreans whom I met across my research sites seemed to share similar preferences for certain destinations, different individuals may have different views according to what they seek, their possibilities, and changing circumstances in those locations and across their pathways. Refugees I met in Ethiopian camps seemed to pattern their preferences on the basis of their contacts and the structural openings of legal channels and migration corridors. Reaching certain destinations also had a different meaning for different informants according to their gender, contacts, age, religion, and political orientation, among other things. Moreover, not all of the Eritreans I encountered in my research wanted to migrate. Although I have touched only briefly on Eritrean patriotism here, it is important to highlight that there are some Eritreans who believe in the national project followed by the government and are ready to stay there to contribute to it.[7] Another instance of chosen immobility is the case of Eritrean Kunamas living in Shimelba camp. As with many other refugees who strive for repatriation, their example shows that a cosmology can also be retrospective, projecting the future back into the homeland, rather than toward further destinations. In sum, the notion of cosmologies of destinations does not define a specific set of preferences, but rather refers to the shifting relationship between collective imaginaries, normative expectations, and personally felt moral obligations connected to certain migration destinations.

Cosmologies of destinations imply specific moral understandings of national borders and legitimate ways to cross them. While the international asylum regime and the visa policies of different Western states are unable to provide solutions to protracted displacement, unauthorized mobility and those who enable it assume a positive role in the eyes of many refugees. Contrary to the current claims of the international community, smugglers are not specifically blamed for fatalities at sea or in the desert. In my informants' accounts, it is instead the lack of long-term solutions for refugees and those who restrict their access to regular migration who are responsible for them. Facilitators of unauthorized migration are no more than service providers, who can be judged by the quality of their services. Transnational marriages, either arranged or paid, represent ways to help each other out of the stasis young Eritreans experience at home and in Ethiopia and Sudan.

The idea of cosmologies of destinations provides a framework to analyze perceptions of risks as embedded in emic understanding of the world, and the subject's views of his/her own position within it. However, to understand refugees' determination to move on in spite of dangers, it is of key importance to consider the cumulative aspect of migrants' efforts. Here is where the metaphor of *The Big Gamble* becomes an analytical tool to advance the understanding of high-risk migration.

Drawing on studies of gamblers, I have advanced the idea of entrapment to make sense of my informants' repeated attempts to move on. My informants "gambled"—often more than once—when they fled Eritrea, then when they left Ethiopia and Sudan, again when they journeyed through Libya, and finally when they sought to move forward from Italy. These attempts should be considered as cumulative. The sacrifices they had made to attain the migration goal increased the further they went from home. This leads to a sense of "entrapment" similar to what gamblers experience. To turn all the losses into gains, the goal of migration—be it a specific geographic destination or the social recognition of families and peers—has to be reached.

Migrants, thus, are trapped into trying again and again to overcome the obstacles that separate them from their desired goal. When these obstacles are represented by migration policies, it is likely they will not produce the results expected by policy makers. This unexpected interaction between structural obstacles and migrants' motivations to move on could be one factor explaining why migration policies often fail.[8] With border controls becoming increasingly restrictive and European states doing their best to keep asylum seekers out, the above considerations about perception of risks suggest that there is no easy way to stop the refugee flow. When what is at stake in migration is such a deep-rooted moral and socially shared goal, policies aiming at deterring flows are unlikely to be successful.

POSTSCRIPT

I went back to Eritrea in October 2018. Many things had changed since my last visit. Many others had not. In July, the newly established Ethiopian president, Abyi Mohammed, had extended his hand to President Isaias Afwerqi. After twenty years of conflict and diplomatic silence, their peace agreement has led to what seems to be a new era of cooperation between the two countries. Now merchandise and people freely move across the border. Separated families have managed to see each other again after decades apart. Markets were flooded with cheap products produced by the booming Ethiopian economy. The cost of living went down—even if only for a few months—and local salaries increased just enough for families to breathe a sigh of relief. In December, the United Nations finally suspended sanctions that had contributed to isolating Eritrea and made the everyday lives of its people even more complicated.

Revolution came to the market, but the political atmosphere remained unchanged. Political and religious prisoners were still detained, and there was no sign of democratic evolution. Some people argued that change takes time, but others believed that no real change can come while the current ruling class is in power. National service was still obligatory. In December, young people eagerly watched a televised interview of the president looking for some hint of a possible change, but in vain. Many did not wait to hear what President Afwerqi had to say: they already knew Eritrea was not for them. Between July and December, it is estimated, over ten thousand Eritreans, mostly young people, crossed into Ethiopia seeking asylum.[1]

Most of my friends in Asmara left, and their families continually struggle with separation and worry about the few prospects for their children in Ethiopia and in Sudan, in a time of extreme instability for both countries. Ethiopia is strug-gling with a revived ethnic conflict across the country, and the Sudanese dicta-torship of Omar Al-Bashir has ended, leaving the place to a transitional military council. These political scenarios, unravelling as we speak, open a wide range of questions not only for the citizens of these countries, but for the security and long-term prospects of their numerous refugee populations. Meanwhile, the European Union has made deals and established border enforcement measures that block aspiring asylum seekers in Libya or even prevent rescue ships from reaching Ital-ian coasts. Many reports denounce systematic abuses and torture in detention centers in Libya,[2] but European national governments boast of their successes in curbing migrants' invasion.

Notwithstanding all these shifting geopolitical events, the fact remains, now as at the beginning of my research, that most Eritreans are trapped in protracted displacement, as 78 percent of the total refugee population—who now number twenty-six million. Not only is it impossible for them to return home, but it is also extremely difficult for them to migrate in a regular fashion from their first place of refuge, where they usually have little prospect of long-term integration. For those who can move on in irregular ways along the Libyan corridor, the risks remain huge, if not higher than before.

These unchanged structural conditions demonstrate how wrong it is to talk about these phenomena as "crises" and "emergencies," words that have been con-tinually repeated by politicians, humanitarian actors, and the media over the past five years (the phrase "European refugee crisis" is the key example here). The nor-malized aspect of migration, even in its most tragic implications, points to the importance of inscribing migrants' histories in political and institutional contexts that reproduce the stratification of rights and the conditions for mobility and im-mobility. It is my hope that *The Big Gamble* will contribute to orient the public debate in this direction.

Backstage

Notes on Methodology and Ethics

There are three main problems for researchers of refugees and asylum seekers: how to access them and their settings; how to deal with the complex power dynamics produced within the discursive and political context of the international asylum regime; and how to address vulnerability and justify one's research with respect to it. These three main issues intersect with a wide range of other methodological concerns that have long occupied social scientists and are by no means exclusive to refugee or forced-migration studies, such as the role of trust in qualitative research, the influence of the researcher's positionality on his/her data, the gendered nature of every encounter in the field, and personal distance and engagement in the lives of informants. In narrating obstacles, encounters, and dilemmas of my own fieldwork, this methodological note revisits these wider methodological discussions in relation to the specific challenges of doing research with refugees in environments characterized by authoritarian regimes, paternalistic humanitarian structures, widespread lack of trust, and irregularity. In particular, I discuss the unavoidably covert nature of research in authoritarian regimes, the choice among multiple loyalties in the field, as well as in writing, and the complex web of reciprocal, and often unparalleled expectations that researchers need to navigate. Here, I account for the *microphysics of participation,* as Giorgia Donà called it,[1] that characterized my fieldwork. By describing the shifting power dynamics that informed my fieldwork and the variable—more or less vulnerable—positions occupied by different actors, such as the researcher, my refugee informants, other participants, and helpers, this note works against essentialist methodological accounts that reify refugees as the "vulnerable other." In line with the rest of the book, this methodological note aims to overcome more or less explicit paternalistic attitudes that shape ways of thinking about and doing research with refugees. Drawing on these considerations, I also advance some reflections on what research on refugees should ultimately aim for and the intrinsic importance of representation in it.

DANGEROUS, REMOTE, AND ENCLOSED: ACCESSING THE FIELD

Researchers' access to refugees can be hindered in many different ways. First of all, refugees' contexts of departure have generally remained outside researchers' scope. As refugees are by definition escaping from areas marked by violence, war, and lack of freedom, the possibilities of studying them are undoubtedly limited. Although social scientists have recently started debating the role of researchers in settings of war, and violence,[2] it is hard to deny that, in some contexts, the risks for scholars and their informants can be too high. Dangers are not necessarily connected to open war, but can be even more present while doing research under authoritarian regimes,[3] as the death of Giulio Regeni tragically proves.[4]

Yet those who fortuitously found themselves in the right place or were persistent and bold enough to venture into the heart of the crisis managed to provide precious accounts. Among the most notable examples, Stephen C. Lubkemann's ethnographic work during the civil war in Mozambique illustrates how different localized social conflicts within the broader national war influenced specific groups' perceptions of risks and mobility strategies.[5] The importance of "being there" as ethnographers lies[6] in making sense of how individuals, groups, and communities survive in conditions of protracted crisis, and what role mobility assumes in these contexts. Given the fact that most refugees come from areas of chronic crisis, the investigation of their everyday lives in the context of departure is crucial if we are to grasp the commonplace, but no less disrupting, dimension of violence.[7]

Research in refugees' areas of origin is important for investigating, not only the root causes of their mobility/immobility, but also the social embeddedness of their migration projects.[8] This entails exploring how refugees, as well as migrants, engage in transnational relationships with their home country, communities, and families. From this perspective it is possible to consider how these actors contribute to the emergence of migration desires at the outset of the journey, and in subsequent steps. Acknowledging that in practice implies walking refugees' pathways in the opposite direction.

The second main problem in studying refugees involves their isolation from the general population. Not only they are often located in remote areas, but also they are institutionally separated. As Barbara Harrell-Bond and Eftihia Voutira put it, "refugees as persons are subsumed under elaborate bureaucratic structures which control them."[9] These bureaucratic structures can be camps, reception or detention centers. Here, international and national authorities responsible for protecting refugees are also the ones responsible for regulating the access of those who could expose their failing to do so (including but not limited to researchers). Within such paradoxical bureaucratic contexts, researchers are often denied access to refugees and, even when they are allowed to do so, their work is closely monitored and restricted. These are the kinds of situations that I had to face in doing research among Eritreans in camps in Ethiopia. Even in urban areas, however, refugees may be "hidden" populations because they often have no permission to reside there.

Aside from these practical obstacles, one of the main challenges of doing research with refugees is their deeply rooted distrust of strangers, officials, authorities, or anyone associated with authority figures. This is especially the case in communities—Eritreans and Ethiopians being cases in point—in whose home countries the regime maintains extensive espionage networks both at home and abroad.[10] In these contexts, trust building between researcher and researched acquires further theoretical facets and methodological implications. Lack of trust, secrecy, and lies were omnipresent ingredients of my fieldwork in Eritrea, Ethiopia, Sudan, and Italy. This leads us into the second main issue of doing research with refugees: the importance of considering the power dynamics inherent in the bureaucratic and discursive settings of the international asylum regime. However, before I move on to that, let me expand on the complications involved in accessing refugees, drawing from my fieldwork experience.

ERITREA AS *TERRA NULLIUS:* LOW-PROFILING AND SECRECY

In 2000, Kjetil Tronvoll started one of his articles on highland land tenures by saying that Eritrea was *terra incognita* in terms of ethnographic research.[11] Except for Italian and British colonial officers who did some ethnographic investigation,[12] Eritrea has rarely been a fieldwork site for anthropologists, especially over the past fifty years. Lack of freedom, violence, and war have not only caused refugee flows but been the reasons why ethnographers have had a hard time investigating Eritrean society.

Tronvoll's ethnography of a highland Eritrean village (1998), David Bozzini's study of the resistance of young Eritreans to unlimited conscription (2011), Magnus Treiber's research on young Eritreans' coping strategies in Asmara (2009), David O'Kane's research on the impact of war on peasants (2012), and Valentina Fusari's demographic study on postconflict Eritrea (2011) are some of the few recent ethnographic studies available on the region. Many journalists, researchers, and employees of international agencies have long been prohibited from going back to Eritrea because the Eritrean government has considered their work not aligned to the regime's values.[13] Others, even if not blacklisted, would not go back for fear of government reprisals. All the stories I had been told by development workers and other experienced researchers were on my mind when I applied for a tourist visa at the Eritrean consulate in Milan. However, after a month, I found out that against all odds my application had been accepted.

My decision not to officially declare that I was doing research in Eritrea was the result of numerous chats with more experienced scholars of Eritrea and my refugee friends. The extremely sensitive and politically charged nature of the subject I was investigating could have either led Eritrean authorities to reject my visa application, or to put me and the people I encountered under close scrutiny. My semi-covert research in Eritrea was certainly not a first; most of those who have written about the country were arguably there as university lecturers or employees of international organizations, not as declared researchers. However, there is little discussion of what such secrecy entails or of why it may be necessary.

The lack of discussion of this may be due to a general condemnation of covert research in the social sciences. Informed consent and transparency are generally held to be basic elements of any ethical research.[14] However, some authors have remarked how undisclosed research in informal settings should be accepted as a normal practice, inasmuch as it does not breach any entitlement to privacy.[15] Others, such as those who have done "dangerous fieldwork" have contended that the circumstances faced by ethnographers in that context challenge ethical codes. As J. C. Kovats-Bernat argues, transparency implies, first, that the ethnographer is in control in the field; but this is often not the case, for example, with researchers working in dangerous circumstances, where risks cannot be anticipated and usual binary distinctions—a colonial legacy according to this author—between researcher and researched are subverted. Secondly, the calculation of risks and potential advantages—often mentioned as an important prerequisite for conducting research in dangerous fields—is based on the mistaken assumption that data exist independently of the surrounding violence.[16]

In my case, it was hard to separate the risks of the research from the relevance of the data which were embodied by my informants' subtle but omnipresent everyday experience of structural violence. Dangerous fields are not only those in open war or among widespread violence, such as those explored by Kovats-Bernat and other scholars,[17] but also those under authoritarian regimes where ethnographers are under the arbitrary discretion of authorities as much as the citizens. Openly talking about taboo research topics or presenting oneself as researcher in these contexts may not be in the best interest of the ethnographer and his/her informants, as discussed by Marlies Glasius and her colleagues.[18]

I thus followed a rather localized ethic in my fieldwork in Eritrea. To quote Kovats-Bernat, "rather than guide my fieldwork with hegemonic assumptions about uneven power relationships between ethnographer and informants, I took stock of the good advice and recommendations of the local population in deciding what conversations (and silences) were important, . . . , the questions that were dangerous to ask, and the patterns of behavior that were important to follow for the safety and security of myself and those around me."[19]

Even though I managed to enter the country, my movements there were quite limited. Foreigners are generally only allowed to visit certain areas in the country, such as Massawa, Keren, and Mendefera, and even then they need specific permission to do so.[20] Other areas are forbidden. Non-nationals must carry their travel permission to move from one place to the other and show it at the frequent military check points on the way. This is also why most of my time in the country was spent in Asmara where I lived with Ester's family, hung out with its young members and their friends, and connected with other families. However, thanks to some locals, I also managed to reach a few rural areas, where I was able to visit my friends' relatives and observe the manifold effects of migration there. All this was done while trying to avoid institutional figures as much as possible and keep a low profile.

Secrecy and suspicion thus became part of everyday life while doing research in Eritrea. In the coffee shops I used to go to with my friends, it was usual to see someone sitting alone close to us listening in to our conversation. Was that simple curiosity or was he a spy? The country was full of spies, according to my informants. At the beginning of my fieldwork, when I used to go out in the evenings with Salam and her friends, I was surprised that they would order a tea or a soft drink from the car and consume it there. "We have privacy here . . . you know, people like to listen to what other people say," Salam told me once.

Once I asked Lwam and Johanna how spies could be spotted. They told me that it is was hard, but, according to Lwam, some may pretend to hate the government and then will go to the police to denounce their neighbors and colleagues. After that discussion I started suspecting anyone expressing negative views about the government. Sometimes I even doubted my best informants and friends, thinking they might be government spies. I never conducted formal interviews and I never used a voice recorder; I just wrote up my field notes on my laptop every evening, while Ester, Saba, and the girls were watching TV.

For the same reasons, I did not often divulge that I was doing research there. Unless my informants were directly involved with me, I would not present myself as a researcher. Due to their significant contribution in the study and our close relationship, I spoke to Lwam, Sister Lethe Brahne, and Valentina about it, but all of them warmly advised me to keep my research topic to myself. Upon my return to Italy, Gabriel asked me to keep my mouth shut about the fact that I had lived with his family in Asmara: "You know people talk too much and they think too far . . . they may think you are a spy . . . are you?" Although I had explained to him many times that I was a university student, Gabriel still had his doubts about me, and I guess he was not the only one, because most of my informants never really grasped the purpose of my stay. Many times, as I explained my role to them, their looks seemed to say: "How could someone possibly be willing to live as Eritreans live and face several dangers just for research purposes?" I understand it was quite hard for them to believe me.

The above ethnographic instances call into question the possibility of being transparent about our roles and our aims as researchers with our informants. Although there is wide acknowledgement of the importance of being as open as possible with research participants about the scope, aims, and methods of the research,[21] little is said about the fact that in practice, ethnographic research often remains incomprehensible or irrelevant from informants' points of view. Although many of my informants were supportive, others were simply not interested but still helped me out. Their cooperation mostly emerged from personal friendship, sympathy for me, or hope of obtaining benefits unrelated to the research, ranging from financial support to some kind of access to Europe.

Without underestimating the importance of trying at least to make informants active participants in research, I see a need to rethink the possibility of engaging our informants in meaningful ways more humbly. Based on David Turton's statement that all research on human suffering ultimately needs to find justification in trying to alleviate the suffering itself,[22] some authors have argued that research with refugees should be empowering, or even therapeutic.[23] These considerations seem to me the wishful thinking of researchers more rather than what goes on in the field. I sympathize with the considerations that support a participatory approach, such as the need to consider refugees as more than mere sources of data; I likewise appreciate the criticism vis-à-vis the practice of informed consent as the ultimate proof of informants' willingness to be part of a study. However, it seems to me naïve to think of most research as based "on a reciprocal relationship between researcher and participants in which there is a more equal exchange of ideas and of the benefits to be gained by being involved" in it.[24] Although some research may have managed to bring equal benefits to refugee participants and researchers, it would be misleading to overemphasize their interest and gain from the research. In practice, refugees have many more important things to worry about. It seems equally naïve to me to justify research with the idea that it will eventually contribute to social change, since in practice nobody can realistically forecast what a particular study will bring about in terms of practical improvement. Yet the study may still be worth doing not only from the researcher's point of view.

Although some of my informants were not interested in the study, others understood it and enriched it with different meanings. Tsegay, the smuggler, for instance, decided to talk to me precisely because he saw my research as a way to make Eritrean people's suffering known. Likewise, Stephanos, one of the novice priests in Addis Ababa, encouraged me and helped me find key informants because he believed that I might perhaps "make the voice of the voiceless heard." Their perceptions of my research motivated me and enlarged my own understanding of what my research aims should be. However, acknowledging researchers' limited capabilities of sharing their plans with informants and of controlling how they represent "us" in the field is of crucial importance in analyzing data. This is especially vital while conducting research in highly sensitive and institutionalized contexts, such as reception centers and refugees camps, where researchers may be regarded by refugees as authorities, spies, or service providers.

HIDING AND AIDING: ACCESSING REFUGEE CAMPS

Although my research mainly relied on informal and family refugee networks, I sometimes had no alternative but to ask for the help of humanitarian organizations or NGOs working with refugees. This was especially the case when investigating secondary movements from refugee camps in northern Ethiopia to Sudan and Libya. Even here, I knew it would have been hard to get permission from ARRA, the national agency dealing with all refugee affairs, which was well known for being particularly diffident with researchers and journalists. To make things even more complicated, a few months before my arrival in the country, the camps had been the sites of large riots, which had been violently repressed. After those episodes, a sort of state of emergency was declared and all refugee issues suddenly became even more delicate.

I decided to try to get access to the camps anyway and contacted NGOs and international agencies such as the UNHCR, naïvely thinking that they might find the scope of my research interesting for their operations and would assist me in entering the camps. Instead, all of them kindly refused to help me, saying that the subject I wished to research was rather sensitive. Although I understood their concerns, I was also surprised to see how uninterested they were in the topic of the research—the same topic that, some months later, the European Union paid millions of euros to consultancy firms and other research institutions to investigate.[25] This defensive stance was even more surprising when I saw how eager many refugees were to participate in the research, thinking that I could expose their situation more to the world.

Without neglecting the possible ethical intricacies of doing research with refugees,[26] I feel it is important to point out how closely the protective attitude of the humanitarian organizations I approached reflects the paternalistic stance that Michael Barnett identifies as a marker of international humanitarian actions in our contemporary world, defining paternalism as an "attempt by one actor to substitute his judgment for another's on the ground that it is in the latter's best interest or welfare."[27] In my case, the refugees were effectively prevented from having the last say on their being actively involved in the research.[28] Although it may be hard to judge whether paternalism is ethical or unethical, it can nonetheless be debated to what extent refusal to let refugees decide on their own was aimed at safeguarding their well-being, rather than protecting the delicate cooperation between international organizations and the Ethiopian authorities at the cost of transparency.

I then decided to address ARRA directly. Interestingly, the government agency proved less intimidated by my study than the humanitarian organizations in the field. Armed with a few letters of reference and a lot of patience, I went to the ARRA office almost every week for about two months before receiving an answer—ultimately a positive one. The Addis Ababa office apparently communicated my imminent arrival to the Shire office, but as I soon discovered, permission to do research in the camps meant being under the constant control of the authorities.

THREATS AND LOYALTIES: RESEARCH IN HIGHLY CONTROLLED SETTINGS

Although I had gained permission to go to the camps, my freedom to conduct research had to be negotiated with authorities at each location. As soon as I arrived to the local office in Shire, the head officer carefully interrogated me. By that time I already knew that authorities mainly wanted to be reassured about the "nonpolitical nature" of my study. I had never quite understood what that meant, but, from the first moment, it seemed that my statement about the academic nature of my research was sufficient for them to provide me with a car to reach the camps.

However, logistical help was simply another way to keep me under scrutiny. In Shimelba, ARRA offered me a room in their operational compound adjacent to the camp for a week. Almost every day one of the protection officers would come to ask me if I had finished my research. As I quickly realized, in ARRA there was an almost undecipherable difference between a "protection officer" and a "secret security agent."[29] On my first day, I was given a first hurried tour by car around the camp, and I had to sit and listen to an organized meeting with members of the local Refugee Central Committee (RCC). This body, supposed to represent the residents in the camp, was used by authorities to keep informed regarding the underground atmosphere. I then tried to get in touch with my previously established contacts among the refugees in the camp, but I soon gathered that I was not supposed to walk around asking questions. While I was conducting an interview with Noah, my Kunama translator, a protection officer, Philmon, and two of his colleagues suddenly walked in.

"You cannot go around the camp by yourself. It is a question of safety. Why aren't you talking to RCC?"

"I am not alone. Noah is with me. I talked with RCC yesterday."

"Give me the list of the people you are going to talk to."

"I won't. Firstly, I don't have a list, and even if I had I would not give it to you."

"Well, from now on, I will follow you. I do not want to listen to your conversations, but I need to see who you are talking to."

I did not notice anyone following me that day, but the following day Philmon summoned me alone. He took me to a small dark room adjacent to the clinic of the camp. There were only a desk, two chairs and a small window: alarmingly similar to the interrogation rooms I had only seen in movies.

"I want the list of the people you want to speak to," he ordered. I was intimidated by the circumstances, but my answer could not be any different:

"I already told you that I have no list. Subjects are randomly chosen and I guaranteed them anonymity."

"I heard you want to talk to Mebrathu [the name of one of my friends' contacts]. Why do you want to talk to him?"

"He is a friend of a friend and I just thought to meet him for coffee, that's it."

"You know, he called me yesterday. He was very scared because he heard you were asking around about him. You know we've recently had riots in the camps surrounding Shimelba, and people are scared to be involved. Keep doing your research, but do not talk to Tigrinya people."[30] Understood?

The dangerous position ethnographers find themselves in when they have information of interest to the relevant authorities is stressed by B. A. Jacobs.[31] Researchers may run into serious trouble if they are dedicated to protecting their informants' privacy. Since I was not supported by an international organization in the field, my position was even more fragile with respect to the requests of Ethiopian authorities. However, the aggressive nature of the pressure I experienced convinced me even more that the anonymity of my informants was of utmost importance and that I should be extremely careful while asking around. Again, recording seemed too risky for me and my informants, and I decided to write my field notes in private, away from the gaze of security officers and their associates.

Knowing what the right thing to do is rarely straightforward.[32] Doing research in refugee settings often means entering a field of complex power dynamics in which researchers might feel stretched between conflicting loyalties: on the one hand, the predisposition to comply with regulations set by local and international authorities, on the other hand, the commitment to one's own respondents. As Didier Fassin writes, "carrying on an ethnography is cumulating debts."[33] These debts are not only to those who respond to our questions, but also to those who facilitate or allow the research to happen. These debts carry different weights, however, and the ethnographer must often pick a side. In my case I felt indebted to the Ethiopian authorities for allowing me to conduct my research in the camps, but I had little doubt that my loyalty ultimately lay with my research participants, given their vulnerable position vis-à-vis the authorities.[34] Their disadvantaged position and their risk of being questioned or harassed by camp security easily convinced me that the least I could do to protect my research participants was to reject the authorities' requests for their names.

Yet even loyalty to informants vis-à-vis the authorities can be a source of dilemmas when respondents are engaged in criminal activities. For example, in researching people smugglers, was it my duty to report them? Was I making myself complicit by not denouncing Michael or Tsegay to the authorities? Reflecting on her own fieldwork on organ trafficking in Brazil, South Africa, and Israel and the decision to share her information with the U.S. government and other authorities, Nancy Scheper-Hughes argues that at times it is necessary to collaborate. She writes: "Anthropologists are not detectives, and we are trained to hold anthropologist-informant relations as a sacred trust. But surely this does not mean that one has to be a bystander to international crimes against vulnerable populations."[35] In my case, however, the smugglers were not engaged in exploitative activities, as in the case of the organ traffickers interviewed by Scheper-Hughes. Even if ambivalently judged, their actions could have liberating and emancipatory consequences for their customers. Their undertakings may have been seen as criminal by the state and international authorities, but were not intrinsically destructive. Although my informants' activities could possibly entail violence, I neither witnessed nor knew of any violent actions that would have justified my collaboration with authorities. Again, these ethnographic engagements with diverse subjects push us to revisit commonly held ethics of fieldwork and consider the importance of reflecting contextually on the issues of privacy, responsibility, and morality.

My refusal to cooperate with camp authorities, however, had direct consequences on my fieldwork. On the one hand, it hindered productive collaboration with the camp's main managing body; on the other, it won me the trust of my refugee informants. As noted by Jacobs apropos of dangerous fieldwork, by resisting institutional pressures, the ethnographer can increase his/her credibility in the eyes of informants.[36] My unpleasant encounter with Philmon turned out to be positive inasmuch as Noah started seeing me as an enemy of ARRA and thus—since the enemy of the enemy becomes an ally—we became closer and started speaking more freely about the tensions in the Kunama refugee community, threats of the Kunama liberation front to his family, and the corruption involved in Kunama resettlement (see chap. 2).

TRUST OF STRANGERS AND SECRETS AMONG FRIENDS

Access to the field, not only as a physical place, but also as a bundle of relationships,[37] can also be substantially limited by difficulties in winning refugees' trust. Mistrust lies at the heart of many refugees' experience, as E. V. Daniel and J. C. Knudsen note in their edited volume *Mistrusting Refugees*.[38] The conditions that surround their departures—be they ethnic conflicts, state persecution, or generalized violence—often shake the ordinary circumstances in which individuals have some degree of control over their lives. After fleeing, refugees find themselves once again in precarious legal and material conditions and often under the scrutiny of authorities, or the gaze of international workers. In such contexts, researchers—with their looks and questions—can be easily associated with the authorities or with those agencies providing services. It is no wonder that trust is a rather rare and precious ingredient in research with refugees.[39] Throughout my research, I observed the effects of my informants' mistrust of foreigners, be they Ethiopians, Sudanese, or Italians. I have described how lack of trust in local society turned Eritrean squats in Rome into closed enclaves, and how Eritreans' deep-rooted mistrust of Sudanese prevents collaboration with them in Khartoum even given promising openings.

Wariness, suspicion, and distrust characterize Eritreans' everyday lives long before leaving their homeland. In this sense, their flight does not contravene ordinary circumstances where trust is the norm. It rather prolongs their usual mistrust of strangers and insiders. The first question I was asked, not only by refugees in Ethiopia and Sudan before they spoke to me, but by NGO workers and national officialdom as well, was: "Is your research political?" I knew the answer had to be "no," even though that way of articulating the question did not make sense to me. Yet it was clear that the question meant much more than it appeared at first. By posing it, refugees were actually asking: "Is your research going to put me in danger?" "Were you sent by the Eritrean or Ethiopian government or the UNHCR?" Their fears usually disappeared after meeting me in person. I seemed harmless, many told me.

However, it would be wrong to think that strangers were the only objects of my informants' mistrust. I was always amazed to realize how many secrets self-declared "good friends" were keeping from each other. Maria's network of friends was a striking example of this. Seifu, one of Maria's contact in Khartoum, had a son by a man who was not the one with whom she was reuniting in Sweden (nobody seemed to know who the father of the baby was). Seifu's housemate often dressed in revealing clothes, used to receive Sudanese men in her room, but nobody spoke about it. Gebreyesus was a freelance journalist and anti-government blogger, but nobody in the group knew about his "political" activities. Michael was a *semsari* and everyone seemed to ignore it. This lack of openness may be due not only to distrust of fellow Eritreans, but also to a sort of respectful discretion in sharing delicate information about each other. Navigating mistrust and respectful discretion, for me, took time, some cultural learning, and a good dose of acquired mistrust in my informants' narratives.

MEANINGFUL LIES: REFUGEES' REPRESENTATIONS OF THE SELF

Lying informants have a great significance in research, as F. A. Salamone noted over forty years ago.[40] In particular, Salamone maintained that informants' lies should not be discarded as wrong information, but investigated as potentially re-vealing tools for identifying crucial cultural values and underlying rules of social relationships where fieldworker and informants interact. The debate has remained open since then.[41]

In my own experience with Eritreans, I encountered several "lies" and misrep-resentations of the self. My informants in Follonica reception center often nar-rated invented or semi-invented biographies to me, thinking that I could help them in their Refugee Status Determination (RSD) procedures; others, knowing that I was a single woman, hid the fact that they were married, perhaps hoping that an affair with me might develop into something advantageous to their cases. The refugees I interviewed in the Tigrayan camps often sought to conceal the fact that they received support from their relatives in the diaspora, probably think-ing that this would make their cases for resettlement look more urgent. This was because I was often identified with UNHCR resettlement officers, even though I stated my independent role of researcher before every interview. Many Eritreans I met in Italy tended to hide their attempts to move to other European countries, or the fact that they had got married and were preparing their cases for the family reunification process.

Most of the above lies were connected to the refugees' attempts to obtain legal status or present their cases in a way that would increase the likelihood of their being assisted or considered for resettlement. These responses are clearly influ-enced by their position as vulnerable subjects who feel constantly under scruti-ny.[42] However, there is more to it than that. The identification of such fabrications and their examination are of great theoretical significance for analyzing refugees' responses to certain political and humanitarian discourses.[43] On the one hand, my informants' deceits were reflexively aimed at complying with the categories of the international asylum regime, which builds on the distinction between the deserving refugee—the victim and eligible recipient of humanitarian and welfare aid[44]—and the many undeserving migrants. On the other hand, their lies were ac-tive manipulations to circumvent what they saw as "unfair rules".

I am not arguing that there is a truth out there that the ethnographer can dis-cover by overcoming the untruths of his/her informants. However, if these nar-ratives are not duly interpreted based on structural relationships in the field, the understanding of migration strategies, motivations, and trajectories may become biased. I believe that identifying what informants themselves recognize as "lies" may enable the researcher to get closer to his informants' point of view and his/her own positionality in the field, by detecting the webs of power, roles, and re-lated expectations embedded in fieldwork. Ethnography based on long-term en-gagement with informants and with their living environment is particularly well placed, to do that.[45]

Nevertheless, as Karen Jacobsen and Loren Landau remark,[46] it is common to read studies based on interviews originating from extemporaneous encounters with refugees in asylum centers or in structured contexts. This is particularly the case in Europe, where respondents are likely to lie in order to reinforce their asylum case or to construct an image of themselves that helps justify their presence there. If the scope of the study is to analyze refugees' narratives, in-depth interviews may be an important technique, but if the aim of the investigation is to reconstruct real trajectories and the motivations behind the migration decision, interviews may not be enough.

It was by observing and participating in the everyday lives of my informants in the most significant sites of their journeys that I was able to perceive the gap between their narratives and their practices. For instance, observant participation with refugees in Italy and with their families in Eritrea enabled me to grasp the multifaceted relationships between migrants and left-behind kin. Likewise, triangulation and familiarity with different social actors, such as authorities, refugees in different countries, families at home, relatives abroad, and the professionals of unauthorized migration were key in gaining a deeper understanding of transnational marriages and of smuggling among refugees, smugglers, and relatives abroad. Moreover, the more I knew Eritreans, and the more I became acquainted with their tricks and their mind-sets, the easier it was to navigate the varied constellation of images they had of me.

BEYOND VULNERABILITY: ON THE BLURRED BOUNDARIES OF "US" AND "THEM" IN REFUGEE RESEARCH

Refugees are often extremely vulnerable populations.[47] Precarious legal and material circumstances as well as the traumas they experience before and as a result of their flight from home undeniably mark the lives of many of them. Yet the vulnerable condition of refugees should not be essentialized. Throughout this book, I have illustrated prospective refugees' abilities to cope with present adversities and plan the future even in extreme conditions. Even when discussing methodological approaches to refugee studies, it is important to go beyond a crystallization of informants as vulnerable subjects. As a result of this crystallization, the researcher's relationship with his/her informants is typically conceived as an unbalanced one between individuals with incommensurably distant lives, power stances, and possibilities. Without underplaying the difficult conditions most of my informants were facing and the multiple power imbalances that characterized my relationship with them, I attempt here to provide a more nuanced understanding of the shifting power dynamics I experienced in the field.

Here I would stress, paraphrasing Karsten Pærregaard, how often it was my own vulnerability that allowed me to "slip through the native gaze."[48] As Pærregaard convincingly argues, the researcher is caught in a web of overlapping representations by her/his informants. Seen variously as intruders, tourists, and government agents, researchers often have to overcome all these images gain the necessary recognition before their respondents feel ready to share their experiences. As noted earlier, refugees often perceived me as a journalist or a UNHCR official, or feared me as a spy. This was the case, not only with those with whom I had chance encounters in institutional settings, but also with others with whom I had long-term relationships.

There was no standard rapport with my informants. Every meaningful relationship I had in the field was characterized by different levels of indeterminacy, divergent expectations, and misunderstandings on both sides. As opposed to romanticized accounts of fieldwork as an unproblematic terrain,[49] the following sections describe the ambivalent relationships of friendship, care, and desire that marked my fieldwork and the resulting ethical dilemmas.

FRIENDS . . .

Ethnographic literature is rich in examples of friendships between ethnographers and their informants.[50] Some authors highlight how friendship can be a valuable resource insofar as it provides insights based on trust, inside perspective, and depth—especially when doing research in critical situations;[51] others emphasize the possible negative implications of a friendship with informants,[52] such as the deceptive mechanisms it can lead to[53] and the differential power relation that it may mask.[54] Marina de Regt, for instance, gives a poignant account of her long-term relations with her informant Noura and critically discusses what friendship means when it involves continual financial support. Caught in the web of expectations and crucial needs expressed by Noura, de Regt reflects how their relationship became more similar to a fictive kinship rather than a reciprocal friendship.[55]

Equally, my friendships with my informants were imbued with unparalleled expectations and marked by different economic and life possibilities. My relationship with Maria discussed in chapter 2 became more and more unbalanced due to the her continual requests for money and was progressively eroded by different ideas of long-term solutions for her and her child. In other circumstances, what I perceived as friendship was instead romantic interest on the part of my male informants. Nevertheless, among all these ambiguities, friendship—intended as a reciprocal involvement in each other's life beyond the time and the scope of my research—remained a crucial ingredient and unavoidable, natural result of many of my relationships in the field.

In spite of (socioeconomic, citizenship, gender, and racial) differences among us, my relationships with Violetta, with Johanna, and with Alazar were also characterized by reciprocal caring, mutual understanding, and resemblances. Violetta and Johanna were my age-mates, highly educated and unmarried like me. We had similar ways of feeling and understanding things. They were the ones who supported me when things were going wrong in the field, such as when Violetta took care of me for two weeks when I fell sick in Ethiopia. Sharing the everyday lives of our informants not only reveals their vulnerabilities, but also our own. As Cynthia Mahmood observes,[56] every ethnographic encounter, especially in critical contexts, entails a risk for those who let the researcher into their lives, and for the researchers who put their lives in their informants' hands. Power imbalances are shifting and contextual, and do not ultimately prevent us from bridging the gaps with our informants.

Mutual involvement in each other's lives has resulted, in my case, not only in meaningful insights into how Eritreans cope with exile, but with access to social networks that would have been impossible to enter otherwise. It was thanks to my long-term friendship with Alazar, for instance, that I gained entry to buildings occupied by Eritreans at the beginning of my fieldwork in Rome. It was thanks to Gabriel's willingness to help me that I found a family ready to host me for over two months in Asmara. This is not a roundabout way to acknowledge my informants' help. Rather, it is a statement about the unavoidably personal nature of doing ethnographic research.

Involvement, however, implies neither credulity nor lack of reflexivity about the potential impact of our research on the lives of our interlocutors. My involvement in my informants' lives was often complicated with a range of asymmetric and ambivalent expectations, over which I had limited control.

. . . CAREGIVERS . . .

Contrary to the stereotypical power imbalance between a strong researcher and his/her vulnerable subjects, my informants perceived me as vulnerable—as an outsider without family in a unfamiliar setting—and thus felt responsible for my well-being.[57] This sense of responsibility was enhanced by the fact that it was usually a dear friend or relative who had sent me to them. Before going to a site, I would usually ask my informants if they had relatives or friends living there. If they agreed to give me their contacts, it usually meant that the person on the site was going to take care of me. It was a question of respect for the person who had sent me.

For example, in Asmara, Lwam took good care of me because I had been sent to her by her brother. By the same token, she was very surprised that Samuel, Alazar's brother, was avoiding me against his brother's request: "It is not respectful to his brother. If my brother sends you to me, I help you, because I love my brother." This comment was unexpected, since I had not realized that Lwam was sticking around me mostly as a moral obligation to her brother.

This is probably also why my informants have rarely accepted money from me. Gabriel's family did not want me to pay rent in Asmara. Likewise, my informants in Eritrea, Ethiopia, and Sudan wanted to invite more than be invited for dinner or lunch. They mostly felt they had to take care of me as a guest and somebody who had been sent by a loved one. I was rarely left alone, always accompanied everywhere and treated like someone needing protection/guidance rather than the independent researcher I liked to see myself to be.

As the one being taken care of, I also often found myself playing the role of the child. This is because, as an outsider, the researcher has to be acculturated, as Chiara Pussetti points out.[58] He/she has to be warned about possible dangers unknown to him/her, and also taught how to behave properly with others. Due to my role as student and my relatively young age at the time of the fieldwork, I was perceived as especially vulnerable to the often unsafe circumstances we were living in. In their eyes I was to be educated, to be protected, and also to be proud of when I behaved well in front of other members of the group. Maria, for example, often scolded me because I was hesitant to take a shower twice a day due to water shortages, and often forgot to dust my shoes before walking into the room as a good Habesha woman would do. Violetta tried to teach me to speak better Tigrinya, how to cook *shiro,* a typical Eritrean dish, and how to deal with guests politely. Violetta's guests often complimented me on my newly acquired Tigrinya manners, ability to speak a bit of the language, and knowledge of Eritrean history and culture, saying: "She is a real Habesha!"

This does not mean that the differences between them and me could be avoided. As a middle-class white woman with a European passport, I was there by my own choice. I could take a flight anytime to go back to my home and my family. My informants could not say the same. However, my efforts to live like "one of them," eschewing comforts available to me and trying to understand their problems, and the simple fact that I knew the places where they had been, led my informants to trust me more and recognize me as a self-defined subject rather than a "researcher," a "European," or a potential source of benefits. Moreover, my familiarity with their home back in Eritrea and the daily shared experience of difficulties allowed me to achieve more recognition among my informants. Once I had seen their houses, met their beloved parents, and lived the way they had lived before, my informants started to treat me less and less as an external observer and more as part of their clique.

. . . AND SUITORS

Being a relatively young woman conducting fieldwork on my own with mostly male young informants, I sometimes realized that my interlocutors, most of them young single men, were developing romantic interests in me. As noted in chapter 4, I received several marriage proposals while in Ethiopia. Most of them were simply mirroring a desire to reach Europe. Other times, instead, the desire to migrate and romantic feelings seemed to mingle in a way that made me wonder to what extent my presence in the field was influencing their geographic imagination. My "field," configured as a bundle of relationships, was also as a site of emerging desires and flowing imaginaries. I was part of it in one way or another.

Although the issue of the researcher's sexuality in fieldwork has for long time been a taboo, recently scholars have started debating the complex ethical and epistemological implications that sexual encounters, untold desires, and intimate connections can have on research.[59] Some authors have highlighted the value of intimate experiences as sources of knowledge and insights, but Jill Dubisch for one warns against breaching intimate interpersonal boundaries.[60] It is in any case certain that the researcher's sexuality is part of ethnographic fieldwork, either explicitly or implicitly, and, as such, should be rightly acknowledged and reflectively examined. My ethnography was no exception. Although I have never been romantically involved with any of my informants, their expectations and desires have certainly had an impact in allowing me to be part of their lives or in assisting me throughout my fieldwork. No matter how much I tried to be clear with them, stating that my interest in their stories had nothing to do with romance, I had little control over what they expected of me. For example, it became progressively clear that Gabriel, my informant in Milan, did not see me only as a friend. Once I came back from fieldwork in Eritrea, and he asked me whether he could visit me in my hometown, where I was spending some time with family. I naturally accepted, bearing in mind all the generosity and trust he and his family had shown me. However, I did not foresee his expectations. He came to stay with us, and it soon became clear that he wanted me to be his girlfriend. I again had to clarify my position, which led to a small drama: Gabriel drank too much and got lost somewhere in my town. My family became alarmed by our guest's behavior, and I drove around my hometown trying to find him. I finally found him on a bench of the park at 3 a.m. and took him back home. Although he apologized for his conduct in the morning, our friendship was compromised.

That episode left me wondering whether I had unknowingly taken advantage of Gabriel's feelings by involving him in my research, and conversely, what I risked by trusting my male informants. Close relationship with them may have indirectly enabled me to gain insights that would have been hard to attain otherwise, but on other occasions, this has also exposed me to potential harm. This never translated in my case to anything more than dodging sexual advances and enduring sexist proposals by refugees, local gatekeepers, and more or less institutional male figures whom I met throughout my fieldwork.[61]

This brings us back again to the shifting power dynamics in the field and the idea that the researched are exclusively vulnerable. Rather than conceiving research with refugees as ineluctably shaped by an unbalanced relationship between an authoritative researcher and vulnerable refugees, I argue that one's relationships with refugee informants assume many different meanings, according to gender, emotional attitudes, age, and the power dynamics and social ties that inform our presence in the field. All these aspects shape fieldwork relationships well beyond crystallized categories built around the assumption of the "vulnerable other." Nevertheless, in a field of close, but often unbalanced relationships, researchers may face dilemmas regarding reciprocity and responsibility to informants, with no easy solution.[62]

ETHICAL GUIDELINES? SOME UNSOLVED DILEMMAS IN REFUGEE RESEARCH

Managing the expectations of my informants was and still is the hardest part of my fieldwork. After I had already finished my fieldwork, I kept receiving calls from refugees in Libya who wanted my financial support for their journey over the Mediterranean; Michael called me to ask me if he could transfer fifty thousand euros into my account so as to save some of his earnings; and Gabriel came to visit me in my hometown thinking that, after what his family had done for me, he could become my boyfriend.

All these situations have put me in a continuous ethical dilemma in the months since my fieldwork. The hospitality and availability that many of my informants showed me during the research was priceless; it was not only material, but also emotional support. For this reason, my emotional engagement with them has transcended the research site and the ordinary forms of rapport between researcher and informants. Nevertheless, my part in the relationship was not always easy, because of the power imbalance, geographic distance, and discrepancy in expected roles.

Sometimes, a "no" was not a big deal: Michael was not offended, for example, when I explained that it would be hard to answer questions from my bank about a sudden massive transfer of money from a Sudanese account. But in other cases, a "no" could mean a lot: refusing to pay for the journey of someone held by the smugglers in Libya may have significant implications for his/her life. Once, Jacob, one of the refugees I met in Ethiopian camps, called me from Libya to ask for money for continuing his journey to Italy. Although this confronted me with a severe conundrum, my inability to actually raise that money on the spot gave me some time to look for alternatives. I tried to call Jacob's sister in Sweden to consult with her on how to help Jacob, and kept checking on him via phone calls. Jacob's sister did not respond, however, and communication with Jacob became harder due to network failures. After a month Jacob called me to say that he had safely arrived in Italy. The positive epilogue to this story luckily solved my practical doubts, but did not answer my ethical riddles about the role of the researcher in such a case. It is easily understandable how helpless, angry, and worried I felt when something similar happened again with Maria. As I already narrated, a few months after I left Sudan Maria called, asking me for money to pay for her and Anna to get to Libya and then to Italy. Fortunately, in that case I was still in time to discourage her from leaving.

These episodes exemplify the possible tensions between ethically required intervention,[63] and not encouraging actions that would be harmful for informants.[64]

Not paying for some of my interlocutors' trips (assuming I had the money to do so) might put them in danger; paying for them might create a fatal precedent for other informants, motivating them to embark on dangerous journeys in the belief that I could support them. Moreover, by paying their smugglers, I would have contributed to an illegal activity. As yet I have no solution for these ethical dilemmas, which suggest the unavoidable moral and ethical indeterminacy of ethnographic fieldwork.

BEYOND GAZE AND ADVOCACY: REPRESENTING REFUGEES' LIVES

Once I came back from my fieldwork, I started thinking about what my responsibility was as an ethnographer who had been able to share the lives of my informants and to collect their stories. The end of my fieldwork overlapped with the explosion of the "European refugee crisis" across 2014 and 2015, focusing the attention of the whole world precisely on the people and the routes I had been studying for over two years. Although I was not a public intellectual but a mere PhD student, I was often asked how the crisis could be solved. This often left me with little more than superficial policy suggestions about the need for increased resettlement quotas, the unproductive implications of border enforcement, and the importance of acknowledging the legal rights of those who seek asylum in Europe. However, I was left dissatisfied with my own responses. Certainly, these were useful circumstantial solutions to specific issues, but they did not fundamentally address the paradox that lies at the foundation of the asylum crisis: the need of the welfare state to protect the security and social rights of its citizens and the ethical imperative to guarantee prospects to those who seek safety and a decent life.

If my research was not providing solutions and probably had little short-term policy relevance, what was it for? Without overemphasizing the potential impact of research in the "real world," I still needed to be aware of the possible consequences of my writing on the lives of those with whom I worked.[65] Sensitive to the positions of those who argue for a militant role on the part of researchers—including but not limited to migration studies[66]—and to refugee scholars who claim that all work should ultimately aim to promote social justice,[67] I began wondering how I could balance realistic depiction of the social realities I encountered and the safeguarding of the rights of those I studied with a critical stance toward the overall asylum regime. In my case, it seemed especially hard to reconcile these ethical imperatives, since I often felt that protecting Eritrean asylum seekers was somehow in contradiction with the need to criticize the asylum regime and its categories, which protect and exclude at the same time. How could I escape the categories that protected as well as oppressed my informants? How to account for the bravery, the determination, and the dreams of my informants, if I had to keep reproducing the image of the victim so that they could be recognized as legitimate refugees?

These considerations have also led me to think about who I was ultimately accountable to while writing. My informants, the Eritrean people, refugees, migrants, the academic community, truth, or all of them? Even if my debts to my informants made me especially accountable to them, the divides among them still made it hard to decide what perspective to privilege.[68] Eritreans are deeply divided along generational, political, and regional lines. Even if my loyalty mostly lay with those who participated in my research—which does not equate with Eritreans or Eritrean refugees in general—this still meant facing a deeply ambivalent audience divided between appreciation of the actions of the Eritrean government and denunciation of its violence, to mention only one of the many issues dividing them. But even among the closest circle of my informants, perspectives differed: some thought that the manuscript—which I shared with them—should have denounced the human rights violations of the Eritrean government more strongly; some thought I should stay out of political debates; some wanted me to highlight the daily challenges that make refugees' lives so hard in Sudan, Ethiopia, and Italy even more than I did; some thought I should focus on more eminent refugee personalities, rather than on ordinary refugees nobody would be interested in.

The conversations I had with my informants and with the texts of those scholars who had addressed these issues before me left me alone with my own authority, its related responsibilities, and a lot of choices still to make. Although I acknowledge the impossibility of remaining neutral in a deeply political debate such as the one on migration and asylum, I started recognizing that my main responsibility as a researcher was neither militancy nor advocacy. For me, both of these stances betray a paternalism on the part of the researcher, who purports to know what is best for others and to speak on their behalf.

I decided to let my informants' stories largely speak for themselves, but I am not naïve about the choices involved in how I represent my informants and their lives. The rationale that oriented my writing can be summarized by rephrasing Didier Fassin's reflections on the difference between fiction and ethnography: "If the fictional imagination lies in the power to invent a world with its characters, the ethnographic imagination implies the power to make sense of the world that subjects create by relating it to larger structures and events."[69] In this perspective, the researcher's most important responsibility is to provide nuanced representations of the stories, the people, and the situations he/she encountered, making sense of his/her informants' points of view, while explaining the structures of power that shape them. I certainly did not want to serve institutional attempts to map my informants' trajectories; rather, I intended to contribute to understanding the implicit political stance expressed by my informants' ways of countermapping by crossing borders at all costs. The depiction of their aspirations and possibilities, along with the representation of the challenges they faced in different contexts, also aimed at overcoming the depersonalization of forced migration widely criticized by scholars from varied theoretical backgrounds, such as

Thomas Faist and Sandro Mezzadra.[70] The focus on migrants' social, imaginative, and emotional worlds meant restoring their subjectivity beyond stereotypical media portraits and policy categories. Herein lies the most revolutionary contribution that a researcher can bring to the public debate, I believe; it is neither by advocating on behalf of his or her informants nor by attempting to produce research that is directly policy-relevant or primarily aimed at social change. Our task is rather to unveil the everyday lives of refugees, who are often spoken about but mostly misrepresented.

NOTES

INTRODUCTION

1. The concept of "cosmology" has a long-standing history in anthropology (see Barnard and Spencer 1996). Derived from the ancient Greek *cosmos* (order, harmony, world) and *logos* (discourse), cosmology was historically intended as the knowledge of the structure and shape of the world, entailing not only cognitive classifications of the world but "evaluations and moral premises and emotional attitudes translated into taboos, preferences, prescriptions and proscriptions" (Tambiah 1985, 3–4). Much of the relevant literature has focused on religious beliefs and aimed to reconstruct the "traditional" and "original" worldviews of a people. Nevertheless, cosmologies are not necessarily static traditional systems (Powers 1987; Prins and Lewis 1992), but rather continuous elaborations that reflect structural circumstances, social conflicts, and events historically crucial for social groups. In Douglas and Wildavsky 1983, cosmological beliefs encompass the realm of the sacred and inform the classification of natural objects, moral conduct, and behavior toward risk in contemporary technological societies.

2. Abramson and Holbraad (2012) argue that the concept of cosmology is a relevant tool to analyze contemporary globalized societies. In particular, a cosmological approach is useful for understanding the perceived spatiotemporal relocation of contemporary subjects caused by the impact of neoliberalism and by the rhetoric of modernity.

3. Ferguson 2013.

4. Sahlins 1994.

5. Chu 2010.

6. Malkki 1995. As Malkki explains, the emergence of this mythical history is partly the result of cultural and historical elaboration allowed by the structural separation between refugees living in camps and locals. In fact, other Hutu refugees in town had different attitudes about pure identity, as well as different attitudes to the future.

7. Monsutti (2007, 2008).

8. Carling 2002; De Haas 2011; Bal and Willems 2014.

9. Carling and Collins 2018, 915.

10. The idea of a "culture of migration" has been used by anthropologists and sociologists in different ways: the former use it to illustrate the fact that mobility has been an ordinary livelihood strategy for many traditional societies to cope with environmental hardships as well as political instability (Hahn and Klute 2007); the latter employ the same idea to describe the widespread perception of migration as the solution to social stasis and relative deprivation among the members of communities with long-standing emigration histories (Kandel and Massey 2002; Cohen 2004). Migration-related expectations are so deeply rooted in these communities that most individual projects and aspirations for the future turn into the desire to leave, and a socially respected status often overlaps with being an émigré (Ali 2007).

11. Wider notions of economic stability, modernity, freedom, and technology are some of the common ingredients of widespread imaginaries about emigration that result from wider process of global socioeconomic and cultural transformation. However, scholars have also highlighted that each imaginary is locally interpreted—influenced by the specific history of the place and its connections to other places and peoples (Vigh 2006; Bal and Willems 2014). Imaginaries are moreover intrinsically personal and thus greatly depend on the specific position in society (gender, class, ethnic background, etc.). Scholars working with the concept of migration imaginaries have often observed their hierarchical character. For instance, Henrik Vigh describes the social imaginary of his Guinean informants as "an understanding of a world order consisting of societies with different technological capacities and levels of masteries over physical and social environment, as well as the spaces and social options which are open or closed to persons of different social categories within it" (Vigh 2009, 93). Likewise, Ervind Pajo (2007) argues that Albanians order their emigration preferences according to locally interpreted values of progress, modernity and capitalism. Other scholars, instead, observed that the imaginings of the outside world among their informants were often blurred into a collective sort of positive understanding of foreign lands as lands of opportunities. For instance, Salazar 2011 notes that Tanzanians generally refer to Europe and the West as *majuu,* a Swahili word that means "up on top." For a defintion of the concept of imaginaries see e.g. Gaonkar 2002; Salazar 2011 and Vigh 2009.

12. Lubkemann 2008; Bhungalia 2012; Black and Collyer 2014; Hammar et al. 1997; Carling 2002.

13. See Carling 2002 on the immobilizing effects of migration policies and visa systems. About involuntary immobility and war see Lubkemann (2008). He shows how war particularly impacted the lives of women, children, and the elderly who had less capabilities to move. These people became "displaced in place."

14. Appadurai 2013.

15. Different authors have used different terms to define this condition of immobility in transit: In her work on Nigerians in China, H. Ø. Haugen (2012) speaks about a second state of immobility; Núñez and Heyman (2007) in their study of border vigilance at the Mexico-U.S. border talk about the "entrapment processes" (see also Jansen 2009); Brigden and Mainwaring (2016) analyze the interplay between mobility and immobility as constitutive of migrants' journeys as in a matryoshka doll. Hyndman 2012.

16. For statistical purposes, the UNHCR defines protracted displacement, as a situation "in which 25,000 or more refugees from the same nationality have been in exile for five consecutive years or more in a given host country." Many of these situations have become practically permanent—e.g., Palestinians in Lebanon, Afghans in Pakistan, Eritreans in Sudan. For a critical review of the concept of protracted displacement, see Crisp 2003; Hyndman and Giles 2017; and Etzold et al. 2019.

17. Van Hear 2006; Lubkemann 2008.

18. The concept of social immobility is akin to that of liminality in anthropology. Drawn from the study of ritual phases (van Gennep 1960; Turner 1969), this concept has come to designate those temporary statuses that become permanent. However, immobility has also been considered in its more general and existential sense, as representing that "feeling that life is going nowhere" (Hage 2009), perhaps experienced universally at certain stages of everyone's life, but typical of some strata of the population due to structural conditions of society.

19. In particular, Mbembe and Roitman (1995, 324) argue that global developmental models have not only failed, but have arguably weakened local economies and disrupted long-standing social organizations; conflicts, natural disasters, corruption, and inflation have been "the fundamental experiences of African societies for the last several years."

20. Ferguson 2006.

21. Honwana 2012.

22. Vigh 2009.

23. The full text of the Geneva Convention is available at www.unhcr.org/3b66c2aa10.html.

24. These regulations are the Asylum Procedure Directive, the Reception Conditions Directive, the Qualification Directive, the Dublin Regulation, and the Eurodac Regulation. Together, they are the basic elements of the Common European Asylum System (CEAS). More about these juridical tools can be found at http://ec.europa.eu/dgs/home-affairs/what-we-do/policies/asylum/index_en.htm.

25. Goodwin-Gill and McAdam 1996.

26. Kunz 1973.

27. Stein 1981.

28. For a critical consideration of exceptionality, emergency, crisis, and the humanitarian paradigm in refugee studies, see Malkki 1992; Nyers 2006; Lindley 2014; Brun 2016.

29. For a historical examination of how the definition and the discourse surrounding refugees have changed over the past fifty years, see Gatrell 2013.

30. UNHCR 2019.

31. Castles 2003; Castles and van Hear 2005.

32. The notion of mixed migration often used in policy documents referring to the fact that migrants and refugees increasingly make use of the same routes and means of transport to get to an overseas destination. However, the UNHCR states that "migrants are fundamentally different from refugees and, thus, are treated very differently under international law. Migrants, especially economic migrants, choose to move in order to improve their lives. Refugees are forced to flee to save their lives or preserve their freedom" (www.unhcr.org/mixed-migration.html). About the limit of institutional labelling see Crawley and Skleparis 2018.

33. Chimni 2009; Bakewell 2008; Black 2001.

34. Betts 2010.

35. McAdam 2014.

36. E.g. Foster 2007. The category of "forced migration" has had its critics and supporters since its origin. Some argued that its use could be dangerous, since it detracts from the legal specificities and distinct legal protection accorded to refugees under international law (Hathaway 2007). Others have contended that the shift from refugee studies to forced migration studies was not significant in analytical terms, but a simple reflection of an ongoing political agenda of the humanitarian/neocolonial/hegemonic global order (Chimni 2009). Some academics, instead, have welcomed the introduction of the category of forced migration. From a juridical point of view, DeWind 2007 asserts that "the concept of forced migration helps to correct this incongruity between rights and protections," since the refugee definition was too limited to account for the multiplicity of causes that force people to leave their homes. From a sociological point of view, van Hear 2011, 12, supports the analytical significance of forced migration as a category enabling scholars to make sense of the links between the contemporary global migration order and the individual/micro/family level. This author envisions a sort of "matryoshka doll" category in which migration studies would include forced migration studies, which would in turn encompass refugee studies. Placing the field of forced migration in between migration and refugee studies discloses the relationships between different kinds of migration and their connections to global forces. See also Kourula 1997; Moberg 2008; L. Barnett 2002.

37. See further https://refugeesmigrants.un.org/sites/default/files/180713_agreed_outcome_global_compact_for_migration.pdf. and www.unhcr.org/the-global-compact-on-refugees.html.

38. For a critical assessment of the Global Compact for Migration, see Pastore 2019.

39. Important exceptions are the studies by Horst 2006; Monsutti 2008; Lindley 2009b; Fuglerud 2001; and the MEDMIG project (Crawley et al. 2017). Brigden and Mainwaring 2016, portraying the complex negotiations and practices involved in border crossings by asylum seekers who make it to Europe by boat, is remarkable in this respect.

40. Richmond 1993; De Haas 2010; Castles 2003; Crawley and Skleparis 2018; Fitzgerald and Arar 2018.

41. Erdal and Oeppen 2018.

42. Faist 2018, 420. Faist notes that the issue of refugee movements is at the heart of a multilayered dilemma involving moral, political, and social principles. Refugees mobilize both the security concerns of nation-states and their obligation to provide humanitarian protection. Refugee reception creates a conflict between the social rights of citizens in a welfare state and the principle of free movement of goods and labor. Moreover, the widespread human rights narrative has increased migrants' expectations of finding refuge, without actually expanding the opportunities for it.

43. Faist 2018; Erdal and Oeppen 2018; Mezzadra 2010.

44. On the hardships experienced by Eritreans once arrived at their "final" destination, see van Heelsum 2017.

45. On the multifaceted implications of the immobility of social rights in an era of transnationalism, see Levitt et al. 2017 and Boccagni 2016a.

46. Erdal and Oeppen 2018, 9–10. Although this work emerges from the need to overcome labels such as refugees, forced, and voluntary migrants, I often use the word "refu-

gees" to refer to my research participants. This label, in fact, mirrors unavoidable categories of practice (Brubacker 2013), which shape the legal and geopolitical conditions in which mobility as well as immobility are produced. The international asylum regime, its opportunities, its constraints and the discourse related to it are the most pervasive manifestations of these categories or labels (Zetter 1988). These powerfully shape the conditions of millions of people living outside of their countries and of those who aim to flee. The international discourse on asylum influences the way migrants perceive their experience as prospective or actual refugees as well as the way they plan their future. Moreover, as I illustrate in this book, my informants often represented themselves in relation to such a mainstream discourse from the outset of their migration. For these reasons, I will keep using these labels throughout the book.

47. The concept of safe countries is a common tool in national asylum commissions to assess protection claims. This is hardly legitimate from a legal point of view. According to the Geneva Convention, persecution claims should be individually assessed, not judged based on general safety levels in the country of origin. For a critical review of the concept of safe countries see Goodwin-Gill 1992 and Costello 2005.

48. This estimate is calculated adding UNHCR data (2019) on current Eritrean refugees to the number of Eritrean diaspora members declared by the Eritrean government. For a critical assessment of the calculation of the Eritrean diaspora, see Hirt 2015.

49. Butzer 1981; Pankhurst 1997.

50. Tewodoros II unified the region only in the 1850s, after which Yohannes I, a Tigreyan, ruled for a few years until succeeded by the emperor Menelik II, who defeated an Italian invasion in the late nineteenth century (Zewde 1991).

51. Abbay 2001; Reid 2005.

52. Smidt 2010. Highlanders are traditionally Coptic Christians (with the exception of the group called Jeberti, who are Muslims, and Catholics in the Segeneiti area) and sedentary agriculturalists. They speak a Semitic language called Tigrinya. Tigrinya as well as Amharic, the official language of Ethiopia, derives from the ancient Ge'ez language and uses the Ge'ez alphabet. Eritrean Tigrinya speakers belong to the same ethnic group as the Tigreyans who live around Axum, Makallé, and shire in Northern Ethiopia.

53. Donham and James 1986.

54. In 1869, a Genovese shipping company, Rubattino, bought the area surrounding the port of Assab from Egypt. This was proclaimed an "Italian colony" in 1881, which was gradually extended to surrounding areas, to Massawa (1885), and to other parts of the highlands. In spite the defeats by the Ethiopian army, such as at Dogali in 1887, the Italians managed to push their occupation as far as the Mereb River, and under the Treaty of Wichale (Uccialli) between Italy and Menelik II, the emperor of Ethiopia, the Italian colony called "Eritrea" was established in 1889.

55. Palumbo 2003; Negash 1987; Markakis 1988 ; Bereketeab 2002.

56. Many aspects of Eritrean contemporary history cannot be understood without taking into account the deep impact of colonialism on Eritrean society. Treiber 2010 shows, for instance, that many developmental measures implemented by the current Eritrean government are inspired by ideals of cleanliness and modernity deriving from Italian colonial rule. The first wave of international migration for Eritreans was then directed towards Italy due to the long-term contacts between colonial employers and indigenous domestic workers. Even in Italy, however, unequal colonial relationships were reproduced,

also symbolically, by deep-rooted conceptions, shared by Eritrean workers and their Italian employers, of modernity and backwardness, cleanliness and dirtiness (S. Marchetti 2011, 2014).

57. E.g., Markakis 1987; Iyob 1995.

58. About Eritrean migration to the Gulf and the Middle East see Thiollet 2007; 2011 and Kifleyesus 2012.

59. The emergence and establishment of a separate Eritrean identity have long occupied historians and other regional experts. Some have argued that Eritrea has always had a distinct history (Pateman 1998); others have considered the impact of colonization on its development (Negash 1987); still others examine the many different ethnic, religious, and political factors leading to the Eritrean nationalist struggle (e.g., Markakis 1988). For a critical review of historiography on Eritrean nationalism, see also Gilkes 1991.

60. The ELF leadership was based in Cairo and the movement was mainly constituted by Muslim Eritreans until the mid-1960s. This changed after 1965, when many Christians joined the struggle because of increasing repression of political opposition by the imperial police.

61. In May 1967, there were already 25,500 refugees in the camps established in Sudan. Military operations against the ELF became even more violent in 1969–70 in the eastern Akele Guzai and the area of Keren. Massacres of civilians in those areas were repeatedly reported. These acts of violence could be interpreted in continuity with the history of conflict and domination between Christian highlanders and lowlanders (Pankhurst 1992; Zewde 1991; Naty 2002a and b). In fact, those who fled in 1967 were mainly Muslim pastoralists from the Beni Amer, Maria (a subgroup of Tigre), and Saho ethnic groups. The ethnic composition of the refugee population started to vary in the 1970s when the repression started to spread to Asmara as well as to the highlands (Kibreab 1987).

62. In that period, Christian Tigrinya started to flee to Sudan, and some proceeded thence to Europe, the United States, or Australia. Some managed to reach Germany, owing to a breach in its migration policy. A number of Eritreans, regarded as "Ethiopian" refugees and in Cold War logic considered as such to be victims of a communist regime (i.e., the Derg), were variously resettled in Australia, Denmark, Sweden, or the United States (Getahun 2007). When Eritrea formally gained independence in 1993, many refugees, mainly those who lived in refugee camps in Sudan, chose to be repatriated through a UNHCR program. Many others who had settled in Europe, the United States, Canada, and Australia did not come back, but continued to support the government politically and economically. During the war, the political and economic connection between the liberation fronts and the increasing number of Eritreans fleeing the country became stronger. Sources from the 1970s and 1980s report solidarity campaigns through which Eritrean communities in Italy and other countries in Europe and the United States showed their moral and economic support for the fighters. Nationalistic feelings were flourishing among the Eritreans abroad at the time and are still strong in the contemporary diaspora, despite growing internal divisions. The financial and political role of the diaspora in supporting the government has been so crucial that some authors have defined Eritrea as a "diasporic state" (Iyob 2000). Remittances, which are more or less voluntary, remain one of the most important economic resources of the Eritrean government. The mythology of the heroic diaspora publicly disseminated in Eritrea today originated in this historical linkage between the diaspora and the future Eritrean government (Bernal 2004; Conrad 2006).

63. For an in-depth analysis of what led to the conflict, see Negash and Tronvoll 2000. See also Jacquin-Berdal and Plaut 2005; Abbink 2003.

64. On the deep-rooted resentment of the international community, see Reid 2005. International NGOs and organizations have been expelled from the country on several occasions; diplomatic relations in international meetings have been tense or absent, and foreign investment in the country rigorously restricted. However, this strategy of self-sufficiency seems unrealistic given the country's limited environmental, human, and industrial resources.

65. Connell 2005.

66. On multi-sited ethnography, see Marcus 1995; Coleman and von Hellermann 2009; Falzon 2009.

67. On migrant transnationalism and media, see Dekker and Engbersen 2014; Wilding 2006; Panagakos and Horst 2006.

68. Boccagni 2014.

69. This methodology, moreover, matches, but at the same time surpasses, the agenda set by scholars such as David FitzGerald (2006), who argues for a theoretical ethnography of migration, and Gadi BenEzer and Roger Zetter (2014), who call for more attention to refugees' journeys. First, by being a highly multi-sited form of fieldwork, the ethnography of a corridor enables a researcher to explore how different sites are linked to each other. In doing so, it "removes national blinders" and shows "the effect of place on a variety of outcomes" (Fizgerald 2006, 2). Second, by following the path of many refugees, the ethnography of a corridor provides experiential insights into their journeys as a "profoundly formative and transformative experience" (BenEzer and Zetter 2014, 6), while avoiding the pitfalls of a merely narrative approach. In chapter 5, I highlight the importance of looking at refugees' decision-making as a cumulative and sequential process that progressively compels them to risk more and more—like gamblers—to move forward.

70. On the emergence and closing of migration corridors, see Ciabarri 2014 and Bredeloup and Pliez 2011. The central Mediterranean route has been the most used by Eritreans and many other migrants over the past ten years, but intergovernmental agreements have periodically redirected migration pathways. In 2008, for instance, the Italian government struck a deal with the Libyan dictator Muammar al-Gaddafi to stem arrivals from Libya, leading to a drastic decrease in the number of migrant crossings in the following two years (Paoletti 2011). More recently, in 2017, the leftist Italian government reached several agreements with different emerging Libyan political and military leaders to prevent migrants' arrival in Italy. The memorandum of understanding between Italy and Libya has then been endorsed by the EU (Palm 2017). This effort could be inscribed in the larger European strategy inaugurated in the so-called Khartoum Process, which aims to engage transit countries in more efficient control of their borders and combat illicit migration. The Khartoum Process and recent deals with Libyan authorities have led to huge human rights abuses and had significant impacts on the lives of migrants in Libya and in other transit countries. On this, see Giacomo Zandonini's reportage on Niger at www.newsdeeply.com/refugees/articles/2018/05/22/niger-europes-migration-laboratory.

71. E.g. Sabar and Posner 2013.

72. E.g. Thiollet 2007. About Eritreans migrating to other African destinations see e.g. Jourdan 2012a.

73. Salamone 1979; Condominas 1973.

74. Harrell-Bond et al. 1992; Daniel and Knudsen 1995.

75. See E. Goffman 1959.

CHAPTER 1. WHEN MIGRATION BECOMES THE NORM

1. Vigh 2008, 10.

2. This reluctance was often due to the fact that many of my informants had not kept in touch with their families (Belloni 2019b). In other cases, they did not want to attract the attention of neighbors or officials. Alazar's family were refused to accommodate me in Asmara because they planned to escape the country.

3. Cf. Wilson 1998.

4. See Bernal 2014; Hirt 2015.

5. Eritrean women working in Italy, for instance, were called "mothers of Eritrea," since they offered much of their income to support the struggle (S. Marchetti 2011) See also Kifleyesus 2012 for female migration to the Gulf and the Middle East.

6. Even speaking about one's own desire to leave the country can be sufficient reason to be jailed. "The first time I was arrested, it was because I was trying to collect some information about the possible ways to leave Eritrea through my Yahoo," Kudus, a thirty-year-old Eritrean whom I met in Addis Ababa in 2014, explained. "Even the thought of escaping the country is a crime over there." He was subsequently incarcerated twice for attempting to flee Eritrea illegally. He spent eight years in prison and then finally managed to cross over to Ethiopia.

7. The consequences of their failed flight can be different depending on their individual circumstances. Military officers and soldiers run the highest risks—if caught trying to cross the border, especially into Ethiopia, they can be shot, or otherwise imprisoned for at least a year, and even tortured, depending on the head of their original military unit.

8. If the family cannot pay (fines were around 50,000 nakfa per escapee), a member of the household who is held "responsible" for the deserter's conduct is imprisoned. These measures are not systematic and can vary from place to place, and from case to case. See also HRW 2009.

9. The song "Zemen" was released in 1985, when the independence struggle was more furious than ever and Yemane was an exile in Sudan. The song's title, "Time," refers to the period under the Ethiopian oppressor. On Eritrean art and theater, see Matzke 2002, 2004.

10. Ambivalence about migration is a specific characteristic of the Eritrean migration context as observed by Belloni 2018b and Riggan 2013.This ambivalence is multifaceted. First, while condemning current generations of migrants and labeling them traitors, the government cultivated a strong connection with its historic diaspora. Second, although it tries to prevent the outflow of young people at all costs, the Eritrean nation-state heavily depends on migrant remittances. Not only family survival but also the Eritrean state's existence would not be possible without the contribution of Eritreans abroad (A. Poole 2013; Woldemikael 2009), which may approach 40 percent of the national GDP. Eritrean citizens abroad (more or less willingly) in fact contribute to the development of their homeland by paying the 2 percent of their annual income to the government. This tax is practically compulsory for those who want to preserve their right to visit and own property in the country (A. Poole 2013). This suggests that the current political status quo relies on the

fact that Eritreans keep migrating, circumventing the rules established by those in power. This leads us to the another major aspect of government's ambivalence. Although it publicly denounces the refugees as deserters and traitors, the state allows those who leave the country illicitly to recover their passports and rights provided they officially admit guilt and promise to support the development of the homeland economically (Hirt and Mohammad 2017). Emigrants given rights as external citizens and residents denied their basic citizenship rights by reason of compulsory national service are thus treated differently.

11. Eritrea's currency is the nakfa. The exchange rate between nakfa and euro set by the Eritrean government was 20 to 1, but this was far above the rate on the international money market. A U.S. dollar was worth 50 nakfa on the black market when I was in Eritrea, and I have used that rate in the book.

12. Remittance architecture is one of the marks of a "culture of migration," where migration has become the most desired channel for social mobility, according to the literature (e.g., Timmermann 2008; Lopez 2010).

13. Remittance houses and their manifold meanings have been studied e.g. in Ghana (Smith and Mazzucato 2009), Mexico (Lopez 2010, 20), and Somaliland (Ciabarri 2011).

14. "Absences are a necessary precondition for migrants to realise their dream houses" (Lopez 2010, 34).

15. As scholars have observed in other contexts, memories of migrants are often reified in things like photograph albums, underlining both the absence of the migrant and his/her continued presence in the life of the family (Tolia-Kelly 2004; Rose 2003; Boccagni 2014).

16. Comparing the cost of living and official salaries in Eritrea clearly indicates that the majority of families depend on remittances from abroad for their survival. In 2013, the highest salary in the public sector was around 2,500 nakfa—around 50 U.S.$, which is what specialized doctors earn. However, the majority of people working in the public sector earned 700 nakfa (about 14 U.S.$) a month at most. In the poor area where I was living, houses rented for around 5,000 nakfa (about 100 U.S.$); a pair of jeans in the market near our house cost around 1,000 nakfa (about 20 U.S.$); a shirt, or a chicken, 500; a kilo of coffee beans, around 200; and a kilo of bananas, the cheapest produce, sold for 25 nakfa. Unless families had someone abroad to help them or had their own private business, survival was a daily challenge.

17. T. M. Woldemikael 2009, 3; Brahne Tewolde, 2008; Fessehatzion 2005.

18. Kandel and Massey 2002; Ali 2007.

19. Migration has been widely portrayed as a rite of passage to adulthood in the literature (see Aguilar 1999; Ali 2007; Monsutti 2007).

20. Van Gennep 1960; Turner 1969.

21. Treiber 2009.

22. Patterson 1982.

23. Mauss [1926] 1950.

24. Peter 2010.

25. Vigh 2006.

26. See, e.g., Stark and Bloom 1985. Recently, FitzGerald and Arar (2018) argued that the new economics of labor migration be also be applied in the context of refugee movements. By taking a household perspective, researchers may be able to by analyzing how families collectively manage different kinds of risks related to war, displacement and migra-

tion. These considerations partly apply to the case of the Eritrean families I met, even if, as I show elsewhere (Belloni 2019), migration is rarely a collective decision.

27. In general, the parents I met assumed three main attitudes to their children's plans to migrate: some promoted them and helped finance them; some indirectly endorsed them, without being actively involved; others opposed them out of patriotic loyalty (see Belloni 2019a).

28. Belloni 2016b; Belloni 2019a.

29. See http://popstats.unhcr.org/en/demographics.

30. Muller 2008; O'Kane and Hepner 2009.

31. For more information about Eritrean national service, see Human Rights Watch 2009; Kibreab 2009; Bozzini 2011.

32. There used to be another, even harder training camp, called Ueah, for those unable to reach eleventh grade. Many young men died there because of the lack of food, the heat, and the workload, which pushed the government to close the center some years ago and replace it with other training centers across the country.

33. This year used to be divided into six months of intensive military training and six months of teaching. Today, military training is mostly been limited to three months, with the exception of the students of the Italian school, who after finishing school in Asmara go to Sa'wa for up to four months' training.

34. By means of the "experiment of social engineering" (Bereketeab 2002) that Sa'wa represents, the government seeks to mold the diverse Eritrean population into one people sharing a sense of belonging to the same nation and a spirit of self-sacrifice for the common good. Minority groups are thus obliged to contribute to a national project they do not necessarily share.

35. Riggan 2009; Muller 2008.

36. In 2016, public sector salaries were upgraded. Even if most Eritreans have still not been released from their public duties, their became as those of civilians. Today (2018), those with a degree, depending on their specialization, may earn between 2,000 and 4,000 nakfa a month. Those with lower education earn around 1,000–1,500 nakfa a month.

37. The upper middle class in Eritrea is mainly represented by older generations—usually the generation of the freedom fighters—or by those who have a release document, often thanks to their family connections with high-up government officials. These Eritreans can open private businesses and travel to import goods and foreign exchange into the country.

38. On Eritrean political humor, see Bozzini 2013 and Bernal 2013.

39. Lubkemann 2008.

40. See Belloni 2018b.

41. Draft-dodging is well documented in the literature on Eritrea; see Bozzini 2011; Treiber 2009; Hirt and Mohammad 2013.

42. Treiber 2009; Bozzini 2011.

43. Goffman 2014.

44. Bozzini 2011.

45. This sense of "immobility" is also documented in other African contexts where many young people have been left with limited socioeconomic prospects and often in a position of economic dependence on older generations (Ferguson 2006; Christiansen 2006; Vigh 2006; Cutolo 2015).

46 E.g. Hirt and Mohammad 2013; Treiber 2009

47. Madianou and Miller 2013; Vacchiano 2012; Bal and Willems 2014.

48. "Modernity" has come to be part of African local traditions, reproduced in new alternative, parallel forms, widely discussed by anthropologists (Larkin 1997; Fabian 1983, 1998; Comaroff and Comaroff 1993; Ferguson 2006, 2002; Piot 1999; Bal and Willems 2014). As Piot puts it (1999, 22), African societies can no longer be represented as "small, bounded, static . . . at some remove from the tumult of global history". This literature has positively contributed to overcoming the idea of a primitive, ahistorical Africa, although perhaps partly neglecting existing global socioeconomic hierarchies (Ferguson 2006; Castells 2000). When an ethnographer eventually goes into the field, possibly aiming to showcase Africa's alternative modernity, he/she may face informants' disenchantment about their own "backwardness," together with their claim to a conventional form of "modernity." My informants' desires for modernity were also in a way quite conventional (see Belloni 2018a). Their aspirations to be part of the modern world directly emerge from their daily experience of deprivation and inequalities between them and their peers in the outside world.

49. Appadurai 2013.

50. Aspirations have recently become central in migration theories, as one of the subjective factors that affect the individual decision to migrate (Carling 2002). Desires to migrate "are not simply generated by rationalist choices based on economic calculations," but are embedded in "translocal processes that concern people's ideas about the good and the right life" (Åkesson 2008, 269). De Haas 2011 outlines an analytical framework of migration as a function of aspirations and capabilities, the first being subjective desires and the second being the (structure-affected) possibility of achieving them. More recently, on aspirations and desire, see Carling and Collins, 2018

51. Miller 1995.

52. Appadurai 1996; Larkin 1997.

53. On gender and media in Eritrea, see Indira and Vijayalakshmi, 2015.

54. Arnone 2011.

55. About the impact of social remittances on local aspirations and life styles see Levitt 1998; Sayad 2000; Åkesson 2008.

56. On the shifting, negotiable character of migrants' journeys, see Schapendonk 2012b.

57. Although the young Eritreans who were often thinking of leaving the country were at times well informed about life in different destination countries, my older interlocutors had a more blurred image of life in Europe. Even if they were in touch with close relatives abroad, they rarely knew the exact city where they lived, what work they did, or their housing conditions (see chap. 3).

58. Pajo 2007.

59. Vigh 2009, 93.

60. Ferguson (2006, 183) writes that "underdeveloped" countries were expected to move progressively closer to the level of the First World, but as stages of the developmental hierarchy have become permanent statuses, this model has lost credibility. The only way forward that Africans can see is "not by 'patience' and the progress of national or societal development, but by leaving, going elsewhere, even in face of terrible danger".

61. This does not mean that First Worlders are esteemed in every respect. Europeans' lack of care for the elderly, coldness, and attitude to homosexuality were sometimes condemned by my interlocutors.

62. On stereotypes of Ethiopians, see, e.g., Sorenson 1990; Bereketeab 2010. On the complex interethnic relations between Eritreans and Sudaneses and the challenges faced by Eritrean refugee women in Khartoum, see Kibreab 1995. On the legacy of colonial categories of dirty/clean and developed/underdeveloped, see S. Marchetti 2014 (labor relationships), Treiber 2010 (urban development in Asmara) and Andall and Duncan 2005. See discussion on ethnic stereotypes in chap. 2.

63. See, e.g. Palumbo, 2003.

64. On Eritrean women and how their aspirations for migration are connected to their desire of emancipation, see Belloni 2019a and Grabska et al. 2018.

CHAPTER 2. HYPERMOBILE AND IMMOBILE

1. See, e.g., the following statement by the UNHCR in 2014 "Eritrean refugees, including unaccompanied minors who continue to arrive in increasing numbers, tend to move on from Ethiopia to a third country, a situation which presents a major challenge in providing protection" (accessed 2014, page discontinued).

2. Among the most notable exceptions among studies on refugees, see Zimmermann 2009 and Moret et al. 2006. Besides the studies exclusively focusing on refugees, it is important to highlight a growing number of studies addressing migrants' journeys (Schapendonk et al. 2018; Khosravi, 2010). These studies highlight that migrants' trajectories are far from being linear; they are often multi-directional and characterized by complex temporalities. Schapendonk (2012, 2008), for instance, examines the trajectories of West Africans on their way to Europe, and shows how these are continually reshaped by migrants' volatile networks and shifting aspirations.

3. Sudan and Ethiopia are, today, the largest recipients of Eritrean refugees worldwide (UNHCR 2016; UNHCR 2019). They respectively host 121,000 and 170,000 Eritrean refugees (http://popstats.unhcr.org/en/persons_of_concern), but both countries provide shelter for many other nationalities as well. In Sudan, the refugee population totals 160,000, not counting 1,873,300 internally displaced people. Ethiopia hosts about half a million refugees. Sudan has historically been the first refuge for Eritreans, whereas Ethiopia has also formally become a shelter for many Eritreans only in the past decade. Walter Kok reported in 1989 that Eritreans in Sudan had mostly self-settled in Kassala state. Only a small portion of them were assisted by the UNHCR in camps. All the others have been living outside camps for decades and are usually locally integrated with the local Sudanese population given their ethnic and religious homogeneity. Self-settled Eritrean refugees were usually Muslim lowlanders and belong to the Beni Amer and the Nara ethnic groups. However, many Christian highlanders also settled in Kassala town and others moved to cities, mainly Khartoum and Port Sudan (Weaver 1985). From the 1960s to the 1990s, Eritreans were fighting against Ethiopia in order to secede from it, and they tended to flee to Sudan, the Middle East, and European countries. However, after the 1998–2000 border conflict with Ethiopia, the situation changed, and Eritreans have progressively started to seek asylum in Ethiopia. Both countries actively cooperate with the UNHCR for the assessment of refugee status and the assistance and protection of refugees. Although refugees receive formal protection in Sudan and Ethiopia, these two countries have severely limited their freedom of movement. This means that refugees tend to be kept in camps; local integration in rural and urban en-

vironment is officially not facilitated (Crisp 2003; Kibreab 1996). Nevertheless, in practice, refugees have long circumvented these policies and settled in urban and rural areas, often in significant numbers.

4. To my knowledge, there is no reliable estimate of the rate of secondary movement from Ethiopian camps, but it is hard to keep track of refugees there. However, around 2015, IOM and UNHCR declared that some 80 percent of Eritreans in Sudanese camps, many of whom had previously been in Ethiopian camps, moved on within the first few months. This gives an idea of their hypermobility. https://sudan.iom.int/sites/default/files/docs/FINAL%20Joint%20Anti-trafficking%20smuggling%20strategy%20UNHCR_IOM.pdf.

5. I spent most of my time in Shimelba and Adi Harush because I was subject to less control by the Ethiopian authorities and could spend the night there.

6. Refugees slept in tents and communal shelters in Hintstas, but those in Adi Harush and Mai Aini, respectively established in 2010 and 2008, had houses, which they built on their own or were provided by NGOs. Being the last of the camps established in Tigray (2013), Hintstas lacked most of the facilities of other camps, such as schools, clinics, and proper housing. Not only was there no NGO presence there, but the UNHCR also had no stable basis there. Housing areas were still under construction. Nevertheless, refugees were quickly organizing and had already established barber shops and small food stores.

7. In 2017, the total population of these camps was stated to be around 38,000 (www.refworld.org/country,,UNHCR,,ETH,,59e5aae94,0.html). Shimelba was the least populous in 2013, with 6,000 refugees. The other camps ranged between 10,000 to 15,000 inhabitants. On the idea of city camps, see Agier 2002. See also Crisp and Jacobsen 1998 on the different policy and academic debates on refugee camps.

8. Eritrean security could not easily infiltrate into Ethiopia, though it was known that Eritrean security agents could wander undisturbed across the Sudanese border to arrest individuals of interest to the government. Moreover, whereas bandits were not operating in Ethiopian territory, camps in Eastern Sudan were known among refugees for frequent kidnappings by traffickers.

9. At that time Israel had already become almost inaccessible because of its no-tolerance approach at the Sinai border. Other African countries instead started to emerge as possible destinations among my informants. Some, for instance, thought to reach Angola or Juba in South Sudan, which seemed to offer some prospect for business opportunities in spite of the high level of insecurity.

10. Since the camps are mostly in remote and dry areas, firewood has become a rarity there. Refugees travel long distances to fetch it, even if this is formally forbidden by the local authorities.

11. Samuel Hall Consulting 2014.

12. For specific demographic data on refugee population in the camps, see the UNHCR statistical database at http://popstats.unhcr.org/en/demographics.

13. See "UNHCR Projected Global Resettlement Needs" (2018), www.unhcr.org/protection/resettlement/593a88f27/unhcr-projected-global-resettlement-needs-2018.html.

14. See the 2018 UNHCR resettlement handbook, www.unhcr.org/protection/resettlement/4a2ccf4c6/unhcr-resettlement-handbook-country-chapters.html.

15. On the complex interactions between refugees and their relatives in the diaspora, see Belloni 2016b; 2018.

16. Three refugees—forty-year-old Jeremiah; Jacob, a young engineer from Asmara; and fifty-year-old Tekeste—assisted me throughout the survey, translating and providing me with useful insights about life in the camp. The main questions concerned the size of the household, mobility, desired destinations, and the support received from abroad.

17. This partly conflicts with the MEDMIG project's finding that "when the migrants and refugees on the Central Mediterranean route initially set out from their place of origin they often did not have very clear plans about where their final destination would be. Only one third (37.5%) of the interviewees [500 in all] who spoke about their intentions said that they had been intending to move to Europe when they set out, and even then they often had little specific knowledge about a particular European country" (McMahon and Sigona 2016, 8). The differences between my observations and what was found by the MEDMIG researchers mainly emerge from the variety of national groups interviewed as part of that project. Different national groups of migrants often have different migration histories, aspirations, and also different prospects of legalization in Europe, making it hard to generalize.

18. On the feminization of the refugee population in the camps in protracted displacement, see Hyndman and Giles 2011.

19. Black and Collyer 2014.

20. Tronvoll and Mekonnen 2014.

21. Noah, Bartholomeus, and their families were resettled to Texas just two months after I met them in the camp.

22. Tronvoll and Mekonnen 2014, 130.

23. First settled in Wallanabi, the first refugee camp ever established in Tigray, Kunama refugees were moved for security reasons—Wallanabi was apparently too close to the Eritrean border—to Shimelba in 2004. Many families came right after the Ethiopian army evacuated Barentu in northwestern Eritrea and brought their camels, cows, and goats with them.

24. One instance of this strong relationship with the land is represented by the care for the dead. Although monotheistic religions have become prevalent among Kunamas, traditional beliefs are still widespread and syncretically practiced in wedding ceremonies, baptisms, funerals, and initiation rituals. Once a loved one dies in the camp and is buried there, the family is somehow bound to be in the same place so as not to betray the spirit of the dead person (Dore 2012).

25. Naty 2002a and b.

26. Although I cannot go into detail, there is a long-standing debate in refugee studies (see, e.g., Malkki 1992; Kibreab 1999; Brun 2001; Hammond 2004; Turton 2005) critically reflecting on the relationship between people, place, and identity. Some argue that roots and identity should not be thought as anchored in only one place (Malkki 1992; Hammond 2004); others stress the importance of territory and place for refugees' self-understanding (Brun 2001) and realistic prospects for the future (Kibreab 1999).

27. Malkki 1994.

28. For a reflection on the terminology surrounding illegal/irregular/undocumented/unauthorized migration see Paspalanova 2008.

29. As mentioned in the introduction, not all sectors of Eritrean society have participated equally in international migration throughout over the past fifty years (see Kibreab 1987; Getahun 2007).

30. Urban refugees can be generally said to be better off than the stable population of camps. Those who can afford to live outside the camp without UNHCR assistance usually count on remittances of relatives from abroad. Moreover, if they are allowed to live in Addis Ababa, they typically have some kind of "process" (family reunification procedure, sponsor visa, etc.) that requires their presence in the city and therefore also have potential access to a "regular" or "almost regular" migration option. Nevertheless, urban life also has its challenges.

31. UN High Commissioner for Refugees (UNHCR), Ethiopia: Refugees and Asylum-seekers in Ethiopia, 31 December 2014, 31 December 2014. available at: https://www.refworld.org/docid/54b4e2784.html [accessed 19 September 2019]. Estimates of urban population have hugely shifted in recent times. In September 2018, Eritreans in Addis Ababa were over 18,000 accounting for about 79% of urban refugee population of the Ethiopian capital. Of these, 17,217 are beneficiaries of the Government's Out-Of-Camp Policy (https://reliefweb.int/report/ethiopia/unhcr-ethiopia-urban-refugees-factsheet-september-2018).

32. The "out-of-camp" policy, implemented since 2011, allows Eritrean refugees to study at different universities in Ethiopia or to live outside a camp if an Ethiopian sponsor will take responsibility for supporting him/her. (Samuel Hall Consulting 2014).

33. Over 73,000 Eritrean refugees who previously lived in camps have settled in urban areas in Ethiopia, according to recent UNHCR estimates, www.refworld.org /country,COI,,,ETH,,59e5aae94,0.html.

34. Karadawi 1987. At that time Ethiopians and Eritreans could hardly be differentiated in statistics, because Eritrea was not an independent state yet.

35. There are around 64,000 refugees and displaced people in Khartoum, according to the latest UNHCR estimates (www.refworld.org/country,,,,SDN,,573ad3274,0.html), but figures on distribution by nationality are not available.

36. COR, a branch of the Ministry of Interior and the Security Department, is the main Sudanese government agency dealing with legal status determination, security service, issue of travel permit, and management of refugee camps, with the collaboration and full economic support of UNHCR.

37. See, e.g., www.ibtimes.co.uk/eritrea-ethiopia-lampedusa-dead-refugee-camps-511960.

38. The long-term participation of Eritrean women and men in the Sudanese labor market is documented by Kibreab 1995, 1994.

39. Gaonkar 2002; Salazar 2011.

40. On the role of the mall in Africans' imagination, see Mbembe and Nuttall 2004; Jackson et al. 2005; Dolby 2006. Such spaces can simultaneously be "material sites for commodity exchange and symbolic and metaphoric territories" (Crewe 2000, 275).

41. Reid 2003.

42. Smidt 2010.

43. Sorenson 1990.

44. This does not mean that all Eritreans I met thought the same way about Sudanese. Some also praised their generosity and affability. However, that attitude was less widespread among the refugees I encountered.

45. For a more detailed account of the impact of colonial categories and distinctions on Eritrean societal understanding and political discourse, see Treiber 2010 and Marchetti 2014.

46. Massa 2016; Kibreab 1995, 1996; Kok 1989.

47. Kibreab 1991 observes that the strict gender segregation of Sudanese society is not
common in Eritrean society. This among other factors (Kibreab 1995) has led Sudanese to
think of Eritrean women as more accessible and sexually available than Sudanese women
and has increased the risk of sexual harassment.

48. There is a rich literature on the topic of collective emotions ranging from anthropology to sociology and psychology (see, e.g., Maffesoli [1988] 1995; Collins 2014), which
I am not able to fully address here. However, it is important here to observe that the role
of emotions in migration has rarely been taken into account. About this see Boccagni and
Balsassar 2015.

49. Eritreans use the term "process" to refer to a legal procedure for regular migration.

50. This sense of longing is somehow akin to the feeling of *buufi* that Cindy Horst
(2006) encountered in Somali refugee camps in Kenya. Buufis is the term used by Somali
refugees not only to refer to 'resettlement' in general, but also to indicate the longing and
desire for it. This longing, at times, becomes almost like an illness or possession. Horst defines it as 'a new phenomenon' emerging from the transnational flow of information, desires
and money which connects refugees in camps and their co-nationals in diaspora reinforcing their relative sense of deprivation and their desire for resettlement.

51. Van Hear 2006; Belloni 2016b.

52. Seare was referring to the Italian "Mare Nostrum" operation in 2014–15, in which
the Italian Navy patrolled the Mediterranean to find and assist endangered migrant vessels
headed for Italy.

CHAPTER 3. AN ENDLESS JOURNEY

1. Southern European countries such as Spain, Greece, and Italy are usually the first safe
places in Europe where asylum seekers can formalize their asylum requests. Italy was the first
European country reached by African and other asylum seekers, by way of the Libyan corridor, until 2017, when Italy signed a memorandum of understanding with Libya on development cooperation, illegal immigration, human trafficking, fuel smuggling and reinforcement
of border security (http://eumigrationlawblog.eu/the-italy-libya-memorandum-of-under-
standing-the-baseline-of-a-policy-approach-aimed-at-closing-all-doors-to-europe). This
has been endorsed by the EU. (See Palm 2017 for a critical review of the memorandum.)
This agreement has not stopped the flow of people trying to reach Europe. Some of it has
been redirected to Spain and Greece. Many migrants are trapped in prisons and detention
centers in Libya, where it is reported migrants live in inhuman conditions (www.dw.com
/en/widespread-torture-and-rape-documented-in-libyas-refugee-camps/a-48070588).

2. International acknowledgement that Eritrean applicants could face torture and persecution if sent home has led Italy, as well as most European countries, to grant legal protection (mostly in a '"subsidiary" form) to the great majority of them. According to the
data of the Italian Ministry of Interior Affairs (http://www.libertaciviliimmigrazione.dlci.
interno.gov.it/it/documentazione/statistica/i-numeri-dellasilo), Eritreans have one of the
highest rates of recognition among applicants (around 95–98 percent). Those not granted
protection are usually identified as "fake Eritreans"—Tigrayan Ethiopians pretending to be
Eritreans to gain asylum. For a critical analysis of asylum claims based on nationality, see
Campbell 2011, 679.

3. See Papadimitriou and Papageorgiou 2005; Sidorenko 2007; Schuster 2011. The so-called Dublin Regulation governs refugees' movements in Europe, requiring them to apply for asylum in the first European country they reach, which is responsible for processing the application. Refugees who seek asylum in another European country after being identified in Italy are to be returned there. The first Dublin Convention, which aimed to prevent multiple applications from the same individuals in different European countries and to ensure that countries take responsibility for processing asylum seekers' cases, was signed on June 15, 1990, and came into force on September 1, 1997. An amended regulation, Dublin II, was adopted in 2003 and updated in 2013 (Dublin III).

4. These estimates are calculated on the basis of the data from the Italian Ministry of the Interior available at www.ismu.org/irregolari-e-sbarchi-presenze. Since the 2000s, Eritreans have progressively become one of the most numerous national groups in asylum flows to Italy. A drop in arrivals was registered only in 2009 and 2010 after the signing of a "Treaty of Friendship, Partnership and Cooperation" between Italy and Libya in August 2008 and related push-back policies (Paoletti 2011; Cuttitta 2014).

5. In sociological literature on migration (e.g., Bryce-Laporte 1972; Carter 2010; Puggioni 2005), "invisibility" usually refers to institutional lack of recognition and neglect, but in the case of Eritrean refugees in Italy, it is an actively pursued survival strategy rather than a handicap. More on invisibility as a tactic can be found in Tazzioli 2015.

6. The fingerprinting policy has changed frequently over the past ten years. Asylum seekers are sometimes forced to provide their fingerprints upon arrival, sometimes only later. In the latter case, which was what happened more systematically in 2014, many individuals actively try to avoid the procedure in order to seek asylum in other European countries. Fingerprinting has been a very thorny issue. Asylum seekers have often refused to cooperate with police officers in the procedure and have been forced to do so. This has attracted media and NGO attention and Italian police were accused of degrading treatment of the asylum seekers. However, in 2013, several informants told me that the police had often turned a blind eye and let them go. When the fingerprinting policy became more relaxed in 2014, other European countries criticized Italy's neglect of the Dublin directives.

7. See Belloni 2016a

8. Irregular secondary migration by Eritreans in Europe usually does not involve physical risks comparable to those the refugees have had to face earlier. However, some journeys can be extremely dangerous, such as the one from France (Calais) to England (Dover). Alexander, a young Eritrean refugee in Rome, told me that the Channel crossing was the worst he had ever experienced (and he had traveled illicitly from Eritrea into Sudan, then crossed the Sahara desert to Libya, and reached Italy from there in a rubber boat). Moreover, even if refugees do not risk much in legal terms, their failed attempts generate psychological stress, a significant waste of time, and, to a lesser extent, loss of money. On the pitfalls of the Dublin Regulation, see European Council on Refugees and Exiles 2013; Association for Juridical Studies on Immigration 2012; and Schuster 2011.

9. Comparative studies about reception systems, refugee integration policies, and welfare regimes include Brekke and Brochmann 2014 and Korac 2003.

10. On several occasions, the official Sistema protezione richiedenti asilo e rifugiati, or SPRAR (System for the Protection of Asylum Seekers and Refugees) has been supple-

mented by initiatives that involve humanitarian agents, like the Red Cross and Protezione Civile as well as private individuals like hotel owners providing basic assistance to asylum seekers, such as in the North African Emergency system (2011). Civil society associations and especially religious organizations, such as Caritas and the Jesuit Refugees Service, also play an important role in providing legal and practical help.

11. On the complexities of the Italian refugee reception system, see Hein 2001 and Ambrosini 2014; Campomori 2018.

12. See, e.g., Andall 1999; Schuster 2005; Lindley and van Hear 2007; van Liempt 2011; Toma and Castagnone 2015.

13. Established social networks, colonial linkages, common language, political discourse, welfare arrangements, and asylum policies in destination countries are factors often cited in studies of refugees' choices (Robinson and Segrott 2002; Koser and Pinkerton 2002; Neumayer 2005; Thielemann 2004 ; Havinga and Bocker 1999). These studies—typically policy-oriented—are concerned less with the distinction between primary and secondary mobility. They highlight that that policies have a limited effect on asylum flows, since refugees' choices are often constrained. Even when they do make a choice, this seems to depend essentially on long-term social links and perceived economic prospects in the country of destination. However, secondary movement occurs to countries without significantly different employment rates or policies on refugees. Van Liempt 2011 notes, for example, that Somali refugees in Denmark and Sweden continued to aspire to move on to the United Kingdom

14. Explanations based on historical and cultural linkages appear inadequate in other cases. It seems improbable that Eritreans, Iraqis, and Somalis would choose to go to Scandinavian countries on linguistic or cultural grounds. Collyer 2004 cites Algerians who refused to go to France because of the historically negative relationship between the two countries but turned to the United Kingdom as an alternative notwithstanding the language barrier.

15. On refugees and transnationalism, see Al-Ali et al. 2001; Cheran 2006; Horst 2006; Brees 2010.

16. Horst 2006.

17. Koser and Pinkerton, 2002.

18. Brekke and Brochmann,2014.

19. See Capalbo 1982; Melotti 1988; Scalzo 1984.

20. Under the original Geneva Convention, states can choose whether to apply it only to European citizens (geographic limitation) or extend it to all individuals in need of protection, no matter what their origin. Italy accepted the Geneva Convention in 1951, but the geographic limitation was retained until 1990, when it was removed by the so-called Martelli law (Hein 2001).

21. On the history of Eritrean migration to Italy, see Marchetti 2014; Mottura and Altieri 1992; Caputo 1983; Melotti 1988; Capalbo 1982.

22. On generational and political divisions in the Eritrean diaspora, see Arnone 2008; Hirt and Mohammad 2017; Hepner 2015.

23. A lively debate on the old and new Eritrean diasporas in the literature highlights the contradictory attitudes of Eritreans, divided by their loyalty to the government, their fear of reprisal, and their desire for change. See, e.g., Hirt and Mohammad 2017; Muller 2012; Riggan 2016; Belloni 2018b.

24. See also Al-Ali et al. 2001.

25. Cf. SPRAR 2012–13, 17.

26. On the effect of the economic crisis on the migrant labor force in Italy, see Reyneri 2010; Fullin 2011.

27. Gastaldi 2013.

28. Belloni 2016c.

29. Since the late 1960s, Rome has been interested by a grassroots political movement that proclaims the universal right to have a house and has actively occupied buildings that were abandoned or had not been used yet (Daolio 1974). Initially, the movement was close to workers' unions and mainly comprised Italian migrants from Southern Italy. Progressively, the movement has included more and more foreigners, mainly from Africa and Latin America; recently, refugees have become a consistent part of it (Vereni 2016).

30. This squat became the focus of international media attention in 2017 when authorities decided to clear the settlement. This decision produced clashes between refugees and local police and resulted in many refugees being homeless, stranded on the streets of Rome for several weeks. See, e.g., the analysis by Aurora Massa https://homing.soc.unitn.it /2017/09/29/aurora-massa-homemaking-of-eritreans-and-ethiopians-after-eviction-in-rome/. In international media: www.latimes.com/world/europe/la-fg-italy-refugees-crackdown-20170824-story.html and www.theguardian.com/world/2017/aug/24/italian-police-water-cannon-refugees-rome-square.

31. Winchester and White 1988; Squats are also common in other Italian cities. See e.g. Manocchi 2012; Quassoli 2004.

32. To some extent, the informal settlements and squats that I investigated in Italy correspond to M. Z. Bookman's definition (2002) of an "encampment" and have similar characteristics: their involuntary nature, since inhabitants of encampments "would rather be elsewhere"; the fact that encampments are meant to be temporary (as seen by institutions and by their inhabitants), but tend to become permanent; the ethnic concentration of minority groups; and the scarcity of economic resources.

33. Brekke and Brochmann 2014; Schapendonk 2012a; Mathews 2011; Zijlstra 2014; Papadopoulou 2003.

34. For a conceptual analysis of precariousness see Grabska and Fanjoy 2015.

35. Schapendonk 2012a, 579.

36. Hage 2009, 97.

37. Mathews 2011; Papadopoulou 2003; Grabska and Fanjoy 2015.

38. Panagakos and Horst 2006; Opas 2012; Harney 2013; Madianou and Miller 2013.

39. Parry and Bloch 1989; Carling 2008; McKenzy and Menjivar 2011; Baldassar and Merla 2014; Tazanu 2015.

40. Lindley 2010. Akuei 2005 notes that the inability to meet the economic obligations to kin and friends back home may lead to social exclusion. These studies are relevant in the case of Eritrean refugees in Italy, who often find it impossible to fulfil their family expectations (Belloni 2019b).

41. See, e.g., Hannaford 2015; Lindley 2009; Tazanu 2015; Akuei 2005.

42. See, e.g., Akesson 2011; Addo and Besnier 2008.

43. Malinowski 1920.

44. Small 2012.

4. MORALITIES OF BORDER CROSSING

1. For a critical review of state responses and media images on people smuggling see Sharma 2003; Mountz 2004; Van Liempt and Sersli 2013; Zhang et al. 2018.

2. De Genova et al. 2015.

3. Ryo 2013.

4. In their investigation of the conditions underpinning mistrust among refugees and aid workers, Eftihia Voutira and Barbara Harrel-Bond (1995, 216), for instance, report one of their refugee informants' saying, "To be a refugee means to learn to lie."

5. Kibreab 2004.

6. For theoretical attempts to define the concept of "moralities," see Howell 2005; Zigon 2007.

7. As Samson A. Bezabeh (2017) illustrates, border crossing entails huge ethical challenges for the individual and his/her community. Witnessing women prostituting themselves to cross the border or waiting in vain for a relative to send money can weaken one's trust in romantic relations, as well as in relations with other community members.

8. For a critical appraisal of the Ethiopian out-of-camp policy, see Samuel Hall Consulting 2014.

9. Hagos referred to a sinking on October 3, 2013, when 366 migrants died just a few hundred meters from the Italian island of Lampedusa, most of them Eritreans, many of whom had come from Ethiopian camps in Tigray.

10. The term "process" is often used by Eritreans to refer to different legal ways to migrate. A "process" is usually a family reunification visa procedure or a resettlement process.

11. On migrants' right to escape, see Mezzadra 2015.

12. Sharma 2003 and Spener 2008 illustrate how the portrait of smugglers as inhuman exploiters has been used to endorse more restrictive border controls and restrictive migration policies. The criminalization of the informal agents of irregular migration often leads to worse traveling conditions for smuggled migrants, who have to pay more, embark on more dangerous routes, and rely on smugglers with whom they have no relationship nor trust. As both authors emphasize, the criminalization of smugglers does not hinder irregular migration and does not address the root causes of the problem itself. For these reasons, decriminalizing smuggling has been suggested (see Zhang et al. 2019 and Gerver 2015). For a critical review of EU criminalization of human smuggling, see also van Liempt and Doomernik 2006.

13. "EU Action Plan against migrant smuggling (2015–2020)," https://ec.europa.eu/anti-trafficking/sites/antitrafficking/files/eu_action_plan_against_migrant_smuggling_en.pdf.

14. Spener 2008.

15. On the protests, see http://asmarino.com/press-releases/1878-ethiopian-authorities-shoot-at-refugees-at-mai-ayni-and-adiharush.

16. More considerations on the postcolonial aspect of Eritrean migration can be found in Triulzi 2006.

17. Salt and Stein 1997; Salt 2000; Kyle and Dale 2001; Pastore et al. 2006; Triandafyllidou 2012; Iselin and Adams 2003.

18. Spener 2004; Sanchez 2017. On the concept of embeddedness see Polanyi 1968.

19. Zhang et al. 2018; Majidi 2018; Achilli 2018.

20. Tekalign Ayalew 2018, 58

21. For a review see Getahun 2007.

22. Avraham and Kushner 1986.

23. E.g. Spener 2004.

24. Punishment of "pilots" is especially harsh in Eritrea. If the pilot is a soldier, and thus a "deserter" and "traitor" in the eyes of the authorities, he may be executed on the spot or imprisoned and tortured.

25. For a more detailed report on smuggling along the central Mediterranean route, see and Aziz, Monzini, and Pastore 2015.

26. About this see also my intervention on RMMS website at http://regionalmms.org /index.php/research-publications/feature-articles/item/2-anything-new-under-the-sun-analysing-the-shifting-flow

27. This system is called *xawilaad* in Somalia, *fei-ch'ien* in China, *hund* in Pakistan and Bangladesh, *hawala* in India and the Middle East. About it see Ismail 2007; El Qorchi et al. 2003; Maimbo and Passas 2004.

28. Schaeffer 2008; Lindley 2010; Ballard 2005.

29. Lindley 2009a and b.

30. Lindley 2010, 2.

31. To counter the currency black market, the Eritrean government issued a new currency in 2015. As the issuance of new notes rendered the old ones valueless, the population had no other option than to deposit their cash savings in national banks. The government then stipulated that monthly bank withdrawals cannot surpass 20,000 nakfa (U.S.$1,000 at the official exchange rate). This has not only led to a contraction of the currency black market, but has also decreased the purchasing power of most of the population, making basic products less accessible. Moreover, the withdrawal limit forms an obstacle for the hawalas who used to manage most remittances from the diaspora.

32. *Delalai* and *semsari* are the singular forms of *delelti* and *senserti.*

33. The middleman I met in Khartoum had rented a small house in the city to "host" his customers while they waited to proceed to Libya. However, I was told that in Libya Eritrean brokers were in touch with Libyans who owned or rented big warehouses, where migrants were kept while waiting for payments and the preparation of their journey to be finalized. In these warehouses, migrants could be victims of violence and threats, especially if payments had not been successful.

34. Article 3a of the UN *Protocol to Prevent, Suppress and Punish Trafficking in Persons, Especially Women and Children* defines trafficking as "the recruitment, transportation, transfer, harboring or receipt of persons, by means of the threat or use of force or other forms of coercion, of abduction, of fraud, of deception, of the abuse of power or of a position of vulnerability or of the giving or receiving of payments or benefits to achieve the consent of a person having control over another person for the purposes of exploitation." Exploitation may include sexual exploitation, forced labor, slavery, and organ harvesting. Article of the *Protocol against the Smuggling of Migrants by Land, Sea and Air* defines smuggling differently as "procurement, in order to obtain, directly or indirectly, a financial or other material benefit, of the illegal entry of a person into a State Party of which the person is not a national or a permanent resident." www.unodc.org/documents/treaties/UNTOC /Publications/TOC%20Convention/TOCebook-e.pdf.

35. See, e.g., Gallagher 2001; Aronowitz 2001; Baird 2014.

36. See Spener 2004 and 2009; Achilli 2018.

37. Humphris 2013. Such kidnapping has to some extent decreased owing to the restriction of the Egypt–Israel migration corridor and combined actions by UNHCR-IOM and national police in Sudan and Egypt. https://sudan.iom.int/sites/default/files/docs/FINAL%20Joint%20Anti-trafficking%20smuggling%20strategy%20UNHCR_IOM.pdf.

38. Lijnders and Robinson 2013; van Reisen et al. 2012.

39. About the estimation of smuggling business see International Organization for Migration (IOM), https://migrationdataportal.org/themes/smuggling-migrants. UN Office on Drugs and Crime 2010; and Frontex data at http://frontex.europa.eu/trends-and-routes. For general review see McAuliffe and Laczko (2016).

40. On the potlatch concept, see Barnett 1938.

41. About Eritreans' complex relations with homeland politics see Hepner 2013; Treiber 2015 and Belloni 2018b.

42. Zhang and Chin 2002 and Webb and Burrows 2009 also note that people smugglers express little sense of wrongdoing.

43. E.g., Chin 1999; Charrière and Frésia 2008.

44. See, e.g., Içduygu and Toktas 2002; Pastore et al. 2006; Sanchez 2017.

45. See appendix.

46. Constable 2003; see also Del Rosario, 2005; Mai and King 2009.

47. On family-arranged marriages, see, e.g., Shaw 2001; Shaw and Charsley 2006. On transnational marriages in the context of forced migration see Grabska 2010. On the commodification of marriage, see Wang and Chang 2002.

48. Beck-Gernsheim 2007.

49. European Council Directive 2003/86/EC, Article 16(2b).

50. Modernity produced the idea of the "pure relationship" in which partners are bound together by love and sexual intimacy, Giddens (2013) argues, but Lindholm (2006) shows that the concept of romantic love is by no means exclusive to the Western world.

51. See Eggebø 2013 in the Norwegian context; Zampagni 2016.

52. Infantino 2014.

53. Ibid.; Charsley and Benson 2012.

54. About the cultural relativity of romantic love see Jankowiak and Fisher 1992; Lindholm 2006.

55. Organized criminal networks are more a fantasy than a reality; people smuggling and related services are usually performed by small-scale, individual enterprises or loose networks (see, e.g., Zhang and Chin 2002; Pastore et al. 2008).

56. On the shifting representation of migration in the Italian context, see Marchetti 2014 and Colombo 2013.

57. Moral preconceptions about who the deserving refugee is and how he/she should behave influence juridical proceedings (Walaardt 2013), bureaucratic procedures (Zampagni 2016; Infantino 2016), the organization of assistance (Casati 2018), and the overall political atmosphere surrounding refugee reception and rejection (Holmes and Castaneda 2016).

58. Moreover, while most states grant recognized refugees and other beneficiaries of protection the right to reunite with already existing spouses through a facilitated procedure, those who arrive in Europe as single individuals are usually required to provide

evidence of sufficient income, a stable work contract, and housing. These requirements are extremely difficult to meet for newly arrived refugees and make transnational marriages almost impossible for them. This makes it hard for many young Eritrean men to achieve one of their main aspirations—to have a family and become respected family providers. However, this is not the case in Italy, where refugees are allowed to reunite with new spouses too.

59. Most of the money would go to the spouse, with a percentage for the broker who facilitated the transaction.

60. As far as I know, this has since changed, and fingerprinting is now done at the consulate.

CHAPTER 5. ENTRAPPED

1. See inter alia UNHCR 2017.

2. The definition of risk has been at the center of a complex and interesting theoretical debate between social scientists and philosophers. I understand risk here as exposure to a potential danger. The crucial implicit counterpart of the negative idea of risk as danger is the notion of risk as opportunity. Both these dimensions are fundamental in migrants' decision-making. The adjective "high" refers to the magnitude of the possible danger more than to the likelihood of it happening.

3. Hernández-Carretero and Carling 2012.

4. Hernández-Carretero 2008. Once the busiest entryway to Europe, the West African route from Senegal to the Canary Islands has progressively lost its centrality over the past ten years owing to bilateral agreements between Spain and Senegal in 2007 and the emergence of the central Mediterranean route.

5. Koser and Pinkerton, 2002; Hernández-Carretero 2008. For a critical assessment of information campaigns to deter irregular migration see e.g. Nieuwenhuys and Pécoud 2007 and Andrijasevic and Anderson 2009.

6. Douglas 2003 and 2013; Luhmann 1987; Lupton 1999. Larger debates on risk perception and risk attitudes at individual and societal levels are relevant here. Constructivist approaches have been key in understanding how certain risks become acceptable to migrants depending on social contexts and living conditions. Common misperceptions in risk evaluation include suspicion and the tendency to overestimate the significance of striking but rare events (see, e.g., Kahneman and Tversky 1974).

7. E.g., Carling 2008; Hernández-Carretero 2008; Sheridan 2009.

8. Slovic 1987.

9. Sheridan 2009.

10. The idea of migration as a rite of passage has been extensively discussed in the literature (e.g., Aguilar 1999). In the context of forced migration studies, see Monsutti 2007.

11. Hayenhjelm 2006, 190.

12. Hernández-Carretero and Carling 2012; Massey and Kandel 2002; Christensen et al. 2006; Vigh 2006.

13. Belloni 2016a.

14. About the dynamic of structure and agency along the complex pathways of contemporary migrants see the work by Schapendonk et al. 2018; Schapendonk 2012b; Brigden and Maiwaring 2016.

15. About trafficking in the Sinai see Van Reisen et al. 2012.

16. When investigating the determination of refugees to leave Ethiopia and Sudan, I was often faced with a similar fatalistic attitude: "What is written will happen." So there is no reason to worry, many of my informants seemed to imply. However, it would be wrong to interpret this as a passive acceptance of one's own destiny. As Gaibazzi 2012 argues in the context of Gambian high-risk migration, fatalistic statements are used instead to justify a proactive attitude to risk in a culturally accepted way.

17. Sheridan 2009.

18. See, e.g., Connell 2005 on eminent political prisoners of the Eritrean government.

19. It is calculated that over 150,000 migrants were saved by Mare Nostrum, an Italian rescue operation in the Mediterranean in 2013–14 that searched for all migrant boats in trouble, even if they were still in Libyan waters. However, owing to the cost and limited financial collaboration between EU and Italy, the operation was concluded at the end of 2014 and replaced by more limited Frontex interventions. The result of this was a surge in fatalities at sea. For a precise assessment of the relationship between search and rescue perations and mortality rates at sea, see Steinhilper and Gruijters 2017.

20. Belloni 2016a.

21. Collyer 2010. In his work on the trajectories of West African migrants to Europe, Joris Schapendonk (2012) defines these journeys as turbulent. According to this author, the idea of turbulence highlights "the multi-causality and multi-directionality of contemporary migration" and can then be seen as a welcome alternative to the often-used migration metaphors of *flows* and *waves* that suggest that migration patterns are unidirectional, possibly invasive, and encounter little resistance from supra-state and state authorities (Schapendonk, 2012, 29).

22. See Belloni 2016b, 2019; Achtnich 2016.

23. As the narratives of the Eritreans I met in Italy suggest, many of them are caught while trying to embark by Libyan police patrolling the beaches. Sometimes the boat's engine cuts out and they have no choice but to go back into the hands of the police, who will imprison them until they can bribe someone to let them out. One of the Eritrean refugees I met in Genoa had tried four times before succeeding. This was the situation in Libya before the ongoing civil war. On post-Gadhafi Libya, see also Achtnich 2016.

24. However, as much scholarship has shown, gambling is more pervasive among socioeconomically marginalized populations, who see it as their only hope of escaping from poverty. Thus, in a number of cases, the inclinations both to gamble and to engage in high-risk migration can be seen as the result of constrained agency.

25. Judging by unauthorized border crossings in the United States and Europe, migrants have better odds than gamblers do. In 2016, the "deadliest year of all," over 5,000 migrants died in the Mediterranean, out of 362,000 arrivals, a 98 percent success rate. The percentage is lower for the route through Libya to Italy, by far the most dangerous (see Steinhilper and Gruijters 2017 on death rates by year and route), and even lower if one estimates the number who die in the Sahara, but such a high success rate would nonetheless be unthinkable in gambling. Success at blackjack, considered the game with the best odds, does not exceed 48 percent, and other games offer dramatically lower odds (Chau and Phillips 1995).

26. Like high-risk migration, gambling has always attracted attention not only for its social and human costs, but also for the difficulties in grasping the rationale driving gamblers' choices. Innumerable books and articles have tried to solve the puzzle of why people would gamble at all, considering the expected negative returns and the mounting losses. Philosophers, psychologists, sociologists, anthropologists, and economists have been debating the motivations of gambling for centuries. In one of his most famous passages, Pascal ([1670] 1999) wrote that people gamble to escape existential ennui. Some authors have argued that individuals gamble for a variety of motives, ranging from the desire to hurt oneself (Bergler 1936), to attaining higher self-esteem (Martinez 1983). Although some scholars have argued that gambling is perfectly rational behavior in line with utility maximization (Becker and Murphy 1988), most authors would rather compare gambling with some kind of addiction characterized by weakness of the will (Elster and Skog 1999). A number of authors (Smith 1984; Rosecrance 1988) have in turn highlighted that gambling is deeply social—its main motivations are rooted in the social environment where gamblers live. Other authors have instead focused on cognitive mechanisms leading gamblers to keep betting despite expected losses, unrealistic optimism, perceived luckiness, the illusion of control, and superstitious thinking among them (Kahneman and Tversky 1979; Wagenaar 1988; Rogers 1998). Research on Senegalese pirogue migration also mentions these as factors perhaps contributing to migrants' risk-prone attitudes (Hernández-Carretero 2008, 57).

27. Rogers 1998; Griffiths and Wood 2001.

28. Elster 2003.

29. Jansen 2009.

30. Núñez and Heyman 2007.

31. Stoll 2010; O' Connel Davidson 2013.

32. Brigden and Mainwaring 2016.

CONCLUSION

1. On the importance of overcoming an emergency/humanitarian paradigm in refugee studies, see, e.g., Nyers 2006; Brun 2016; Hyndman and Giles 2017.

2. Brigden and Mainwaring 2016, 408.

3. On the tension between refugee deservingness victimhood and agency, see Sales 2002; Walaardt 2013; Holmes and Castaneda 2015; Lems et al. 2019.

4. Carling 2002; Lubkemann 2008.

5. Cf. Bauman 1998.

6. On the tension between geographic mobility and immobility in migrants' journeys, see Schapendonk et al. 2018; Brigden and Mainwaring 2016.

7. On Eritrean patriotism and migration, see Bernal 2014; Belloni 2018b; Hirt and Mohammad 2017.

8. I refer here to the factors analyzed in Castles 2004, which emphasizes three kinds of factor that lead to policy failures: those emerging from the social dynamics of the migratory process, those linked to increasing global inequalities, and those emerging from the political system of the receiving state. My considerations mostly refer to the first range of causes.

POSTSCRIPT

1. See, e.g., The Migrant Project, www.themigrantproject.org/eritrean-ethiopia.

2. See, e.g., Palm 2017; www.amnesty.org/download/Documents/MDE1975612017 ENGLISH.PDF; www.dw.com/en/new-report-highlights-tragedy-of-migrant-slave-markets-in-libya/a-38466216, and www-cdn.oxfam.org/s3fs-public/file_attachments/mb-migrants-libya-europe-090817-en.pdf.

APPENDIX

1. Doná 2007.

2. Boyden and de Berry 2004; Nordstrom and Robben 1995.

3. On doing research in authoritarian regimes, see Glasius et al. 2017.

4. Giulio Regeni, a Cambridge PhD student doing research on independent trade unions in Egypt, was tortured and killed by secret service agents in Egypt in 2015. See www.nytimes.com/2017/08/15/magazine/giulio-regeni-italian-graduate-student-tortured-murdered-egypt.html.

5. Lubkemann 2005.

6. Borneman and Hammoudi 2009.

7. For an analysis of different forms of violence see Bourgois and Scheper-Hughes 2004.

8. Sayad 2000.

9. Harrell-Bond and Voutira 2007, 284.

10. Massa 2016; Bozzini 2013; Vaughan and Tronvoll 2003.

11. Tronvoll 2000

12. Conti-Rossini 1916, Pollera 1935, and Nadel 1946 are among the most notable colonial studies.

13. A BBC team was allowed into the country again in 2015, but their movements were strictly controlled during their stay.

14. On the pros and cons of covert research, see Calvey 2008.

15. Spicker 2011.

16. Kovats-Bernat 2002.

17. Nordstrom and Robben 1995; Lubkemann 2010; Waterstone 2008.

18. Glasius et al. 2017.

19. Kovats-Bernat 2002, 214.

20. In general, all foreigners must apply for a permit, at the ministry that facilitated their entry, to travel outside Asmara. The permit is often limited in time (only a couple of days depending on the site), aside from travel to Massawa.

21. See, e.g., McLaughlin and Alfaro-Velcamp 2015; Pittaway et al 2010.

22. Turton 1996, 96.

23. See Doná 2007; Harrell-Bond and Voutira 2007; Block et al. 2012.

24. Hugman, Pittaway, and Bartolomei 2011 , 1279.

25. See, e.g., https://ec.europa.eu/trustfundforafrica/region/horn-africa/regional/research-and-evidence-facility_en.

26. Leaning 2001; Jacobsen and Landau 2002.

27. Barnett 2017, 13.

28. For a critical account of institutional protective attitudes, see Lange et al. 2007.

29. For more about Ethiopian policing strategies under the EPRDF led the government, see Di Nunzio 2014.

30. Tigrinya refugees were especially feared by the Ethiopian authorities because they were deemed to be more politicized and more easily assailable to spies of the Eritrean government sent to trigger turmoil in Ethiopia.

31. Jacobs 2006.

32. On the complications of being ethical in research, see Robins and Scheper-Hughes 1996.

33. Fassin 2013, 640. In his study on the work of police in Parisian banlieus, Fassin reports having felt incompatibly both loyal to the police, with whom he spent significant amounts of time, and to the youth of the banlieues who were the target of the police interventions.

34. My position, here does not differ from those who argue that researchers are most accountable to those who are most oppressed and are in line with the mainstream ethical guidelines set by the American Anthropological Association. See inter alia Scheper-Hughes 1995.

35. Scheper-Hughes 2009, 14.

36. Jacobs 2006.

37. See, e.g., Cook et al. 2009.

38. Daniel and Knudsen 1995.

39. See also Miller 2004 and Massa 2016 on the difficulty of gaining trust in research with refugees.

40. Salamone 1977.

41. Bleek 1987; Obligacio 1994; Fujii 2010.

42. See also, e.g., Shuman and Bohmer 2004; Hynes 2003.

43. The paternalism of humanitarian regimes does not function through coercion but through dominance, reproduced in a convergence of the interests of the dominant and the dominated (Fassin 2017). The process of selecting legitimate refugees based on proof of victimhood satisfies both parties. In seeking protection, the asylum seeker often performs a role implying the cultural and moral inferiority of the society he comes from in order to gain the benevolence of hospitality. See also Ticktin 2006 and Fassin and Rechtman 2009.

44. De Voe 1981; Zetter 1991, Holmes and Castaneda 2016.

45. See Goffman 1959 and, with reference to refugee studies, Miller 2004.

46. Jacobsen and Landau 2003.

47. E.g., Hugman et al. 2011; Pittaway and Bartolomei 2013.

48. Pærregaard 2002, 329.

49. See Falzon 2009 and, in particular, Gallo 2009.

50. See Gay y Blasco and de La Cruz Hernández 2012 for one of the most interesting essays on friendship between anthropological researchers and participants.

51. Tillmann-Healy 2003; Taylor 2011.

52. Nowicka 2012.

53. Glesne 1989.

54. Driessen 1998.

55. De Regt 2015.

56. Mahmood 2002.

57. This relationship is not uncommon in ethnographic studies. Pærregaard reports, e.g., being treated by informants as an "orphan" who was unable to count on anyone for care when in need (Pærregaard 2002, 328).

58. E.g., Pussetti 2005.

59. Newton 1993; Kulick and Wilson 2003.

60. See Dubisch 1995.

61. Scholars who fear for their own reputations or the credibility of their studies often avoid mentioning sexual harassment and implicit violence inflicted on female researchers by male interlocutors. See, e.g., Green et al. 1993; Sharp and Kremer 2006; Kloß 2017.

62. E.g. Pearson and Paige 2012.

63. Hugman et al. 2011.

64. Jacobsen and Landau 2003; Mackenzie et al. 2007.

65. Cf. Fassin 2017; Hodgson 1999.

66. De Genova 2013, Scheper-Hughes 1995.

67. See, e.g., Turton 1996; Doná 2007.

68. As Dorothy Hodgson 1999, 202, argues, we can "no longer presume . . . that 'communities', however isolated or subsistence-oriented, are homogenous, undifferentiated collectivities, but recognize the possibility of conflicting structural positions, interests, and perspectives."

69. Fassin 2014, 53.

70. Faist 2018; Mezzadra 2004.

REFERENCES

Abbay, A. 2001. "'Not with Them, Not without Them': The Staggering of Eritrea to Nationhood." *Africa: Rivista trimestrale di studi e documentazione dell'Istituto italiano per l'Africa e l'Oriente* 56 (4): 459–91.

Abbink, J. 2003. "Ethiopia–Eritrea: Proxy Wars and Prospects of Peace in the Horn of Africa." *Journal of Contemporary African Studies* 21 (3): 407–26.

Abramson, A., and M. Holbraad. 2012. "Contemporary Cosmologies, Critical Reimaginings." *Religion and Society* 3 (1): 35–50.

Achilli, L. 2018. "The 'Good' Smuggler: The Ethics and Morals of Human Smuggling among Syrians." *Annals of the American Academy of Political and Social Science* 676 (1): 77–96.

Achtnich, M. 2016. "Migrants and the 'business' of the Boat Journey from Libya to Europe." Africa at LSE blog entry. http://eprints.lse.ac.uk/id/eprint/76176.

Addo, P. A., and N. Besnier. 2008. "When Gifts Become Commodities: Pawnshops, Valuables, and Shame in Tonga and the Tongan Diaspora." *Journal of the Royal Anthropological Institute* 14 (1): 39–59.

Agamben, Giorgio. 1998. *Homo sacer: Sovereign Power and Bare Life.* Stanford, CA: Stanford University Press.

Agier, M. 2002. "Between War and City: Towards an Urban Anthropology of Refugee Camps." Ethnography 3 (3): 317–41.

Aguilar, F. V., Jr. 1999. "Ritual Passage and the Reconstruction of Selfhood in International Labour Migration." *Sojourn: Journal of Social Issues in Southeast Asia* 14 (1): 98–139.

Åkesson, L. 2008. "Cape Verdeans in Sweden." In *Transnational Archipelago: Perspectives on Cape Verdean Migration and Diaspora,* ed. L. Batalha and J. Carling. Amsterdam: Amsterdam University Press.

———. 2011. "Remittances and Relationships: Exchange in Cape Verdean Transnational Families." *Ethnos* 76 (3): 326–47.

Akuei, S. R. 2005. *Remittances as Unforeseen Burdens: The Livelihoods and Social Obligations of Sudanese Refugees.* Geneva: Global Commission on International Migration.

Al-Ali, N., R. Black, and K. Koser. 2001. "The Limits to 'Transnationalism': Bosnian and Eritrean Refugees in Europe as Emerging Transnational Communities." *Ethnic and racial studies* 24 (4): 578–600.

Ali, S. 2007. "'Go west young man': The Culture of Migration among Muslims in Hyderabad, India." *Journal of Ethnic and Migration Studies* 33 (1): 37–58.

Ambrosini, M. 2014. "Better Than Our Fears? Refugees in Italy: Between Rhetoric of Exclusion and Local Projects of Inclusion." In *Refugee Protection and the Role of Law: Conflicting Identities,* ed. Susan Kneebone, Dallal Stevens, and Loretta Baldassar. London: Routledge: 235–51.

Andall, J. 1999. "Cape Verdean Women on the Move: 'immigration shopping' in Italy and Europe." *Modern Italy* 4 (2): 241–57.

Andall, J., and D. Duncan. 2005. *Italian Colonialism: Legacy and Memory.* London: Peter Lang.

Andrijasevic, R., & Anderson, B. 2009. Anti-trafficking campaigns: decent? honest? truthful?. Feminist Review, 92(1), 151–155.

Appadurai, A. 1996, *Modernity at Large: Cultural Dimensions of Globalization.* Minneapolis: University of Minnesota Press

———. 2013. *The Future as Cultural Fact: Essays on the Global Condition.* New York: Verso.

Arendt, H. [1951] 1973. *The Origins of Totalitarianism.* New ed. New York: Harcourt Brace Jovanovich .

Arnold, P. 1977. *The Encyclopedia of Gambling: The Game, the Odds, the Techniques, the People and Places, the Myths and History.* Secaucus, NJ: Chartwell Books.

Arnone, A. 2008. "Journeys to Exile: The Constitution of Eritrean Identity through Narratives and Experiences." *Journal of Ethnic and Migration Studies* 34 (2): 325–40.

———. 2011. "Tourism and the Eritrean Diaspora." *Journal of Contemporary African Studies* 29 (4): 441–54.

Aronowitz, A. A. 2001. "Smuggling and Trafficking in Human Beings: The Phenomenon, the Market That Drive It and the Organisations That Promote It." *European Journal on Criminal Policy and Research* 9 (2): 163–95.

Associazione Giuridica per gli Studi sull'Immigrazione [ASGI; Association for Juridical Studies on Immigration]. 2012. *Il sistema Dublino e l'Italia: un rapporto in bilico.* www.asgi.it/card-regolamento-dublino/il-sistema-dublino-e-litalia-un-rapporto-in-bilico.

Avraham, S., and A. Kushner. 1986. *Treacherous Journey: My Escape from Ethiopia.* New York: Shapolsky.

Aziz, A., P. Monzini, and F. Pastore. 2015. "The Changing Dynamics of Cross-border Human Smuggling and Trafficking in the Mediterranean." Downloadable article. www.iai.it/sites/default/files/newmed_monzini.pdf. Rome: Istituto Affari Internazionali.

Baird, T. 2014. "Human Smuggling and Violence in the East Mediterranean." *International Journal of Migration, Health and Social Care* 10 (3): 121–33.

Bakewell, O. 2008. "Research beyond the Categories: The Importance of Policy Irrelevant Research into Forced Migration." *Journal of Refugee Studies* 21 (4): 432–53.

Bal, E., and R. Willems. 2014. "Introduction: Aspiring Migrants, Local Crises and the Imagination of Futures 'away from home.'" *Identities* 21 (3): 249–58.

Baldassar, L., and L. Merla. 2014. *Transnational Families, Migration and the Circulation of Care: Understanding Mobility and Absence in Family Life.* New York: Routledge

Ballard, R. 2005. "Remittances and Economic Development in India and Pakistan." In *Remittances: Development Impact and Future Prospects,* ed. Dilip Ratha and Samuel Munzele Maimbo, 103–18. Washington, DC: World Bank.

Barnard, A., and J. Spencer, eds. 1996. *Encyclopedia of Social and Cultural Anthropology.* New York: Taylor & Francis.

Barnett, H. G. 1938. "The Nature of the Potlatch." *American Anthropologist* 40 (3): 349–58.

Barnett, L. 2002. "Global Governance and the Evolution of the International Refugee Regime." *International Journal of Refugee Law* 14 (2–3): 238–62. https://doi.org/10.1093/ijrl/14.2_and_3.238.

Barnett, M. N., ed. 2017. *Paternalism beyond Borders.* New York: Cambridge University Press.

Bascom, J. B. 1989. "Social Differentiation among Eritrean Refugees in Eastern Sudan: The Case of Wad el Hileau." *Journal of Refugee Studies* 2 (4): 403–18.

———. 1990. "Border Pastoralism in Eastern Sudan." *Geographical Review,* 416–30.

Bauman, Z. [2003] 2004. *Wasted Lives: Modernity and Its Outcasts.* Oxford: Polity Press.

Becker, G. S., and K. M. Murphy. 1988. "A Theory of Rational Addiction." *Journal of Political Economy* 96 (4): 675–700.

Beck-Gernsheim, E. 2007. "Transnational Lives, Transnational Marriages: A Review of the Evidence from Migrant Communities in Europe." *Global Networks* 7 (3): 271–88.

Belloni, M. 2016a. "Refugees as Gamblers: Eritreans Seeking to Migrate through Italy." *Journal of Immigrant and Refugee Studies* 14 (1): 104–19.

———. 2016b. "'My uncle cannot say no if I reach Libya': Unpacking the Social Dynamics of Border-Crossing among Eritreans Heading to Europe." *Human Geography* (Bolton, MA) 9 (2): 47–56.

———. 2016c. "Learning How to Squat: Cooperation and Conflict between Refugees and Natives in Rome." *Journal of Refugee Studies* 29 (4): 506–27.

———. 2018a. "Becoming Unaccustomed to Home: Young Eritreans' Narratives about Estrangement, Belonging, and the Desire to Leave Home." In *Contested Belonging: Spaces, Practices, Biographies,* ed. Kathy Davis, Halleh Ghorashi, and Peer Smets, 161–74. Bingley, England: Emerald Publishing.

———. 2018b. "Refugees and Citizens: Understanding Eritrean Refugees' Ambivalence towards Homeland Politics." *International Journal of Comparative Sociology* 60 (1–2): 55–73. https://doi.org/10.1177%2F0020715218760382.

———. 2019a. "Family Project or Individual Choice? Exploring Agency in Young Eritreans' Migration." *Journal of Ethnic and Migration Studies,* 1–18. https://doi.org/10.1080/1369183X.2019.1584698

———. 2019b. "When the Phone Stops Ringing: On the Meanings and Causes of Disruptions in Communication between Eritrean Refugees and Their Families back Home." *Global Networks* 2 (2): 143–59. https://doi.org/10.1111/glob.12230.

BenEzer, G., and R. Zetter. 2014. "Searching for Directions: Conceptual and Methodological Challenges in Researching Refugee Journeys." *Journal of Refugee Studies* 28 (3): 297–318.

Bereketeab, R. 2002. "Supra-ethnic Nationalism: The Case of Eritrea." *African Sociological Review/Revue africaine de sociologie* 6 (2): 137–52.

———. 2010. "The Complex Roots of the Second Eritrea-Ethiopia War: Re-examining the Causes. *African Journal of International Affairs* 13 (1–3): 15–60.

Bergler, E. 1936. "On the Psychology of the Gambler." *American Imago* 22: 409–41.

Bernal, V. 2004. "Eritrea Goes Global: Reflections on Nationalism in a Transnational Era." *Cultural Anthropology* 19 (1): 3–25.

———. 2013. "Please Forget Democracy and Justice: Eritrean Politics and the Powers of Humor." *American Ethnologist* 40 (2): 300–309.

———. 2014. *Nation as Network: Diaspora, Cyberspace, and Citizenship.* Chicago: University of Chicago Press.

Betts, A. 2010. "Survival Migration: A New Protection Framework." *Global Governance: A Review of Multilateralism and International Organizations* 16 (3): 361–82.

Bezabeh, S. A. 2017. "Africa's Unholy Migrants: Mobility and Migrant Morality in the Age of Borders." *African Affairs* 116 (462): 1–17.

Bhungalia, L. 2012. "Im/Mobilities in a 'Hostile Territory': Managing the Red Line." *Geopolitics* 17 (2): 256–75.

Bisaillon, L., L. Montange, A. Zambenedetti, P. Frasca, L. El-Shamy, and T. Arviv. 2019. "Everyday Geographies, Geographies in the Everyday: Mundane of Mobilities Made Visible." *ACME: An International Journal of Critical Geographies.* In press.

Black, R. 2001. "Fifty Years of Refugee Studies: From Theory to Policy." *International Migration Review* 35 (1): 57–78.

Black, R., and M. Collyer. 2014. "'TRAPPED' POPULATIONS." In *Humanitarian Crises and Migration: Causes, Consequences and Responses,* ed. Susan Forbes Martin, Sanjula S. Weerasinghe, and Abbie Taylor, 287. London: Routledge.

Bleek, W. 1987. "Lying Informants: A Fieldwork Experience from Ghana." *Population and Development Review* 13 (2): 314–22.

Bloch, M., and J. P. Parry, eds. 1989. *Money and the Morality of Exchange.* Cambridge: Cambridge University Press.

Block, K., D. Warr, L. Gibbs, and E. Riggs. 2012. "Addressing Ethical and Methodological Challenges in Research with Refugee-Background Young People: Reflections from the Field." *Journal of Refugee Studies* 26 (1): 69–87.

Bø, B. P. 1998. "The Use of Visa Requirements as a Regulatory Instrument for the Restriction of Migration." In *Regulation of Migration: International Experiences,* ed. Anita Böcker, 191–202. Amsterdam: Het Spinhuis.

Boccagni, P. 2014. "What's in a (Migrant) House? Changing Domestic Spaces, the Negotiation of Belonging and Home-making in Ecuadorian Migration." *Housing, Theory and Society* 31 (3): 277–93.

———. 2016a. "Addressing Transnational Needs through Migration? An Inquiry into the Reach and Consequences of Migrants' Social Protection across Borders." *Global Social Policy* 17 (2): 168–87.

———. 2016b. "From the Multi-sited to the In-between: Ethnography as a Way of Delving into Migrants' Transnational Relationships." *International Journal of Social Research Methodology* 19 (1): 1–16.

Boccagni, P., and L. Baldassar. 2015. Emotions on the move: Mapping the emergent field of emotion and migration. Emotion, Space and Society, 16, 73–80.

Bookman, M. Z. 2002. *After Involuntary Migration: The Political Economy of Refugee Encampments.* Lanham, MD: Lexington Books.

Borneman, J., and A. Hammoudi, eds. 2009. *Being There: The Fieldwork Encounter and the Making of Truth.* Berkeley: University of California Press.

Bourgois, P., and N. Scheper-Hughes. 2004. "Introduction: Making Sense of Violence." In *Violence in War and Peace: An Anthology*, 1–31. Oxford: Blackwell.

Boyden, J., and J. de Berry, eds. 2004. *Children and Youth on the Front Line: Ethnography, Armed Conflict and Displacement*. London: Berghahn Books.

Bozzini, D. 2011. *En état de siège: Ethnographie de la mobilisation nationale et de la surveillance en Erythrée*. Neuchâtel: Université de Neuchâtel.

———. 2013. "The Catch-22 of Resistance: Jokes and the Political Imagination of Eritrean Conscripts." *Africa Today* 60 (2): 38–64.

Brahne [Berthane] Tewolde. 2008. *A Socio-Economic Analysis of Migration and Remittances in Eritrea*. Rome: Ganeditions.

Bredeloup, S., and O. Pliez. 2011. *The Libyan Migration Corridor*. European University Institute research report. http://cadmus.eui.eu/handle/1814/16213?show = full.

Brees, I. 2010. "Refugees and Transnationalism on the Thai–Burmese Border." *Global Networks* 10 (2): 282–99.

Brekke, J.-P., and G. Brochmann. 2014. "Stuck in Transit: Secondary Migration of Asylum Seekers in Europe, National Differences, and the Dublin Regulation." *Journal of Refugee Studies* 28 (2):145–62. http://dx.doi.org/10.1093/jrs/feu028.

Brigden, N., and C. Mainwaring. 2016. "Matryoshka Journeys: Im/mobility during Migration." *Geopolitics* 21 (2): 407–34.

Brubaker, R. 2013. "Categories of Analysis and Categories of Practice: A Note on the Study of Muslims in European Countries of Immigration." *Ethnic and Racial Studies* 36 (1): 1–8.

Brun, C. 2016. "There is no Future in Humanitarianism: Emergency, Temporality and Protracted Displacement." *History and Anthropology* 27 (4): 393–410.

Bryce-Laporte, R. S. 1972. "Black Immigrants: The Experience of Invisibility and Inequality." *Journal of Black Studies* 3 (1): 29–56.

Butzer, K. W. 1981. "Rise and Fall of Axum, Ethiopia: A Geo-archaeological Interpretation." *American Antiquity* 46 (3): 471–95.

Calvey, D. 2008. "The Art and Politics of Covert Research: Doing 'Situated Ethics' in the Field." *Sociology* 42 (5): 905–18.

Campbell, J. R. 2011. "The Enduring Problem of Statelessness in the Horn of Africa: How Nation-States and Western Courts (Re)Define Nationality." *International Journal of Refugee Law* 23 (4): 656–79.

Campomori, F. 2018. Criticità e contraddizioni delle politiche di ricezione dei richiedenti asilo in Italia. Social Policies, (3), 429–436.

Capalbo, G. 1982. "Indagine sui lavoratori eritrei a Roma." *Affari sociali internazionali* 10 (3): 61–71.

Caputo, P. 1983. "Il ghetto diffuso." In *L'immigrazione straniera a Milano*. Milan: Franco Angeli.

Carling, J. 2002. "Migration in the Age of Involuntary Immobility: Theoretical Reflections and Cape Verdean Experiences." *Journal of Ethnic and Migration Studies* 28 (1): 5–42.

———. 2007. "Unauthorized Migration from Africa to Spain." *International Migration* 45 (4): 3–37.

Carling, J., and F. Collins. 2018. "Aspiration, Desire and Drivers of Migration." *Journal of Ethnic and Migration Studies* 44 (6): 909–26

Carter, D. M. 2010. *Navigating the African Diaspora: The Anthropology of Invisibility*. Minneapolis: University of Minnesota Press.

Castles, S. 2003. "Towards a Sociology of Forced Migration and Social Transformation." *Sociology* 37 (1): 13–34.

——. 2004. "Why Migration Policies Fail." *Ethnic and Racial Studies* 27 (2): 205–27.

Castles, S., and N. van Hear. 2005. "The Migration-Asylum Nexus: Definition and Significance." Lecture at COMPAS, 27.

Charrière, F., and M. Frésia. 2008. *West Africa as a Migration and Protection Area.* Geneva: UN High Commissioner for Refugees [UNHCR]. www.refworld.org/docid/4a277db82. html.

Charsley, K., and M. Benson. 2012. "Marriages of Convenience, and Inconvenient Marriages: Regulating Spousal Migration to Britain." *Journal of Immigration, Asylum and Nationality Law* 26 (1): 10–26.

Chau, A. W., and J. G. Phillips. 1995. "Effects of Perceived Control upon Wagering and Attributions in Computer Blackjack." *Journal of General Psychology* 122 (3): 253–69.

Cheran, R. 2006. "Multiple Homes and Parallel Civil Societies: Refugee Diasporas and Transnationalism." *Refuge: Canada's Journal on Refugees* 23 (1): 4–8.

Chimni, B. S. 1998. "The Geopolitics of Refugee Studies: A View from the South." *Journal of Refugee Studies* 11 (4): 350–74.

——. 2009. "The Birth of a 'Discipline': From Refugee to Forced Migration Studies." *Journal of Refugee Studies* 22(1): 11–29.

Chin, K. 1999. *Smuggled Chinese: Clandestine Immigration to the United States.* Philadelphia: Temple University Press.

Christiansen, C., M. Utas, and H. Vigh. 2006. *Navigating Youth, Generating Adulthood: Social Becoming in an African Context.* Uppsala, Sweden: Nordiska Afrikainstitutet.

Chu, J. Y. 2010. *Cosmologies of Credit: Transnational Mobility and the Politics of Destination in China.* Durham, NC: Duke University Press.

Ciabarri, L. 2011. "Estroversione della società e produzione di un paesaggio diasporico: la transformazione dei luoghi di partenza nella migrazione somala." In *Migrazioni: dal lato dell'Africa,* ed. Alice Bellagamba, 103–26. Lungavilla, Pavia, Italy: Edizioni Altravista.

——. 2014. "Dynamics and Representations of Migration Corridors: The Rise and Fall of the Libya–Lampedusa Route and Forms of Mobility from the Horn of Africa (2000–2009)." *ACME: An International Journal for Critical Geographies* 13 (2): 246–62.

Cohen, J. H. 2004. *The Culture of Migration in Southern Mexico.* Austin: University of Texas Press.

Cohen, R., and G. Jónsson, eds. 2011. *Migration and Culture.* Cheltenham, England: Edward Elgar.

Coleman, S., and P. von Hellermann, eds. 2009. *Multi-sited Ethnography: Problems and Possibilities in the Translocation of Research Methods.* New York: Routledge.

Collins, R. 2014. *Interaction Ritual Chains.* Princeton, NJ: Princeton University Press.

Collyer, M. 2005. "When Do Social Networks Fail to Explain Migration? Accounting for the Movement of Algerian Asylum-Seekers to the UK." *Journal of Ethnic and Migration Studies* 31 (4): 699–718.

——. 2010. "Stranded Migrants and the Fragmented Journey." *Journal of Refugee Studies* 23 (3): 273–93.

Colombo, M. 2013. "Discourse and Politics of Migration in Italy: The Production and Reproduction of Ethnic Dominance and Exclusion." *Journal of Language and Politics* 12 (2): 157–79.

Comaroff, J., and Comaroff, J. L., eds. 1993. *Modernity and Its Malcontents: Ritual and Power in Postcolonial Africa.* Chicago: University of Chicago Press.

Condominas, G. 1973. "Ethnics and Comfort: An Ethnographer's View of His Profession." In AAA Annual Report, 1972: 1–17. Washington, DC: American Anthropological Association.

Connell, D. 2001. "Inside the EPLF: The Origins of the People's Party'& Its Role in the Liberation of Eritrea." *Review of African Political Economy* 28 (89): 345–64.

———. 2005. *Conversations with Eritrean Political Prisoners.* Trenton, NJ: Red Sea Press.

Conrad, B. 2006. "Out of the 'memory hole': Alternative Narratives of the Eritrean Revolution in the Diaspora." *Africa Spectrum* 41(2): 249–71.

Constable, N. 2003. *Romance on a Global Stage: Pen Pals, Virtual Ethnography, and Mail Order Marriages.* Berkeley: University of California Press.

———. 2009. "The Commodification of Intimacy: Marriage, Sex, and Reproductive Labor." *Annual Review of Anthropology* 38: 49–64.

Cook, J., J. Laidlaw, and J. Mair. 2009. "What If There Is No elephant? Towards a Conception of an Unsited Field." In *Multi-sited Ethnography: Theory, Praxis and Locality in Contemporary Research,* ed. Mark-Anthony Falzon, 47–72. Burlington, VT: Ashgate.

Costello, C. 2005. "The Asylum Procedures Directive and the Proliferation of Safe Country Practices: Deterrence, Deflection and the Dismantling of International Protection?" *European Journal of Migration and Law* 7 (1): 35–69.

Crawford, N., J. Cosgrave, S. Haysom, and N. Walicki. 2015. "Protracted Displacement: Uncertain Paths to Self-Reliance in Exile." London: ODI Humanitarian Policy Group. www.odi.org/publications/9906-protracted-displacement-uncertain-paths-self-reliance-exile.

Crawley, H., and D. Skleparis. 2018. "Refugees, Migrants, Neither, Both: Categorical Fetishism and the Politics of Bounding in Europe's 'migration crisis.'" *Journal of Ethnic and Migration Studies* 44 (1): 48–64.

Crawley, H. 2010. *Chance or Choice? Understanding Why Asylum Seekers Come to the UK.* London: Refugee Council.

Crawley, H., F. Düvell, K. Jones, S. McMahon, and N. Sigona. 2017. *Unravelling Europe's "migration crisis": Journeys over Land and Sea.* Bristol, England: Policy Press.

Crewe, L. 2000. "Geographies of Retailing and Consumption." *Progress in Human Geography* 24 (2): 275–90.

Crisp, J. 1999. *Policy Challenges of the New Diasporas: Migrant Networks and Their Impact on Asylum Flows and Regimes.* Geneva: UN High Commissioner for Refugees [UNHCR].

———. 2003. *No Solution in Sight: The Problem of Protracted Refugee Situations in Africa.* Center for Comparative Immigration Studies, Working Paper No.68.

Crisp, J., and K. Jacobsen. 1998. "Refugee Camps Reconsidered." *Forced Migration Review* 3 (12): 27–30.

Cupples, J. 2002. "The Field as a Landscape of Desire: Sex and Sexuality in Geographical Fieldwork." *Area* 34 (4): 382–90.

Cutolo, A. 2015. "Giovani, cadetti e vieux pères. Guerra e riproduzione sociale in Costa d'Avorio." *Antropologia*, n.s., 2 (1).

Cuttitta, P. 2014. "'Borderizing' the Island Setting and Narratives of the Lampedusa 'Border Play.'" *ACME: An International Journal for Critical Geographies* 13 (2): 196–219.

Daniel, E. V., and J. C. Knudsen, eds. 1995. *Mistrusting Refugees*. Berkeley: University of California Press.

Danish Refugee Council. 2013. *"We Risk Our Lives for Our Daily Bread"—Findings of the Danish Refugee Council Study of Mixed Migration in Libya*. www.refworld.org/docid/53158b7d4.html.

Daolio, A., ed. 1974. *Le lotte per la casa in Italia: Milano, Torino, Roma, Napoli*. Florence: Feltrinelli.

Day, K., and P. White. 2002. "Choice or Circumstance: The UK as the Location of Asylum Applications by Bosnian and Somali Refugees." *GeoJournal* 56 (1): 15–26.

De Genova, N. 2013. "'We are of the connections': Migration, Methodological Nationalism, and 'militant research.'" *Postcolonial Studies* 16 (3): 250–58.

De Genova, N., S. Mezzadra, and J. Pickles. 2015. "New Keywords: Migration and Borders." *Cultural Studies* 29 (1): 55–87.

De Haas, H. 2010. "Migration and Development: A Theoretical Perspective." *International Migration Review* 44 (1): 227–64.

———. 2011. "The Determinants of International Migration." International Migration Institute, Working Paper, 32.

De Regt, M. 2015. "Noura and Me: Friendship as Method in Times of Crisis." *Urban Anthropology and Studies of Cultural Systems and World Economic Development* 44 (1–2): 43–70.

De Voe, D. M. 1981. "Framing Refugees as Clients." *International Migration Review* 15 (1–2): 88–94.

DeWind, J. 2007. "Response to Hathaway." *Journal of Refugee Studies* 20 (3): 381–85.

Dekker, R., and G. Engbersen. 2014. "How Social Media Transform Migrant Networks and Facilitate Migration." *Global Networks* 14 (4): 401–18.

Del Rosario, T. C. 2005. "Bridal Diaspora Migration and Marriage among Filipino Women." *Indian Journal of Gender Studies* 12 (2–3): 253–73.

Di Nunzio, M. 2014. "Thugs, Spies and Vigilantes: Community Policing and Street Politics in Inner City Addis Ababa." *Africa* 84 (3): 444–65.

Dimitriadi, A. 2018. "Afghans in Greece: Transit, Immobility and Return." In Dimitriadi, *Irregular Afghan Migration to Europe*, 117–65. New York: Palgrave Macmillan.

Dolby, N. 2006. "Popular Culture and Public Space in Africa: The Possibilities of Cultural Citizenship." *African Studies Review* 49 (3): 31–47.

Doná, G. 2007. "The Microphysics of Participation in Refugee Research." *Journal of Refugee Studies* 20 (2).

Donham, D. L., and W. James, eds. 1986. *The Southern Marches of Imperial Ethiopia: Essays in History and Social Anthropology*. Cambridge: Cambridge University Press.

Doomernik, J., and D. J. Kyle, eds. 2004. *Organized Migrant Smuggling and State Control: Conceptual and Policy Challenges*. Edmonton, AB: Prairie Centre of Excellence for Research on Immigration and Integration, 2004. Special issue of the *Journal of International Migration and Integration* 5 (3): 265–384.

Dore, G. 2012. "Sui rituali funebri kunama. Alcuni testi inediti." *Ethnorêma* 8: 23–35.

Dorman, S. R. 2006. "Post-liberation Politics in Africa: Examining the Political Legacy of Struggle." *Third World Quarterly* 27 (6): 1085–1101.

Douglas, M. 1966. *Purity and Danger: An Analysis of Concepts of Pollution and Taboo.* London: Routledge & Kegan Paul, 1966.

———. 1992. *Risk and Blame: Essays in Cultural Theory.* London: Routledge.

Douglas, M., and A. Wildavsky. 1983. *Risk and Culture: An Essay on the Selection of Technological and Environmental Dangers.* Berkeley: University of California Press.

Driessen, H. 1998. "Romancing Rapport: The Ideology of Friendship in the Field." *Folk* 40: 123–36.

Dubisch J. 1995. "Lovers in the Field: Sex, Dominance, and the Female Anthropologist." In *Taboo: Sex, Identity and Erotic Subjectivity in Anthropological Fieldwork,* ed. D. Kulick and M. Willson, 34–50. New York: Routledge.

Durieux, J. F. 2009. "A Regime at a Loss?" *Forced Migration Review* 33: 60–61.

Durkheim, E. 1912. *Les formes élémentaires de la vie religieuse.* Paris: Presses universitaires de France.

Eggebø, H. 2013. "A Real Marriage? Applying for Marriage Migration to Norway." *Journal of Ethnic and Migration Studies* 39 (5): 773–89.

El Qorchi, M., S. M. Maimbo, and J. F. Wilson. 2003. *Informal Funds Transfer Systems: An Analysis of the Informal Hawala System.* Washington, DC: International Monetary Fund.

Elster, J. 2003. "Gambling and Addiction." In *High Culture: Reflections on Addiction and Modernity,* ed. Anna Alexander and Mark S. Roberts, 322. Albany: State University of New York Press.

Elster, J., and O. J. Skog. 1999. *Getting Hooked: Rationality and Addiction.* Cambridge: Cambridge University Press.

Erdal, M. B., and C. Oeppen. 2018. "Forced to Leave? The Discursive and Analytical Significance of Describing Migration as Forced and Voluntary." *Journal of Ethnic and Migration Studies* 44 (6): 981–98. https://doi.org /o.1080/1369183X.2017.1384149.

Essed, P., G. Frerks, and J. Schrijvers. 2004. *Refugees and the Transformation of Societies: Agency, Policies, Ethics, and Politics.* New York: Berghahn Books.

Etzold, B., M. Belloni, R. King, A. Kraler, and F. Pastore. 2019. "Transnational Figurations of Displacement: Conceptualising Protracted Displacement and Translocal Connectivity through a Process-Oriented Perspective." TRAFIG working paper 1/2019. Bonn: BICC [Internationales Konversionszentrum Bonn—Bonn International Center for Conversion].

European Council on Refugees and Exiles [ECRE]. 2013."Dublin II Regulation: Lives on Hold." European Comparative Report. www.refworld.org/docid/513ef9632.html.

Fabian, J. 1983. *Time and the Other: How Anthropology Makes Its Object.* New York: Columbia University Press.

———. 1998. *Moments of Freedom: Anthropology and Popular Culture.* Charlottesville: University Press of Virginia.

Faist, T. 2018. "The Moral Polity of Forced Migration." *Ethnic and Racial Studies* 41 (3): 412–23.

Falzon, M.-A., ed. 2009. *Multi-sited Ethnography: Theory, Praxis and Locality in Contemporary Research.* Burlington, VT: Ashgate.

Fassin, D. 2006. "La biopolitique n'est pas une politique de la vie." *Sociologie et sociétés* 38 (2): 35–48.

——. 2013. "Why Ethnography Matters: On Anthropology and Its Publics." *Cultural Anthropology* 28 (4): 621–46.

——, ed. 2017. *If Truth Be Told: The Politics of Public Ethnography.* Durham, NC: Duke University Press.

Fassin, D., and R. Rechtman. 2009. *The Empire of Trauma: An Inquiry into the Condition of Victimhood.* Princeton, NJ: Princeton University Press.

Ferguson, J. G. 2006. *Global Shadows: Africa in the Neoliberal World Order.* Durham, NC: Duke University Press.

——. 2013. "Cosmologies of Welfare: Two Conceptions of Social Assistance in Contemporary South Africa." In *Radical Egalitarianism: Local Realities, Global Relations,* ed. Felicity Aulino, Miriam Goheen, and Stanley J. Tambiah. New York: Fordham University Press.

Fessehatzion, T. 2005. "Eritrea's Remittance-Based Economy: Conjectures and Musings." *Eritrean Studies Review* 4 (2).

Feyissa, D., and M. V. Hoehne, eds. 2010. *Borders and Borderlands as Resources in the Horn of Africa.* Rochester, NY: James Currey.

FitzGerald, D. 2006. "Towards a Theoretical Ethnography of Migration." *Qualitative Sociology* 29 (1): 1–24.

FitzGerald, D. S., and Arar, R. 2018. "The sociology of refugee migration." *Annual Review of Sociology* 44: 387–406.

Fontanari, E. 2017. "Afterword. An ethnographic gaze on power and refugees." *Etnografia e ricerca qualitativa* 10 (1): 143–58.

Fortier, A. M. 1996. "The Use of Personal Experiences as Sources of Knowledge." *Critique of Anthropology* 16 (3): 303–23.

Foster, M. 2007. *International Refugee Law and Socio-economic Rights: Refuge from Deprivation.* New York: Cambridge University Press.

Fuglerud, Ø. 2001. "Time and Space in the Sri Lanka–Tamil Diaspora." *Nations and Nationalism* 7 (2): 195–213.

Fullin, G. 2011. "Tra disoccupazione e declassamento professionale: la condizione degli stranieri nel mercato del lavoro italiano." *Mondi migranti,* no. 1: 195–228. https://doi.org/10.3280/MM2011-001010.

Fusari, V. 2011. "Dinamiche etnodemografiche all'interno dello spazio geopolitico eritreo." PhD diss., Università di Siena

Gaibazzi, P. 2012. "'God's time is the best': Religious Imagination and the Wait for Emigration in The Gambia." In *The Global Horizon: Expectations of Migration in Africa and the Middle East,* ed. K. Graw and J. S. Schielke, 121–36. Leuven: Leuven University Press.

Gallagher, A. 2001. "Human Rights and the New UN Protocols on Trafficking and Migrant Smuggling: A Preliminary Analysis." *Human Rights Quarterly* 23 (4): 975–1004.

Gallo, E. 2009. "The Unwelcome Ethnographer, or What 'Our' People (May) Think of Multisited Research." In *Multi-sited Ethnography: Theory, Praxis and Locality in Contemporary Research,* ed. M. A. Falzon, 62–80. London: Routledge.

Gammeltoft-Hansen, T., and N. N. Sørensen, eds. 2013. *The Migration Industry and the Commercialization of International Migration.* New York: Routledge.

Gaonkar, D. P. 2002. Toward new imaginaries: An introduction. Public Culture, 14(1), 1–19.

Gardner, K. 1995. *Global Migrants, Local Lives: Travel and Transformation in Rural Bangladesh: Travel and Transformation in Rural Bangladesh.* Oxford: Oxford University Press.

Gastaldi, F. 2013. "Immigrazione straniera a Genova: dalla concentrazione nel centro storico a nuove geografie insediative." *Mondi migranti*, no 2: 73–89. https: doi.org//10.3280/MM2013-002005.

Gatrell, P. 2013. *The Making of the Modern Refugee.* Oxford: Oxford University Press.

Gay y Blasco, P., and L. de la Cruz Hernández. 2012. "Friendship, Anthropology." *Anthropology and Humanism* 37 (1): 1–14.

Gerver, M. 2015, "Why the EU Should Consider Decriminalising People Smuggling." London School of Economics and Political Science, EUROPP [European Politics and Policy] blog. http://bit.ly/1Kdcvg8.

Getahun, S. A. 2007. *The History of Ethiopian Immigrants and Refugees in America, 1900–2000: Patterns of Migration, Survival, and Adjustment.* New York: LFB Scholarly Publishing.

Giddens, A. 2013. *The Transformation of Intimacy: Sexuality, Love and Eroticism in Modern Societies.* New York: Wiley.

Gilkes, P. 1991. "Eritrea: Historiography and Mythology." *African Affairs* 90 (361): 623–28.

Glasius, M., M. de Lange, J. Bartman, E. Dalmasso, A. Lv, A. Del Sordi, M. Michaelsen, and K. Ruijgrok. 2017. *Research, Ethics and Risk in the Authoritarian Field.* New York: Palgrave Macmillan.

Glesne, C. 1989. "Rapport and Friendship in Ethnographic Research." *International Journal of Qualitative Studies in Education* 2 (1): 45–54.

Goedde, P. 2013. "Global Cultures." In *Global Interdependence: The World after 1945*, ed. A. Iriye and J. Osterhammel, 537–678. Vol. 6 of *A History of the World.* Cambridge, MA: Belknap Press of Harvard University Press.

Goffman, E. 1959. *The Presentation of Self in Everyday Life.* New York: Doubleday.

Goffman, A. 2014. *On the Run: Fugitive Life in an American City.* Chicago: University of Chicago Press.

Goodwin-Gill, G. S. 1992. "Safe Country? Says Who?" *International Journal of Refugee Law* 4 (2): 248–50.

Goodwin-Gill, G. S., and J. McAdam. 1996. *The Refugee in International Law.* Oxford: Clarendon Press.

Grabska, K. 2010. "Lost boys, invisible girls: stories of Sudanese marriages across borders." *Gender, Place & Culture* 17 (4): 479–497.

Grabska, K., M. De Regt and N. Del Franco N. 2018. *Adolescent Girls' Migration in The Global South.* Cham: Palgrave MacMillan.

Grabska, K., and M. Fanjoy. 2015. " 'And when I become a man': Translocal Coping with Precariousness and Uncertainty among Returnee Men in South Sudan." *Social Analysis* 59 (1): 76–95.

Green, G., R. S. Barbour, M. Barnard, and J. Kitzinger. 1993. " 'Who wears the trousers?': Sexual Harassment in Research Settings." *Women's Studies International Forum* 16 (6): 627–37.

Griffiths, M., and R. Wood. 2001. "The Psychology of Lottery Gambling." *International Gambling Studies* 1 (1): 27–45.

Hage, G. 2009. *Waiting.* Melbourne: Melbourne University Press.

Hahn, H. P., & Klute, G. 2007. *Cultures of migration: African perspectives*. Münster: LIT Verlag.

Hammar, T. 1995. "Development and Immobility: Why Have Not Many More Emigrants Left the South." In *Causes of International Migration: Proceedings of a Workshop, Luxembourg, 14–16 December 1994*, 173–86. Luxembourg: Office for Official Publications of the European Communities.

Hammar, T., G. Brochmann, K. Tamas, and T. Faist. 1997. *International Migration Immobility and Development: Multidisciplinary Perspectives*. New York: Berg.

Hammond, L. 2004. "Tigrayan Returnees Notions of Home: Five Variations on a Theme." In *Homecomings: Unsettling Paths of Return*, 1: 36–53. Oxford: Lexington Books.

Hannaford, D. 2015. "Technologies of the Spouse: Intimate Surveillance in Senegalese Transnational Marriages. *Global Networks* 15 (1): 43–59.

Harney, N. 2013. "Precarity, Affect and Problem Solving with Mobile Phones by Asylum Seekers, Refugees and Migrants in Naples, Italy." *Journal of Refugee Studies* 26 (4): 541–57. doi: 10.1093/jrs/feto17.

Harrell-Bond, B., and E. Voutira. 2007. "In Search of 'invisible' Actors: Barriers to Access in Refugee Research." *Journal of Refugee Studies* 20 (2): 281–98.

Harrell-Bond, B., E. Voutira, and M. Leopold. 1992. "Counting the Refugees: Gifts, Givers, Patrons and Clients." *Journal of Refugee Studies* 5 (3–4): 205–25.

Hathaway, J. C. 2007. "Forced Migration Studies: Could We Agree Just to 'Date'?" *Journal of Refugee Studies* 20 (3): 349–69.

Haugen, H. Ø. 2012. "Nigerians in China: A Second State of Immobility." *International Migration* 50 (2): 65–80.

Havinga, T., and A. Böcker. 1999. "Country of Asylum by Choice or by Chance: Asylum-Seekers in Belgium, the Netherlands and the UK." *Journal of Ethnic and Migration Studies* 25 (1): 43–61.

Hayenhjelm, M. 2006. "Out of the Ashes: Hope and Vulnerability as Explanatory Factors in Individual Risk Taking." *Journal of Risk Research* 9 (3): 189–204.

Hedru, D. 2003. "Eritrea: Transition to Dictatorship, 1991–2003." *Review of African Political Economy*, 30 (97): 435–44.

Hein, C., ed. 2001. *Rifugiati: vent'anni di storia del diritto d'asilo in Italia*. Rome: Donzelli Editore.

Hepner T. R. 2009. *Soldiers, Martyrs, Traitors and Exiles: Political Conflict in Eritrea and the Diaspora*. Philadelphia: University of Pennsylvania Press.

———. 2015. "Generation Nationalism and Generation Asylum: Eritrean Migrants, the Global Diaspora, and the Transnational Nation-State." *Diaspora: A Journal of Transnational Studies* 18 (1): 184–207.

Hernández Carretero, M. 2008. "Risk-Taking in Unauthorised Migration." MA thesis, University of Oslo.

Hernández-Carretero, M., and J. Carling. 2012. "Beyond 'Kamikaze migrants': Risk Taking in West African Boat Migration to Europe." *Human Organization* 71 (4): 407–16.

Herring, M., and T. Bledsoe. 1994. "A Model of Lottery Participation." *Policy Studies Journal* 22 (2): 245–57.

Hirt, N. 2015. "The Eritrean Diaspora and Its Impact on Regime Stability: Responses to the Imposition of UN Sanctions." *African Affairs* 144 (454): 115–35.

Hirt, N., and A. S. Mohammad. 2013. "'Dreams don't come true in Eritrea': Anomie and Family Disintegration Due to the Structural Militarisation of Society." *Journal of Modern African Studies* 51 (1): 139–68.

———. 2017. "By Way of Patriotism, Coercion, or Instrumentalization: How the Eritrean Regime Makes Use of the Diaspora to Stabilize Its Rule." *Globalizations* 15 (2): 232–47.

Hodgson, D. 1999. "Critical Interventions: Dilemmas of Accountability in Contemporary Ethnographic Research." *Identities* 6 (2–3): 201–24.

Holmes, S. M. 2013. "'Is it worth risking your life?' Ethnography, Risk and Death on the US–Mexico Border." *Social Science and Medicine* 99 (July): 153–61.

Holmes, S. M., and H. Castañeda. 2016. "Representing the 'European refugee crisis' in Germany and Beyond: Deservingness and Difference, Life and Death." *American Ethnologist* 43 (1): 12–24.

Honwana, A. M. 2012. *The Time of Youth: Work, Social Change, and Politics in Africa.* Sterling, VA: Kumarian Press.

Horst, C. 2006. "Buufis amongst Somalis in Dadaab: The Transnational and Historical Logics behind Resettlement Dreams." *Journal of Refugee Studies* 19 (2): 143–57.

Howell, S., ed. 2005. *The Ethnography of Moralities.* London: Routledge.

Hugman, R., E. Pittaway, and L. Bartolomei. 2011. "When 'Do no harm' Is Not Enough: The Ethics of Research with Refugees and Other Vulnerable Groups." *British Journal of Social Work* 41 (7): 1271–87.

Human Rights Watch (HRW). 2009. *Service for Life: State Repression and Indefinite Conscription in Eritrea.* www.hrw.org/report/2009/04/16/service-life/state-repression-and-indefinite-conscription-eritrea.

Humphris, R. 2013. *Refugees and the Rashaida: Human Smuggling and Trafficking from Eritrea to Sudan and Egypt.* Geneva: UN High Commissioner for Refugees [UNHCR], Policy Development and Evaluation Service.

Hyndman, J. 1997. "Border Crossings." *Antipode* 29 (2): 149–76.

———. 2012. "The Geopolitics of Migration and Mobility." *Geopolitics* 17 (2): 243–55.

Hyndman, J., and W. Giles. 2000. *Managing Displacement: Refugees and the Politics of Humanitarianism.* Minneapolis: University of Minnesota Press.

———. 2011. "Waiting for What? The Feminization of Asylum in Protracted Situations." *Gender, Place & Culture* 18 (3): 361–79.

———. 2017. *Refugees in Extended Exile: Living on the Edge.* London: Routledge.

Hynes, P. 2003. *The Issue of "trust" or "mistrust" in Research with Refugees: Choices, Caveats and Considerations for Researchers.* UNHCR Working Paper No. 98. www.unhcr.org/3fcb5cee1.html.

İçduygu, A., and S. Toktas. 2002. "How Do Smuggling and Trafficking Operate via Irregular Border Crossings in the Middle East? Evidence from Fieldwork in Turkey." *International Migration* 40 (6): 25–54.

Indira, M., and P. Vijayalakshmi. 2015. "Gender Matters: Eritrean Women and Mediated Messages of Foreign Television Channel." *Journal of Mass Communication & Journalism* 5 (242): 2.

Infantino, F. 2014. "Bordering 'fake' Marriages? The Everyday Practices of Control at the Consulates of Belgium, France and Italy in Casablanca." *Etnografia e ricerca qualitativa* 7 (1): 27–48.

International Crisis Group. 2014. "Eritrea: Ending the Exodus?" *Africa Briefing* 100 (August 8). https://d2071andvipowj.cloudfront.net/eritrea-ending-the-exodus.pdf.

Iselin, B., and M. Adams. 2003. *Distinguishing between Human Trafficking and People Smuggling.* UN Office on Drugs and Crime, Regional Centre for East Asia and the Pacific, Bangkok. www.embraceni.org/wp-content/uploads/2006/06/Distinguishing[1]1.pdf.

Ismail, A. A. 2007. "Lawlessness and Economic Governance: The Case of [the] *Hawala* System in Somalia." *International Journal of Development Issues* 6 (2): 168–85.

Iyob, R. 1995. *The Eritrean Struggle for Independence: Domination, Resistance, Nationalism, 1941–1993.* Cambridge: Cambridge University Press.

———. 2000. "The Ethiopian–Eritrean Conflict: Diasporic vs. Hegemonic States in the Horn of Africa, 1991–2000." *Journal of Modern African Studies* 38 (4): 659–82.

Jackson, P., M. Rowlands, and D. Miller. 2005. *Shopping, Place and Identity.* London: Routledge.

Jacobs, B. A. 2006. "The Case for Dangerous Fieldwork." In *The SAGE Handbook of Fieldwork*, ed. D. Hobbs and R. Wright, 157–68. Thousand Oaks, CA: Sage Publications.

Jacobsen, K. 2006. "Refugees and Asylum Seekers in Urban Areas: A Livelihoods Perspective." *Journal of Refugee Studies* 19 (3): 273–86.

Jacobsen, K., and Landau, L. B. 2003. "The Dual Imperative in Refugee Research: Some Methodological and Ethical Considerations in Social Science Research on Forced Migration." *Disasters* 27 (3): 185–206.

Jacquin-Berdal, D., and M. Plaut. 2005. *Unfinished Business: Ethiopia and Eritrea at War.* Trenton, NJ: Red Sea Press.

Jankowiak, W. R., and E. F. Fischer. 1992. "A Cross-cultural Perspective on Romantic Love." *Ethnology* 31 (2): 149–55.

Jansen, S. 2009. "After the Red Passport: Towards an Anthropology of the Everyday Geopolitics of Entrapment in the EU's 'immediate outside.'" *Journal of the Royal Anthropological Institute* 15 (4): 815–32.

Jasanoff, S., and S. H. Kim. 2015. Dreamscapes of modernity: Sociotechnical imaginaries and the fabrication of power. Chicago: University of Chicago Press.

Jourdan, L. 2012. "Sono l'uomo giusto nel posto e nel momento sbagliato: storia di un rifugiato eritreo a Kampala (Uganda)." *Antropologia* 9 (14): 259–75.

Kahneman, D., and A. Tversky. 1979. "Prospect Theory: An Analysis of Decision under Risk." *Econometrica: Journal of the Econometric Society* 47 (2): 263–91.

Kahsay, W. 2003. "Pastoralism in Eritrea: Herder Responses to Climatic Stress." *African Geographical Review* 22 (1): 15–28.

Kandel, W., and D. S. Massey. 2002. "The Culture of Mexican Migration: A Theoretical and Empirical Analysis." *Social Forces* 80 (3): 981–1004.

Karadawi, A. (1987). "The Problem of Urban Refugees in Sudan." In *Refugees: A Third World Dilemma*, ed. J. R. Rogge. Totowa, NJ: Rowman & Littlefield.

Khan, N. 2016. "Immobility." In *Keywords of Mobility: Critical Engagements,* ed. N. B. Salazar and K. Jayaram. Oxford: Berghahn Books.

Kibreab, G. 1987. *Refugees and Development in Africa: The Case of Eritrea.* Trenton, NJ: Red Sea Press.

———. 1995. "Eritrean Women Refugees in Khartoum, Sudan, 1970–1990." *Journal of Refugee Studies* 8 (1): 1–25.

———. 1996. "Eritrean and Ethiopian Urban Refugees in Khartoum: What the Eye Refuses to See." *African Studies Review* 39 (3): 131–78.

———. 2000. "Resistance, Displacement, and Identity: The Case of Eritrean Refugees in Sudan." *Canadian Journal of African Studies/La Revue canadienne des études africaines* 34 (2): 249–96.

———. 2003a. "Displacement, Host Governments' Policies, and Constraints on the Construction of Sustainable Livelihoods." *International Social Science Journal* 55 (175): 57–67.

———. 2004. "Pulling the Wool over the Eyes of the Strangers: Refugee Deceit and Trickery in Institutionalized Settings." *Journal of Refugee Studies* 17 (1): 1–26.

———. 2009. "Forced Labour in Eritrea." *Journal of Modern African Studies* 47 (1): 41–72.

Khosravi, S. 2010. *"Illegal" Traveller: An Auto-ethnography of Borders.* New York: Palgrave Macmillan.

Kifleyesus, A. 2012. "Women Who Migrate, Men Who Wait: Eritrean Labor Migration to the Arab Near East." *Northeast African Studies* 12 (1): 95–127.

Kleist, N., and S. Jansen. 2016. "Introduction: Hope over Time—Crisis, Immobility and Future-Making." *History and Anthropology* 27 (4): 373–92.

Kloß, S. T. 2017. "Sexual(ized) Harassment and Ethnographic Fieldwork: A Silenced Aspect of Social Research." *Ethnography* 18 (3): 396–414.

Kok, W. 1989. "Self-settled Refugees and the Socio-Economic Impact of Their Presence on Kassala, Eastern Sudan." *Journal of Refugee Studies* 2 (4): 419–40.

Konseiga, A. 2007. "Household Migration Decisions as Survival Strategy: The Case of Burkina Faso." *Journal of African Economies* 16 (2): 198–233.

Korac, M. 2003. "Integration and How We Facilitate it A Comparative Study of the Settlement Experiences of Refugees in Italy and the Netherlands." *Sociology* 37 (1): 51–68.

Koser, K., and C. Pinkerton. 2002. *The Social Networks of Asylum Seekers and the Dissemination of Information about Countries of Asylum.* London: Home Office, Research, Development and Statistics Directorate.

Kourula, P. 1997. *Broadening the Edges: Refugee Definition and International Protection Revisited.* London: Martinus Nijhoff.

Kovats-Bernat, J.C. 2002. "Negotiating Dangerous Fields: Pragmatic Strategies for Fieldwork amid Violence and Terror." *American Anthropologist* 104 (1): 208–222.

Kulick, D., and M. Willson, eds. 2003. *Taboo: Sex, Identity and Erotic Subjectivity in Anthropological Fieldwork.* New York: Routledge.

Kunz, E. F. 1973. "The Refugee in Flight: Kinetic Models and Forms of Displacement." *International Migration Review* 7 (2): 125–46.

Kyle, D., and J. Dale. 2001. "Smuggling the State Back In: Agents of Human Smuggling Reconsidered." In *Global Human Smuggling: Comparative Perspectives,* ed. Kyle and Rey Koslowski, 29–57. Baltimore: Johns Hopkins University Press.

Lange, C., Z. Kamalkhani, and L. Baldassar. 2007. "Afghan Hazara Refugees in Australia: Constructing Australian Citizens. *Social Identities* 13 (1): 31–50.

Larkin, B. 1997. "Indian Films and Nigerian Lovers: Media and the Creation of Parallel Modernities." *Africa* 67 (3): 406–40.

Lauby, J., and Stark, O. 1988. "Individual Migration as a Family Strategy: Young Women in the Philippines." *Population Studies* 42 (3): 473–86.

Lems, A., Oester, K., & Strasser, S. 2019. Children of the crisis: ethnographic perspectives on unaccompanied refugee youth in and en route to Europe. The Journal of Ethnic and Migration Studies. 1–21.

Levitt, P. 1998. Social Remittances: A Local-Level, Migration-Driven Form of Social Diffusion." *International Migration Review* 32 (124): 926–49.

Levitt, P., and N. Glick Schiller. 2004. "Conceptualizing Simultaneity: A Transnational Social Field Perspective on Society." *International Migration Review* 38 (3): 1002–39.

Levitt, P., J. Viterna, A. Mueller, and C. Lloyd. 2017. "Transnational Social Protection: Setting the Agenda." *Oxford Development Studies* 45 (1): 2–19.

Lijnders, L., and Robinson, S. 2013. "From the Horn of Africa to the Middle East: Human Trafficking of Eritrean Asylum Seekers across Borders." *Anti-Trafficking Review,* no. 2: 137–54.

Lindholm, C. 2006. "Romantic Love and Anthropology." *Etnofoor* 19 (1): 5–21.

Lindley, A. 2009a. "Between 'dirty money' and 'development capital': Somali Money Transfer Infrastructure under Global Scrutiny. *African Affairs* 108 (433): 519–39.

———. 2009b. "The Early-Morning Phone Call: Remittances from a Refugee Diaspora Perspective." *Journal of Ethnic and Migration Studies* 35 (8): 1315–34.

———. 2010. "Between Suspicion and Celebration: The Somali Money Transfers Business." *Development Viewpoint*, no. 45 (January).

———. ed. 2014. *Crisis and Migrations: Critical Perspectives*. London: Routledge.

Lindley, A., and N. van Hear. 2007. *New Europeans on the Move: A Preliminary Review of the Onward Migration of Refugees within the European Union.* COMPAS Working Paper No. 57. Oxford: Centre on Migration, Policy and Society.

Lopez, S. L. 2010. "The Remittance House: Architecture of Migration in Rural Mexico." *Buildings and Landscapes: Journal of the Vernacular Architecture Forum* 17 (2): 33–52.

Lubkemann, S. C. 2005. "Migratory Coping in Wartime Mozambique: An Anthropology of Violence and Displacement in 'fragmented wars.'" *Journal of Peace Research* 42 (4): 493–508.

———. 2008. "Involuntary Immobility: On a Theoretical Invisibility in Forced Migration Studies. *Journal of Refugee Studies* 21 (4): 454–75.

———. 2010. *Culture in Chaos: An Anthropology of the Social Condition in War.* Chicago: University of Chicago Press.

Lucht, H. 2011. *Darkness before daybreak: African migrants Living on the Margins in Southern Italy Today.* Berkeley: University of California Press.

Luhmann, N. 1987. "The Morality of Risk and the Risk of Morality." *International Review of Sociology* 1 (3): 87–101.

Lupton, D. 1999. *Risk and Sociocultural Theory: New Directions and Perspectives.* Cambridge: Cambridge University Press.

Lussier, D. 1997. "Local Prohibitions, Memory and Political Judgement among the Kunama: An Eritrean Case Study." In *Ethiopia in Broader Perspective: Papers of the 13th International Conference of Ethiopian Studies,* ed. K. Fukui et al., 2:441. Kyoto: Shokado Book Sellers.

Lutterbeck, D. 2013. "Across the Desert, across the Sea: Migrant Smuggling into and from Libya." In *Migration, Security, and Citizenship in the Middle East: New Perspectives,* ed. P. Seeberg and Z. Eyadat, 137–66. New York: Palgrave Macmillan.

Lyons, T. 2009. "The Ethiopia–Eritrea Conflict and the Search for Peace in the Horn of Africa." *Review of African Political Economy* 36 (120): 167–80.

Mackenzie, C., C. McDowell, and E. Pittaway. 2007. "Beyond 'do no harm': The Challenge of Constructing Ethical Relationships in Refugee Research." *Journal of Refugee Studies* 20 (2): 299–319.

Madianou, M., and D. Miller. 2013. *Migration and New Media: Transnational Families and Polymedia.* London: Routledge.

Maffesoli, M. [1988] 1995. *The Time of the Tribes: The Decline of Individualism in Mass Society.* London: Sage.

Mahmood, C. K. 2002. "Anthropological Compulsions in a World in Crisis." *Anthropology Today* 18 (3): 1–2.

Mai, N., and R. King. 2009. "Love, Sexuality and Migration: Mapping the Issue (s)." *Mobilities* 4 (3): 295–307.

Maimbo, S. M., and N. Passas. 2004. "The Regulation and Supervision of Informal Remittance Systems." *Small Enterprise Development* 15 (1): 53–61.

Malinowski, B. 1920. "Kula: The Circulating Exchange of Valuables in the Archipelagoes of Eastern New Guinea." *Man* 20: 97–105.

Malkki, Liisa H. 1992. "National Geographic: The Rooting of Peoples and the Territorialization of National Identity among Scholars and Refugees." *Cultural Anthropology* 7 (1): 24–44.

———. 1995. *Purity and Exile: Violence, Memory, and National Cosmology among Hutu Refugees in Tanzania.* Chicago: University of Chicago Press.

Majidi, N. 2018. "Community Dimensios of Smuggling: The Case of Afghanistan and Somalia." *Annals of the American Academy of Political and Social Science* 676 (1): 97–113.

Manocchi, M. 2012. *Richiedenti asilo e rifugiati politici: percorsi di ricostruzione identitaria: il caso torinese.* Milano: Franco Angeli.

Marchetti, C. 2014. "Rifugiati e migranti forzati in Italia: il pendolo tra 'emergenza' e 'sistema.'" *Revista interdisciplinar da mobilidade humana* 22 (43): 53–70.

Marchetti, S. 2011. *Le ragazze di Asmara: lavoro domestico e migrazione postcoloniale.* Rome: Ediesse.

———. 2014. *Black Girls: Migrant Domestic Workers and Colonial Legacies.* Leiden: Brill.

Marcus, G. E. 1995. "Ethnography in/of the World System: The Emergence of Multi-Sited Ethnography." *Annual Review of Anthropology* 24 (1): 95–117.

Markakis, J. 1988. "The Nationalist Revolution in Eritrea." *Journal of Modern African Studies* 26 (1): 51–70.

Marras, S. 2009. "Falsi rifugiati? Pratiche di etichettamento di richiedenti asilo alla frontiera." *Mondi migranti*, 3: 79–97. https://doi:10.3280/MM2009-003005.

Martinez, T. M. 1983. *The Gambling Scene: Why People Gamble.* Springfield, IL: Charles C. Thomas.

Massa, A. 2016. Learning not to ask: Some methodological implications of studying Eritrean refugees in Ethiopia. Zeitschrift für Ethnologie, 257–280.

Massey, D. S., J. Arango, G. Hugo, A. Kouaouci, and A. Pellegrino. 1999. *Worlds in Motion: Understanding International Migration at the End of the Millennium.* Oxford: Clarendon Press.

Mathews, G. 2011. *Ghetto at the Center of the World: Chungking Mansions.* Chicago: University of Chicago Press/

Matsouka, A., and J. Sorenson. 1999. "Eritrean Women in Canada: Negotiating New Lives." *Canadian Woman Studies* 19 (3): 104–9.

Matzke, C. 2002. "Comrades in Arts and Arms." *Matatu* 25 (1): 21–54.

———. 2004. "Shakespeare and Surgery in the Eritrean Liberation Struggle: Performance Culture in Orota." *Journal of Eritrean Studies* [Asmara] 3 (1): 26–40.

Mauss, M. [1926] 1950. "Effet physique chez l'individu de l'idée de mort suggérée par la collectivité." In id., *Sociologie et Anthropologie,* 313–32. Paris: Presses universitaires de France.

Mbembe, A., and S. Nuttall. 2004. "Writing the World from an African Metropolis." *Public Culture* 16 (3): 347–72.

Mbembe, A., and J. Roitman. 1995. "Figures of the Subject in Times of Crisis." *Public Culture* 7 (2): 323–52.

McAdam, J. 2014. "The Concept of Crisis Migration." *Forced Migration Review* 45: 10–11.

McAuliffe M.L. and F. Laczko (eds.) (2016), Migrant Smuggling Data and Research: A global review of the emerging evidence base, IOM: Geneva."

McKenzie, S., and C. Menjívar. 2011. "The Meanings of Migration, Remittances and Gifts: Views of Honduran Women Who Stay." *Global Networks* 11 (1): 63–81.

McLaughlin, R.H., and T. Alfaro-Velcamp. 2015. "The Vulnerability of Immigrants in Research: Enhancing Protocol Development and Ethics Review." *Journal of Academic Ethics* 13 (1): 27–43.

McMahon, S., and N. Sigona. 2016. *Boat Migration across the Central Mediterranean: Drivers, Experiences and Responses. Unravelling the Mediterranean Migration Crisis.* MEDMIG Research Brief no. 3. www.medmig.info/wp-content/uploads/2017/02/research-brief-03-Boat-migration-across-the-Central-Mediterranean.pdf.

McSpadden, L.A., and H. Moussa. 1993. "I Have a Name: The Gender Dynamics in Asylum and in Resettlement of Ethiopian and Eritrean Refugees in North America." *Journal of Refugee Studies* 6 (3): 203–25.

Mekonnen, D.R., and M. Estefanos. 2011. "From Sawa to the Sinai Desert: The Eritrean Tragedy of Human Trafficking." Available at SSRN 2055303. https://dx.doi.org/10.2139/ssrn.2055303.

Melotti, U. 1988. *Dal terzo mondo in Italia.* Milan: Centro Studi Terzo Mondo.

Merton, R.K. 1938. "Social Structure and Anomie." *American Sociological Review* 3 (5): 672–82.

Mezzadra, S. 2010. "The Gaze of Autonomy: Capitalism, Migration and Social Struggles." In *The Contested Politics of Mobility,* ed. Vicki Squire, 141–62. London: Routledge.

———. 2015. "The Proliferation of Borders and the Right to Escape." In *The Irregularization of Migration in Contemporary Europe: Detention, Deportation, Drowning,* ed. Y. Jansen, R. Celikates, and J. de Bloois, 121–35. New York: Rowman & Littlefield International.

Mezzadra, S., and Neilson, B. 2013. *Border as Method, or, the Multiplication of Labor.* Durham, NC: Duke University Press.

Miller, K.E. 2004. "Beyond the Frontstage: Trust, Access, and the Relational Context in Research with Refugee Communities." *American Journal of Community Psychology* 33 (3–4): 217–27.

Moberg, K.K. 2008. "Extending Refugee Definitions to Cover Environmentally Displaced Persons Displaces Necessary Protection." *Iowa Law Review* 94: 1107.

Mohammad, A. S. 2013. *The Saho of Eritrea: Ethnic Identity and National Consciousness* . Münster: LIT.

Monsutti, A. 2007. "Migration as a Rite of Passage: Young Afghans Building Masculinity and Adulthood in Iran." *Iranian Studies* 40 (2): 167–85.

——. 2008. "Afghan Migratory Strategies and the Three Solutions to the Refugee Problem." *Refugee Survey Quarterly* 27 (1): 58–73.

Monzini, P. 2007. "Sea-Border Crossings: The Organization of Irregular Migration to Italy." *Mediterranean Politics* 12 (2): 163–84.

——. 2011. "Recent Arrivals of Migrants and Asylum Seekers by Sea to Italy: Problems and Reactions." *Elcano Newsletter,* no. 77: 7.

Moret, J., S. Baglioni, and D. Efionayi-Mäder. 2006. *The Path of Somali Refugees into Exile: A Comparative Analysis of Secondary Movements and Policy Responses.* Neuchâtel, Switzerland: Swiss Forum for Migration and Population Studies.

Mottura, G., and G. Altieri. 1992. *L'arcipelago immigrazione: caratteristiche e modelli migratori dei lavoratori stranieri in Italia.* Rome: Ediesse.

Muller, T. R. 2008. "Bare Life and the Developmental State: Implications of the Militarisation of Higher Education in Eritrea." *Journal of Modern African Studies* 46 (1): 111–31.

——. 2012. From rebel governance to state consolidation–Dynamics of loyalty and the securitisation of the state in Eritrea. Geoforum, 43(4), 793–803.

Nadel, S. F. 1944. *Races and Tribes of Eritrea.* Asmara, Eritrea: British Military Administration.

Naty, A. 2002a. "Environment, Society and the State in Western Eritrea." *Africa* 72 (4): 569–97.

——. 2002b. "The Discourse on Culture and Development in Eritrea." *Journal of Eritrean Studies* 1 (1): 86–95.

Nyers, P. 2006. *Rethinking Refugees: Beyond State of Emergency.* New York: Routledge.

Negash, T. 1987. *Italian Colonialism in Eritrea, 1882–1941: Policies, Praxis and Impact.* Stockholm: Uppsala University.

Negash, T., and K. Tronvoll. 2000. *Brothers at War: Making Sense of the Eritrean-Ethiopian War.* Oxford: James Currey.

Neumayer, E. 2005. "Bogus Refugees? The Determinants of Asylum Migration to Western Europe." *International Studies Quarterly* 49 (3): 389–410.

——. 2006. "Unequal Access to Foreign Spaces: How States Use Visa Restrictions to Regulate Mobility in a Globalized World." *Transactions of the Institute of British Geographers* 31 (1): 72–84.

Newton, E. 1993. "My Best Informant's Dress: The Erotic Equation in Fieldwork." *Cultural Anthropology* 8 (1): 3–23.

"Nieuwenhuys, C., & Pécoud, A. 2007. Human trafficking, information campaigns, and strategies of migration control. American Behavioral Scientist, 50(12), 1674–1695.

Nordstrom, C., and A. C. Robben, eds. 1995. *Fieldwork under fire: Contemporary Studies of Violence and Survival.* Berkeley: University of California Press.

Nowicka, E. 2012. "Friendship in Anthropological Fieldwork: Some Ethical Doubts." *Lud* 96: 109–22.

Núñez, G., and J. Heyman. 2007. "Entrapment Processes and Immigrant Communities in a Time of Heightened Border Vigilance." *Human Organization* 66 (4): 354–65.

O'Connel Davidson, J. 2013. "Troubling Freedom: Migration, Debt, and Modern Slavery." *Migration Studies* 1 (2): 176–95.

Oelgemöller, C. 2011. "'Transit' and 'Suspension': Migration Management or the Metamorphosis of Asylum-Seekers into 'Illegal' Immigrants." *Journal of Ethnic and Migration Studies* 37 (3): 407–24.

O'Kane, D. 2012. "Limits to State-Led Nation-Building? An Eritrean Village Responds Selectively to the Plans of the Eritrean Government." *Studies in Ethnicity and Nationalism* 12 (2): 309–25.

O'Kane, D., and T. M. Redeker Hepner, eds. 2009. *Biopolitics, Militarism, and Development: Eritrea in the Twenty-First Century.* New York: Berghahn Books.

Pærregaard, K. 2002. "The Resonance of Fieldwork: Ethnographers, Informants and the Creation of Anthropological Knowledge." *Social Anthropology* 10 (3): 319–34.

Pajo, E. 2007. *International Migration, Social Demotion, and Imagined Advancement: An Ethnography of Socioglobal Mobility.* New York: Springer.

Palm, A. 2017. "The Italy-Libya Memorandum of Understanding: The Baseline of a Policy Approach Aimed at Closing All Doors to Europe?" http://eumigrationlawblog.eu/the-italy-libya-memorandum-of-understanding-the-baseline-of-a-policy-approach-aimed-at-closing-all-doors-to-europe.

Palriwala, R., and P. Uberoi. 2008. *Marriage, Migration and Gender.* New Delhi: SAGE Publications.

Palumbo, P., ed. 2003. *A Place in the Sun: Africa in Italian Colonial Culture from Post-Unification to the Present.* Berkeley: University of California Press.

Panagakos, A. N., and H. A. Horst. 2006. "Return to Cyberia: Technology and the Social Worlds of Transnational Migrants. *Global Networks* 6 (2): 109–24.

Pankhurst, R. 1992. *A Social History of Ethiopia: The Northern and Central Highlands from Early Medieval Times to the Rise of Emperor Téwodros II.* Trenton, NJ: Red Sea Press.

———. 1997. *The Ethiopian Borderlands: Essays in Regional History from Ancient Times to the End of the 18th Century.* Trenton, NJ: Red Sea Press.

Paoletti, E. 2011. "Power Relations and International Migration: The Case of Italy and Libya." *Political Studies* 59 (2): 269–89.

Papadimitriou, P N., and I. F. Papageorgiou. 2005. "The New 'Dubliners': Implementation of European Council Regulation 343/2003 (Dublin-II) by the Greek Authorities." *Journal of Refugee Studies* 18 (3): 299–318.

Papadopoulou, A. 2003. "'Give us asylum and help us leave the country!': Kurdish Asylum Seekers in Greece and the Politics of Reception." *Immigrants and Minorities* 22 (2–3): 346–61.

Pascal, B. [1670] 1999. *Pensées and Other Writings.* Oxford: Oxford University Press.

Paspalanova, M. 2008. "Undocumented vs. Illegal Migrant: Towards Terminological Coherence." *Migraciones internacionales* 4 (3): 79–90.

Pastore, F. 2019. "Not so Global. Not so Compact. Reflections of the Shitstorm Surrounding the Global Compact for Migration." *IAI Commentaries* 19 (02): 1–4. www.fieri.it/wp-content/uploads/2019/01/f.pastore-jan2019-iaicom1902.pdf.

Pastore, F., P. Monzini, and G. Sciortino. 2006. "Schengen's Soft Underbelly? Irregular Migration and Human Smuggling across Land and Sea Borders to Italy." *International Migration* 44 (4): 95–119.

Pateman, R. 1998. *Eritrea: Even the Stones Are Burning.* Trenton, NJ: Red Sea Press.

Patterson, O. 1982. *Slavery and Social Death.* Cambridge, MA: Harvard University Press.

Pearson, A. L., & Paige, S. B. 2012. Experiences and ethics of mindful reciprocity while conducting research in Sub-Saharan Africa. African Geographical Review, 31(1), 72–75.

Pécoud, A. 2010. "Informing Migrants to Manage Migration? An Analysis of IOM's Information Campaigns." In *The Politics of International Migration Management,* ed. id. and M. Geiger, 184–201. New York: Palgrave Macmillan.

Pedraza, S. 1991. "Women and Migration: The Social Consequences of Gender." *Annual Review of Sociology* 17: 303–25.

Perrotta, D. C. 2011. *Vite in cantiere: migrazione e lavoro dei rumeni in Italia.* Bologna: Il mulino.

Peter, K. B. 2010. Transnational Family Ties, Remittance Motives, and Social Death among Congolese Migrants: A Socio-Anthropological Analysis." *Journal of Comparative Family Studies* 41 (2): 225–43.

Phuong, C. 2005. "The Removal of Failed Asylum Seekers." *Legal Studies* 25 (1): 117–41.

Piot, C. 1999. *Remotely Global: Village Modernity in West Africa.* Chicago: University of Chicago Press.

Pittaway, E., and L. Bartolomei. 2013. "Doing Ethical Research: 'Whose problem is it anyway?'" In *Values and Vulnerabilities: The Ethics of Research with Refugees and Asylum Seekers,* ed. K. Block et al., 151.Toowong, Queensland: Australian Academic Press.

Pittaway, E., L. Bartolomei, and R. Hugman. 2010. "'Stop stealing our stories': The Ethics of Research with Vulnerable Groups." *Journal of Human Rights Practice* 2 (2): 229–51.

Plaut, M. 2005. "The Eritrea Opposition Moves Towards Unity." *Review of African Political Economy* 32 (106): 638–43.

Polanyi, K. [1944] 1968. *The Great Transformation: The Political and Economic Origins of Our Time.* Foreword by Robert M. MacIver. Boston, MA: Beacon Press.

Pollera, A. 1935. *Le popolazioni indigene dell'Eritrea.* Bologna: Licinio Cappelli.

Pool, D. 2001. *From Guerrillas to Government: The Eritrean People's Liberation Front.* Oxford: James Currey.

Poole, A. 2013. "Ransoms, Remittances, and Refugees: The Gatekeeper State in Eritrea." *Africa Today* 60 (2): 66–82.

Porter, G., K. Hampshire, A. Abane, E. Robson, A. Munthali, M. Mashiri, and A. Tanle. 2010. "Moving Young Lives: Mobility, Immobility and Inter-generational Tensions in Urban Africa." *Geoforum* 41 (5): 796–804.

Powers, W. K. 1987. "Cosmology and the Reinvention of Culture: The Lakota Case." *Canadian Journal of Native Studies* 7 (2): 165–80.

Prins, F. E., and H. Lewis. 1992. "Bushmen as Mediators in Nguni Cosmology." *Ethnology* 31 (2): 133–47.

Puggioni, R. 2005. "Refugees, Institutional Invisibility, and Self-Help Strategies: Evaluating Kurdish Experience in Rome." *Journal of Refugee Studies* 18 (3): 319–39.

Pussetti, C. 2005. *Poetica delle emozioni: i Bijagó della Guinea Bissau.* Rome: GLF editori Laterza.

Quassoli, F. 2004. "Making the Neighbourhood Safer: Social Alarm, Police Practices and Immigrant Exclusion in Italy." *Journal of Ethnic and Migration Studies* 30 (6): 1163–81.

Raghallaigh, M. N. 2014. "The Causes of Mistrust amongst Asylum Seekers and Refugees: Insights from Research with Unaccompanied Asylum-Seeking Minors Living in the Republic of Ireland." *Journal of Refugee Studies* 27 (1): 82–100.

Reichert, J. 1981. "The Migrant Syndrome: Seasonal US Wage Labor and Rural Development in Central Mexico." *Human Organization* 40 (1): 56–66.

Reid, R. 2003. "Old Problems in New Conflicts: Some Observations on Eritrea and Its Relations with Tigray, from Liberation Struggle to Inter-state War. *Africa* 73 (3): 369–401.

———. 2005. "Caught in the Headlights of History: Eritrea, the EPLF and the Post-War Nation-State." *Journal of Modern African Studies* 43 (3): 467–88.

———. 2006. "War and Remembrance: Orality, Literacy and Conflict in the Horn." *Journal of African Cultural Studies* 18 (1): 89–103.

———. 2007. "The Trans-Mereb Experience: Perceptions of the Historical Relationship between Eritrea and Ethiopia." *Journal of Eastern African Studies* 1 (2): 238–55.

Richmond, A. H. 1993. "Reactive Migration: Sociological Perspectives on Refugee Movements. *Journal of Refugee Studies* 6 (1): 7–24.

Riggan, J. 2009. "Avoiding Wastage by Making Soldiers." In *Biopolitics, Militarism, and Development: Eritrea in the 21st Century,* ed. D. O'Kane and T. M. Redeker Hepner, 72–91. New York: Berghahn Books.

———. 2013. "Imagining Emigration: Debating National Duty in Eritrean Classrooms." *Africa Today* 60 (2): 85–106.

Robins, S., and N. Scheper-Hughes. 1996. "On the Call for a Militant Anthropology: The Complexity of 'Doing the Right Thing.'" *Current Anthropology* 37 (2): 341–46.

Robinson, V., and J. Segrott. 2002. *Understanding the Decision-making of Asylum Seekers.* London: Home Office.

Rogers, P. 1998. "The Cognitive Psychology of Lottery Gambling: A Theoretical Review." *Journal of Gambling Studies* 14 (2): 111–34.

Rose, G. 2003. "Family Photographs and Domestic Spacings: A Case Study." *Transactions of the Institute of British Geographers* 28 (1) 5–18.

Rosecrance, J. D. 1988. *Gambling without Guilt: The Legitimation of an American Pastime.* Pacific Grove, CA: Brooks/Cole Publishing.

Ryo, E. 2013. "Deciding to Cross Norms and Economics of Unauthorized Migration." *American Sociological Review* 78 (4): 574–603.

Sabar, G., and R. Posner. 2013. Remembering the past and constructing the future over a communal plate: Restaurants established by African asylum seekers in Tel Aviv. Food, Culture & Society, 16(2), 197–222.

Sahlins, M. 1994. "Cosmologies of Capitalism: The Trans-Pacific Sector of 'The World System.'" In *Culture/Power/History: A Reader in Contemporary Social Theory,* ed. N. B. Dirks, G. Eley, and S. B. Ortner, 412–55. Princeton, NJ: Princeton University Press.

Salamone, F. A. 1977. "The Methodological Significance of the Lying Informant." *Anthropological Quarterly* 50 (3): 117–24.

Salazar, N. B. 2011. "The Power of Imagination in Transnational Mobilities." *Identities* 18 (6): 576–98.

Sales, R. 2002. "The Deserving and the Undeserving? Refugees, Asylum Seekers and Welfare in Britain." *Critical Social Policy* 22 (3): 456–78.

Salt, J. 2000. "Trafficking and Human Smuggling: A European Perspective." *International Migration* 38 (3): 31–56.

Salt, J., and J. Stein. 1997. "Migration as a Business: The Case of Trafficking." *International Migration* 35 (4): 467–94.

Samuel Hall Consulting. 2014. *Living out of Camp: Alternatives to Camp-based Assistance for Eritrean Refugees in Ethiopia.* http://samuelhall.org/wp-content/uploads/2014/05/Living-Out-of-Camp-Alternative-to-Camp-based-Assistance-in-Ethiopia.pdf.

Sanchez, G. 2017. "Beyond the Matrix of Oppression: Reframing Human Smuggling through Instersectionality-Informed Approaches." *Theoretical Criminology* 21 (1): 46–56.

Sayad, A. 2000. *La double absence: des illusions de l'émigré aux souffrances de l'immigré.* Paris: Seuil.

Scalzo, F. 1984. "Stranieri in Italia: la comunità eritrea e marocchina nell'area romana attraverso racconti biografici." *Dossier Europa Emigrazione* 9.

Schaeffer, E. C. 2008. "Remittances and Reputations in Hawala Money-Transfer Systems: Self-Enforcing Exchange on an International Scale." *Journal of Private Enterprise* 24 (1): 95.

Schapendonk, J., 2008. "Stuck between the Desert and the Sea: The Immobility of Sub-Saharan African 'Transit Migrants' in Morocco." In *Rethinking Global Migration: Practices, Policies and Discourses in the European Neighbourhood*, ed. H. Rittersberger-Tiliç, A. Erdemir, and A. Ergun, 129–43. Ankara: KORA, METU & Zeplin Iletisim Hizm.

———. 2012. "Migrants' Im/mobilities on Their Way to the EU: Lost in Transit?" *Tijdschrift voor economische en sociale geografie* 103 (5): 577–83.

———2012. "Turbulent Trajectories: African Migrants on their Way to the European Union." *Societies* 2 (2): 27–41.

Schapendonk, J., I. van Liempt, I. Schwarz, and G. Steel. 2018. "Re-routing Migration Geographies: Migrants, Trajectories and Mobility Regimes." *Geoforum*. DOI: 10.1016/j.geoforum.2018.06.007.

Scheper-Hughes, N. 1995. "The Primacy of the Ethical: Propositions for a Militant Anthropology." *Current Anthropology* 36 (3): 409–40.

———. 2004. "Parts Unknown: Undercover Ethnography of the Organs-Trafficking Underworld." *Ethnography* 5 (1): 29–73.

———. 2009. "The Ethics of Engaged Ethnography: Applying a Militant Anthropology in Organs-Trafficking Research." *Anthropology News* 50 (6): 13–14.

Schuster, L. 2005. "The Continuing Mobility of Migrants in Italy: Shifting between Places and Statuses." *Journal of Ethnic and Migration Studies* 31 (4): 757–74.

———. 2011. "Dublin II and Eurodac: Examining the (Un)intended(?) Consequences." *Gender, Place and Culture* 18 (3): 401–16.

Seymour-Smith, C. 1986. *Dictionary of Anthropology.* Boston: G. K. Hall.

Sharma, N. 2003. "Travel Agency: A Critique of Anti-trafficking Campaigns." *Refuge: Canada's Journal on Refugees* 21 (3): 53–65.

Sharp, G., and E. Kremer. 2006. "The Safety Dance: Confronting Harassment, Intimidation, and Violence in the Field." *Sociological Methodology* 36 (1): 317–27.

Shaw, A. 2001. "Kinship, Cultural Preference and Immigration: Consanguineous Marriage among British Pakistanis." *Journal of the Royal Anthropological Institute* 7 (2): 315–34.

Shaw, A., and K. Charsley. 2006. "Rishtas: Adding Emotion to Strategy in Understanding British Pakistani Transnational Marriages." *Global Networks* 6 (4): 405–21.

Sheridan, L. M. 2009. *"I know it's dangerous": Why Mexicans Risk Their Lives to Cross the Border.* Tucson: University of Arizona Press.

Shuman, A., and C. Bohmer. 2004. "Representing Trauma: Political Asylum Narrative." *Journal of American Folklore* 117 (466): 394–414.

Sidorenko, O. F. 2007. *The Common European Asylum System: Background, Current State of Affairs, Future Direction.* Cambridge: Cambridge University Press.

Sigona, N. 2014. "The Politics of Refugee Voices: Representations, Narratives, and Memories." In *The Oxford Handbook of Refugee and Forced Migration Studies,* ed. E. Fiddian-Qasmiyeh, G. Loescher, K. Long, and N. Sigona. Oxford: Oxford University Press

Sistema di protezione per richiedenti asilo e rifugiati [SPRAR]. 2012–13. *Rapporto annuale.* www.cittalia.it/images/file/atlante_sprar_completo_2012_2013.pdf.

Slovic, P. 1987. "Perception of Risk." *Science* 236 (4799): 280–85. www.heatherlench.com/wp-content/uploads/2008/07/slovic.pdf.

Small, I. V. 2012. "'Over There' Imaginative Displacements in Vietnamese Remittance Gift Economies." *Journal of Vietnamese Studies* 7 (3): 157–83.

Smidt, W. G. 2010. "The Tigrinnya-Speakers across the Borders." In *Borders and Borderlands as Resources in the Horn of Africa,* ed. D. Feyissa and M. V. Hoehne, 61–85. Rochester, NY: James Currey.

Smith, J. F., 1984. "Gambling as Play." *Annals of the American Academy of Political and Social Science* 474 (1): 122–32.

Smith, L., and V. Mazzucato. 2009. "Constructing Homes, Building Relationships: Migrant Investments in Houses." *Tijdschrift voor economische en sociale geografie* 100 (5): 662–73.

Smock, D. R. 1982. "Eritrean refugees in the Sudan." *Journal of Modern African Studies* 20 (3): 451–65.

Sorenson, J. 1990. "Opposition, Exile and Identity: The Eritrean Case." *Journal of Refugee Studies* 3 (4): 298–319.

———. 1991. "Discourses on Eritrean Nationalism and Identity." *Journal of Modern African Studies* 29 (2): 301–17.

Spener, D. 2001. "Smuggling Migrants through South Texas: Challenges Posed by Operation Rio Grande." In *Global Human Smuggling: Comparative Perspectives,* ed. D. Kyle and R. Koslowski, 129–65. Baltimore: Johns Hopkins University Press.

———. 2004. "Mexican Migrant-Smuggling: A Cross-Border Cottage Industry." *Journal of International Migration and Integration/Revue de l'intégration et de la migration internationale* 5 (3): 295–320.

———. 2009. *Some Reflections on the Language of Clandestine Migration on the Mexico-U.S. Border.* Paper presented June 11, 2009, at the 28th International Congress of the Latin American Studies Association, Rio de Janeiro. http://faculty.trinity.edu/dspener/clandestinecrossings/related%20articles/spener%20lasa%202009%20final.pdf.

———. 2011. "Global Apartheid, *Coyotaje,* and the Discourse of Clandestine Migration." In *Global Human Smuggling: Comparative Perspectives,* ed. D. Kyle and R. Koslowski, 157–85. Baltimore: Johns Hopkins University Press.

Spicker, P. 2011. "Ethical Covert Research." *Sociology* 45 (1): 118–33.

Stark, O., and Bloom, D. E. 1985. "The New Economics of Labor Migration." *American Economic Review* 75 (2): 173–78.

Stein, B. N. 1981. "The Refugee Experience: Defining the Parameters of a Field of Study." *International Migration Review* 15 (1–2): 320–30.

Steinhilper, E. and R. Gruijters. 2017. "Border Deaths in the Mediterranean: What We Can Learn from the Latest Data." www.law.ox.ac.uk/research-subject-groups/centre-criminology/centreborder-criminologies/blog/2017/03/border-deaths.

Stoll, D. 2010. "From Wage Migration to Debt Migration? Easy Credit, Failure in El Norte, and Foreclosure in a Bubble Economy of the Western Guatemalan Highlands." *Latin American Perspectives* 37 (1): 123–42.

Tambiah, S. 1985. *Culture, Thought and Social Action: An Anthropological Perspective.* Cambridge, MA: Harvard University Press.

Taylor, J. 2011. "The Intimate Insider: Negotiating the Ethics of Friendship When Doing Insider Research." *Qualitative Research* 11 (1): 3–22.

Tazanu, P. M. 2015. "On the Liveness of Mobile Phone Mediation: Youth Expectations of Remittances and Narratives of Discontent in the Cameroonian Transnational Family." *Mobile Media and Communication* 3 (1): 20–35.

Tazzioli, M. 2015. "Which Europe? Migrants' Uneven Geographies and Counter-mapping at the Limits of Representation. MOVEMENTS: *Journal for Critical Migration and Border Regime Studies* 1 (2).

Tekalign Ayalew, M. 2018. "Refugees Protections from Below: Smuggling in the Eritrea-Ethiopia Context." *Annals of the American Academy of Political and Social Science* 676 (1): 57–76.

Thielemann, E. R. 2004. *Does Policy Matter? On Governments' Attempts to Control Unwanted Migration.* Working Paper 112. UC San Diego Center for Comparative Immigration Studies. http://escholarship.org/uc/item/5jt5v2sw.

Thiollet, H. 2007. *Refugees and Migrants from Eritrea to the Arab World: The Cases of Sudan, Yemen and Saudi Arabia, 1991–2007.* Paper prepared for the Forced Migration and Refugee Studies Program, American University in Cairo, Egypt.

———. 2011. "Migration as Diplomacy: Labor Migrants, Refugees, and Arab Regional Politics in the Oil-Rich Countries." *International Labor and Working-Class History* 79 (1): 103–21.

Ticktin, M. 2006. "Where Ethics and Politics Meet: The Violence of Humanitarianism in France." *American Ethnologist* 33 (1): 33–49.

Tiemoko, R. 2004. "Migration, Return and Socio-economic Change in West Africa: The role of Family." *Population, Space and Place* 10 (2): 155–74.

Tillmann-Healy, L. M. 2003. "Friendship as Method." *Qualitative Inquiry* 9 (5): 729–49.

Timmerman, C. 2008. "Marriage in a 'culture of migration': Emirdag Marrying into Flanders." *European Review* 16 (4): 585–94.

Tolia-Kelly, D. P. 2004. "Materializing Post-Colonial Geographies: Examining the Textural Landscapes of Migration in the South Asian Home." *Geoforum* 35 (6): 675–88.

Toma, S., and E. Castagnone. 2015. "What Drives Onward Mobility within Europe? The Case of Senegalese Migration between France, Italy and Spain." *Population* (English ed.) 70 (1): 65–94.

Treiber, M. 2009. "Trapped in Adolescence: The Post-War Urban Generation." In *Biopolitics, Militarism, and Development: Eritrea in the Twenty-First Century,* ed. D. O'Kane and T. M. Redeker Hepner, 92–114. New York: Berghahn Books.

———. 2010. "The Choice between Clean and Dirty: Discourses of Aesthetics, Morality and Progress in Post-revolutionary Asmara, Eritrea." In *Urban Pollution. Cultural Meanings, Social Practices,* ed. E. Dürr and R. Jaffe, 123–43. New York: Berghahn Books.

———. 2013. "Lessons for Life: Two Migratory Portraits from Eritrea." In *Long Journeys: African Migrants on the Road*, ed. A. Triulzi and R. L. McKenzie, 187–212. Leiden: Brill.

———. 2015. "Informality and Informalization among Eritrean Refugees: Why Migration Does Not Provide a Lesson in Democracy." In *Transitional Justice and Peace Building in Turbulent Regions: Handbook of Research*, ed. H. Quehl and F. Cante, 157–79. Hershey, PA: IGI Global.

Triandafyllidou, A., and Maroukis, T. 2012. *Migrant Smuggling: Irregular Migration from Asia and Africa to Europe*. New York: Palgrave Macmillan.

Triulzi, A. 2006. Displacing the colonial event: Hybrid memories of postcolonial Italy. interventions, 8(3), 430–443.

Tronvoll, K. 1998. *Mai Weini, a Highland Village in Eritrea: A Study of the People, Their Livelihood, and Land Tenure during Times of Turbulence*. Trenton, NJ: Red Sea Press.

———. 2000. "*Meret Shehena*, 'Brothers' Land': S. F. Nadel's *Land Tenure on the Eritrean Plateau* Revisited." *Africa* 70 (4): 595–613.

Tronvoll, K., and D. R. Mekonnen. 2014. *The African Garrison State: Human Rights and Political Development in Eritrea*. Woodbridge, Suffolk, England: Boydell & Brewer.

Turner, V. [1961] 1969. *The Ritual Process: Structure and Anti-structure*. Chicago: Aldine.

Turton, D. 1996. "Migrants and Refugees: A Mursi Case Study." In *In Search of Cool Ground: War, Flight & Homecoming in Northeast Africa*, ed. T. Allen, 96–110. Trenton, NJ: Africa World Press.

UNHCR [Office of the United Nations High Commissioner for Refugees]. UNHCR 2016. *Global Trends: Forced Displacement in 2015*. Geneva: UNHCR. www.unhcr.org/statistics/unhcrstats/576408cd7/unhcr-global-trends-2015.html.

———. 2017. *Desperate Journeys: Refugees and Migrants Entering and Crossing Europe via the Mediterranean and Western Balkans Routes*. https://data2.unhcr.org/en/documents/download/57696.

———2019. *Global Trends: Forced Displacement in 2018*. Geneva: UNHCR.

UN Office on Drugs and Crime. 2010. *The Globalization of Crime: A Transnational Organized Crime Threat Assessment*. Vienna: Office on Drugs and Crime.

Vacchiano, F. 2012. "Giovani in movimento: soggettività e aspirazioni globali a sud del Mediterraneo." *Afriche e Orienti* 14 (3–4): 98–110.

van Gennep, A. 1960. *The Rites of Passage*. Chicago: University of Chicago Press.

van Hear, N. 2006. "'I went as far as my money would take me': Conflict, Forced Migration and Class." In *Forced Migration and Global Processes: A View from Forced Migration Studies*, ed. F. Crépeau et al., 125–58. Lanham, MD: Lexington Books

———. 2011. "Forcing the Issue: Migration Crises and the Uneasy Dialogue between Refugee Research and Policy." *Journal of Refugee Studies* 25 (1): 2–24.

van Heelsum, A. 2017. "Aspirations and Frustrations: Experiences of Recent Refugees in the Netherlands." *Journal of Ethnic and Racial Studies* 40 (13): 1–14.

van Liempt, I. 2011. "'And then one day they all moved to Leicester': The Relocation of Somalis from the Netherlands to the UK Explained." *Population, Space and Place* 17 (3): 254–66.

———. 2016. *A Critical Insight into Europe´s Criminalisation of Human Smuggling*. Swedish Institute for European Policy Studies (SIEPS) policy paper.

van Liempt, I., and J. Doomernik. 2006. "Migrant's Agency in the Smuggling Process: The Perspectives of Smuggled Migrants in the Netherlands." *International Migration* 44 (4): 165–90.

van Reisen, M., M. Estefanos, and C. Rijken. 2012. *Human Trafficking in the Sinai: Refugees between Life and Death.* Oisterwijk, Netherlands: Wolf Legal Publishers.

Vaughan, S., and K. Tronvoll. 2003. *The Culture of Power in Contemporary Ethiopian Political Life.* Stockholm: Swedish International Development Cooperation Agency.

Velayutham, S., and A. Wise. 2005. "Moral Economies of a Translocal Village: Obligation and Shame among South Indian Transnational Migrants." *Global Networks* 5 (1): 27–47.

Vereni, P. 2016. "Cosmopolitismi liminari. Strategie di identità e categorizzazione tra cultura e classe nelle occupazioni a scopo abitativo a Roma." *Anuac* 4 (2): 130–56.

Vigh, H. 2006. "Social Death and Violent Life Chances." In *Navigating Youth, Generating Adulthood: Social Becoming in an African Context,* ed. C. Christiansen, M. Utas, and H. Vigh, 31–60. Uppsala, Sweden: Nordiska afrikainstitutet.

———. 2008. "Crisis and Chronicity: Anthropological Perspectives on Continuous Conflict and Decline." *Ethnos* 73 (1): 5–24.

———. 2009. "Wayward Migration: On Imagined Futures and Technological Voids." *Ethnos: Technologies of the Imagination* 74, no. 1: S. 91–109.

von Scheve, C., and S. Ismer. 2013. "Towards a Theory of Collective Emotions." *Emotion Review* 5 (4): 406–13.

Voutira, E., and B. Harrell-Bond. 1995. "In Search of the Locus of Trust: The Social World of the Refugee Camp." In *Mistrusting Refugees,* ed. E. V. Daniel and J. C. Knudsen, 207–24. Berkeley: University of California Press.

Wagenaar, W. A. 1988. *Paradoxes of Gambling Behaviour.* London: Lawrence Erlbaum Associates.

Walaardt, T. 2013. "From Heroes to Vulnerable Victims: Labelling Christian Turks as Genuine Refugees in the 1970s." *Ethnic and Racial Studies* 36 (7): 1199–1218.

Wang, H. Z., and S. M. Chang. 2002. "The Commodification of International Marriages: Cross-border Marriage Business in Taiwan and Viet Nam." *International Migration* 40 (6): 93–116.

Watanabe, J. M. 1983. "In the World of the Sun: A Cognitive Model of Mayan Cosmology." *Man,* 710–28.

Waterston, A., ed. 2008. *An Anthropology of War: Views from the Frontline.* Oxford: Berghahn Books.

Weaver, J. L. 1985. "Sojourners along the Nile: Ethiopian Refugees in Khartoum." *Journal of Modern African Studies* 23 (1): 147–56.

Webb, S., and J. Burrows. 2009. *Organised Immigration Crime: A Post-conviction Study.* London: Home Office.

Wilding, R. 2006. "'Virtual' Intimacies? Families Communicating across Transnational Contexts." *Global Networks* 6 (2): 125–42.

Wilson, W. P. 1998. "The Deportation of Eritreans from Ethiopia: Human Rights Violations Tolerated by the International Community." *North Carolina Journal of International Law and Commercial Regulation* 24 (2): 451.

Winchester, H. P. M., and P. E. White. 1988. "The Location of Marginalised Groups in the Inner City." *Environment and Planning D: Society and Space* 6 (1): 37–54.

Woldegabriel, B. 1996. "Eritrean Refugees in Sudan." *Review of African Political Economy* 23 (67): 87–92

Woldemikael, T. M. 1993. "The Cultural Construction of Eritrean Nationalist Movements." In *The Rising Tide of Cultural Pluralism: The Nation-State at Bay,* ed. C. Young, 179–99, Madison: University of Wisconsin Press.

———. 2009. "Pitfalls of Nationalism in Eritrea." In *Biopolitics, Militarism and Development: Eritrea in the Twenty-First Century,* ed. David O'Kane and T. M. Redeker Hepner, 1–16. New York: Berghahn Books.

Yohannes, O. 1987. "The Eritrean Question: A Colonial Case?" *Journal of Modern African Studies* 25 (4): 643–68.

Zampagni, F. 2016. "Unpacking the Schengen Visa Regime: A Study on Bureaucrats and Discretion in an Italian Consulate." *Journal of Borderlands Studies* 31 (2): 251–66.

Zetter, R. 1988. "Refugees and Refugee Studies—A Label and an Agenda." *Journal of Refugee Studies* 1 (1): 1–6.

———. 1991. "Labelling Refugees: Forming and Transforming a Bureaucratic Identity." *Journal of Refugee Studies* 4 (1): 39–62.

———. 2011. *Protecting Environmentally Displaced People: Developing the Capacity of Legal and Normative Frameworks.* Research report. Refugee Studies Centre, Oxford University. www.refworld.org/pdfid/4da579792.pdf.

Zewde B. 1991. *A History of Modern Ethiopia. 1855–1991.* Oxford: James Currey.

Zhang, S., and K. L. Chin. 2002. "Enter the Dragon: Inside Chinese Human Smuggling Organizations." *Criminology* 40 (4): 737–68.

Zhang, S., G. E. Sanchez, and L. Achilli. 2018. "Crimes of Solidarity in Mobility: Alternative Views on Migrant Smuggling." *Annals of the American Academy of Political and Social Science* 676 (1): 6–15.

Zigon, J. 2007. "Moral Breakdown and the Ethical Demand: A Theoretical Framework for an Anthropology of Moralities." *Anthropological Theory* 7 (2): 131–50.

Zijlstra, J. 2014. "Stuck on the Way to Europe? Iranian Transit Migration to Turkey." *Insight Turkey* 16 (4): 183–99.

Zimmermann, S. E. 2009. "Irregular Secondary Movements to Europe: Seeking Asylum beyond Refuge." *Journal of Refugee Studies* 22 (1): 74–96.

Zolberg, A. R., A. Suhrke, and S. Aguayo. 1992. *Escape from Violence: Conflict and the Refugee Crisis in the Developing World.* Oxford: Oxford University Press.

Founded in 1893,
UNIVERSITY OF CALIFORNIA PRESS
publishes bold, progressive books and journals
on topics in the arts, humanities, social sciences,
and natural sciences—with a focus on social
justice issues—that inspire thought and action
among readers worldwide.

The UC PRESS FOUNDATION
raises funds to uphold the press's vital role
as an independent, nonprofit publisher, and
receives philanthropic support from a wide
range of individuals and institutions—and from
committed readers like you. To learn more, visit
ucpress.edu/supportus.

Made in the USA
Monee, IL
10 June 2026